MONTH-BY-MONTH GARDENING

ILLINOIS, INDIANA & OHIO

Quarto is the authority on a wide range of topics.

Quarto educates, entertains and enriches the lives of our readers—enthusiasts and lovers of hands-on living.

www.quartoknows.com

First published in 2016 by Cool Springs Press, an imprint of Quarto Publishing Group USA Inc., 400 First Avenue North, Suite 400, Minneapolis, MN 55401 USA.
Telephone: (612) 344-8100 Fax: (612) 344-8692

quartoknows.com
Visit our blogs at quartoknows.com

Cool Springs Press titles are also available at discounts in bulk quantity for industrial or sales-promotional use. For details contact the Special Sales Manager at Quarto Publishing Group USA Inc., 400 First Avenue North, Suite 400, Minneapolis, MN 55401 USA.

10 9 8 7 6 5 4 3 2

ISBN: 978-1-59186-643-5

Library of Congress Cataloging-in-Publication Data

Botts, Beth, 1956- author.
  Illinois, Indiana & Ohio month-by-month gardening : what to do each month to have a beautiful garden all year / Beth Botts.
      pages cm
  Includes index.
  ISBN 978-1-59186-643-5 (pb)
 1. Gardening--Illinois. 2. Gardening--Indiana. 3. Gardening--Ohio. I. Title. II. Title: Illinois, Indiana and Ohio month by month gardening.

 SB450.97.B68 2016
 635.09771--dc23
                                                              2015027878

Acquiring Editor: Billie Brownell
Project Manager: Alyssa Bluhm
Art Director: Cindy Samargia Laun
Layout: Danielle Smith-Boldt

Printed in China

MONTH-BY-MONTH GARDENING

ILLINOIS, INDIANA & OHIO

**What To Do Each Month To Have
A Beautiful Garden All Year**

BETH BOTTS

COOL
SPRINGS
PRESS
Home and Garden Experts™
MINNEAPOLIS, MINNESOTA

Dedication

This book is for my mother, Lee Botts, who taught me to love the garden, the city, the lake, the prairie, the dunes, and the woods.

Acknowledgments

With deepest gratitude to Billie Brownell, my editor at Cool Springs Press, for her patience and guidance. And to the rest of the Cool Springs Press staff—thank you.

Contents

Introduction

The goal of this book is to help gardeners in Illinois, Indiana, and Ohio have attractive, healthy, fruitful gardens by recommending the right timing for common tasks. That's trickier than it may seem. Ultimately, what you can do and when in the garden depends on the weather, and in the Midwest, the weather is especially tricky.

Although Illinois, Indiana, and Ohio are all in what geographers call the "north temperate zone" and share what meteorologists call a "humid continental climate," the big thing they have in common is how much their weather varies. Drought, violent thunderstorms, late freezes, early frosts, blizzards, and melting hot spells with temperatures above 100 degrees Fahrenheit are not anomalies here; they're all within the normal climate of the Midwest.

The weather changes from day to day, of course, but also from year to year. We tend not to remember weather more than a couple of years back, so we often expect each year to be like the last and forget that the range of possibilities is always much wider. Two mild winters with early springs may be followed by a winter of bone-cracking, pipe-busting, bud-killing cold. And so far, the major local effect of global climate change seems to be making the weather even less predictable.

Statisticians help us by supplying numbers such as USDA hardiness zones and first and last frost dates. It's crucial to know these numbers and use them to navigate the garden year. But it's also important for a gardener to remember that they are all based on averages, and that they represent probabilities, not certainties.

HARDINESS ZONES

Hardiness zones are about how cold the winters tend to get in a particular place. They're an essential guide to choosing winter-hardy plants, but they don't tell us everything about the local climate. For example, most of Ohio is in USDA hardiness Zone 5. Yet in Youngstown, in the foothills of the Appalachian Mountains, the median frost-free growing season is about 155 days; in Cleveland, just 75 miles away on the shores of Lake Erie, it's 175 days.

Illinois and Indiana are both very vertical states, running north to south through multiple hardiness zones. Illinois stretches down from Zone 5a in the very north to Zone 7 at its southern tip. Cairo, Illinois, across the Ohio River from Kentucky, has a growing season of 222 days, while in Mount Carroll, up north near Wisconsin, gardeners have only 137 days to get from sowing beans to harvesting pumpkins.

Even gardens just a few miles apart can have very different weather. The local conditions can be affected by winds, elevation, and large bodies of water. They also can be changed by what we build. Large buildings can create wind tunnels, shelter some gardens from frost, or cast shade that keeps the soil cool longer in spring. Masonry, roofs, and paving in a metropolitan area can store the sun's energy, creating a heat island effect that keeps temperatures higher in summer.

The amount of snow and rain your garden gets also can vary. South Bend, Indiana, in the belt of lake-effect snow caused by Lake Michigan, gets, on average, nearly 67 inches of snow a year, while Evansville, down south, averages just 11. But there are years when it scarcely snows in northern Indiana and some years when areas far south of the Great Lakes seem to get all the storms and most of the precipitation.

So what's a gardener to do? Above all, don't expect a garden to run like clockwork. Your plants are part of nature and they respond to nature's signals, flexing with all the variations in warmth, moisture, and sunlight. Pay attention to those same signals as you plan your work, and be flexible.

Use this book as a general guideline, but allow for your garden's geography. See the hardiness zone map on page 19, or you can drill down to your ZIP code on the USDA website at www.planthardiness.ars.usda.gov. Get detailed information on frost dates and the length of the growing season for many cities in your state from NOAA at www.ncdc.noaa.gov.

Or look it up by ZIP code at PlantMaps, www.plantmaps.com.

MICROCLIMATES

Within your garden, note its peculiarities. Are there places where daffodils bloom a week or two later each year because of the shade from a building? Are there spots where the soil dries out faster because they are more exposed to wind?

And above all, watch the weather—not just what's forecast for your general area, but what actually happens in your own yard. Use rain gauges to determine how much rain really fell. Get in the habit of checking how much water is really in the soil; all it takes is sticking a finger in to feel for moisture. Walk through your garden every day, not just on the weekend, and notice things: leaf tips turned brown by frost, buds that are about to open, soil that is so dry it cracks.

Use your common sense. There may be a week of glorious t-shirt weather in early April, but if your location's average last frost date is May 15, you can bet the cold will be back. Don't be tricked into planting the petunias too soon.

■ *Midwestern weather is highly variable, so the wise gardener keeps an eye on the sky as well as the forecast.*

■ *Whether you keep them in a journal or a smartphone app, written records will help you have a better garden.*

One of the best sources of information for any gardener is other gardeners. Seek them out at garden clubs, plant sales, community gardens, or botanical gardens' gardening classes. Or simply take a walk around the neighborhood, look for the best garden, and knock on the door or chat up the person you find weeding the front yard. Nearly every gardener loves to talk about gardening—and the weather. If you're new to gardening or new to the area, local gardeners can provide valuable intelligence about the best approximate dates to sow spinach seed, plant tomatoes, and dig up dahlias. There will be a range of opinions, so talk to two or three people and take an average.

RECORDS

There's one other resource that should supplement this book: your own garden records. Having information from prior years on what happened when, and when you did what, can make your choices clearer and all your jobs easier.

I'm currently keeping my notes in an online calendar, backed up by some online text files and photos. Maybe a spiral-bound notebook or a collection of photos on a smartphone will work better for you. The important thing is to get in the habit of keeping some sort of garden record as a reminder and a reality check.

SOIL

Your success as a gardener will depend largely on how well you match the plants you choose to the conditions that exist in your yard. One of those important conditions is the soil.

The best soil for plants has a good structure, plenty of organic matter, and a healthy underground ecosystem. There are essentially three types of structure: sandy, clay, and loamy/sandy loam.

Structure refers to the mixture of mineral particles in the soil and how they fit together. Soil with mostly large particles is sandy; it drains well and lets plenty of air reach the roots, but it doesn't hold nutrients well. Soil with mostly tiny particles is clay; it's dense and sticky, with poor drainage and little airflow. Some soils right around the shores of Lake Michigan and Lake Erie are sandy, but soil just a mile or so inland tends to be heavy clay.

The happy medium is a mix of particles, with space between them for both air and water to get through. In the Midwest, this ideal is called "sandy

■ *Organic matter improves soil texture and provides food for microorganisms that are essential to healthy soil.*

■ *It's important to top-dress raised beds with organic matter every year.*

Organic matter is a phrase for the remains of plants and animals. In soil, especially after it has decayed a bit, organic matter loosens the texture and holds water like a sponge. It also offers food to all the microorganisms that make up that underground ecosystem, which will break it down and release its nutrients so plants' roots can use them.

loam." Most gardeners have heard about it but few have ever planted in it. The rest of us do our best to improve less-than-ideal soil.

It's always worth having a soil test to understand what your soil is really like (see Plan/All, October, page 142). Some nutrient deficiencies can be addressed by adding fertilizer, but overall, the best way to improve garden soil is by adding organic matter every year.

You can, and should, improve your soil by adding organic matter, which will help it hold moisture and also (interestingly) make it drain better. But it can take years to change soil structure that way. Right now, it's always best to plan for the soil you have, not the soil you wish you had or are working toward. Understand what your current soil conditions are, and choose plants that are able to tolerate them.

The vegetable garden is the exception. It's usually worth a major effort to amend the soil there, because most vegetables require well-drained soil. Even if you build raised beds and fill them with good soil to start with, you'll need to add plenty of organic matter every year.

■ *Grass clippings, leaves, and fruit and vegetable scraps from the kitchen all make good ingredients for homemade compost to improve garden soil.*

There are many ways to add organic matter—for example, by simply leaving the clippings on the lawn when you mow; by tilling last year's mulch or a load of manure into the vegetable garden in fall; by growing a cover crop and tilling it under in early spring; or by spreading mulch over the roots of your trees and letting it slowly decay.

But for most gardeners, the most versatile and convenient form of organic matter is compost. It's simply a version of the humus that naturally forms from the decay of leaves and stalks that fall every year on soils all over the world. We speed up the process by combining a variety of plant materials— fallen leaves, grass clippings, fruit and vegetable scraps from the kitchen—in a small space so the pile can support a large population of bacteria, fungi, bugs, worms, and other organisms that will break it down. (For more information on compost, see Here's How to Make Compost, page 30.)

UNDERGROUND LIFE

All those bugs, worms, fungi, and bacteria are representatives of the unseen ecosystem that lives in the soil with your plants' roots. There are millions of organisms in a teaspoon of healthy soil. They do crucial work, consuming dead plants and animals to release the nutrients from their tissues, making the soil lighter and more porous, and partnering with the roots of trees and other plants for their mutual benefit. The healthier your underground ecosystem, the better for your plants.

One reason it's a good idea to top-dress with compost on garden beds and lawns is that it spreads all those organisms around, to make sure they are available to do their good work in every nook and cranny of your soil.

The biggest threats to your underground ecosystem are too much synthetic fertilizer, too many pesticides, and too much tidiness. If you meticulously rake up all the grass clippings and clean up every last leaf that falls on the lawn, you'll be starving out your worms, bacteria, bugs, and fungi. If you fertilize too much and make a habit of using insecticides, herbicides, and fungicides, you'll kill them off.

The solutions?

■ *Earthworms are one of the many organisms that live in healthy soil and make it a good environment for plants' roots.*

- Resort to chemicals only when you have a problem for which there is no alternative.

- Use slow-release fertilizers, including organic ones.

- Leave the clippings on the lawn; the critters will break them down and return their nitrogen to your grass plants.

- Top-dress with compost to provide organic matter.

- Mulch with shredded leaves and even leave a few on the lawn so nobody goes to bed hungry.

WATERING

Most plants are about 90 percent water. In fact, except for those with a stiff skeleton of wood, water pressure is what holds plants up. Making sure plants have enough water—but not too much—is one of the major tasks for a gardener.

■ *Water slowly, deeply, and not too often for plants to have deep, healthy root systems. Avoid light, frequent watering.*

There are two general rules of thumb for watering. The first is that most plants in the Midwest, from lawns to trees, need the equivalent of 1 inch of rain a week, on average.

In most years, rainfall will be sufficient in spring and fall, although it's the gardener's job to stay alert for years that aren't average. In summer, you will almost certainly need to water many of the plants in your garden.

How do you tell when you've watered 1 inch? Place a straight-sided container, such as a tuna can or a cylindrical water glass, on the lawn underneath the sprinkler you usually use. Check how long it takes to fill with water 1 inch deep. That will tell you about how long you need to run that sprinkler to provide the equivalent of 1 inch of rain.

The second general rule is to water slowly, deeply, and not too often. Light, frequent watering, such as watering a lawn or beds by hand, tends to

encourage roots to stay near the surface of the soil and remain short and feeble. Many lawn problems, from grubs to thatch, are exacerbated by too-frequent watering.

Instead, water for a good long time so the water has time to soak down deep into the soil. Then don't water for a few days. The plants' roots will have to grow down into the soil to seek out water. That will lead them to grow a larger, healthier, deeper root system that can store more water and better resist drought.

Of course, there are exceptions to these general rules. Frequent, light sprinkling is exactly what newly sown seeds need. Containers need frequent watering because their limited soil dries out quickly. Every plant—even native prairie plants that can likely live on rainfall once they're established—needs to be watered often when it is newly planted. Some perennials, such as astilbe, need more frequent watering than others, such as bigroot geranium. You'll need to know the needs of your own plants and check regularly to see how much moisture is actually in your soil. (For more on watering, see Water/All, May, page 91.)

You can reduce watering chores by grouping plants so that those that need the most watering are together, near the hose, and those that can live on rainfall are together, farther away. This is called hydrozoning. Bear in mind too that climate change is bringing more long periods of drought that likely will lead to scarcer, more expensive water, even in the Great Lakes states. So when you choose long-lived plants, such as trees and shrubs, choose them for drought tolerance.

SUN
Sunlight is essential to all plants. They use it to make food through the chemical reaction called photosynthesis, using water, carbon dioxide from the air, and the green-hued chemical called chlorophyll. Some plants can get by with less sunshine than others, although most plants with large and colorful flowers need full sun.

To select the right plants, you need to understand the light situation in your garden. Watch to see how the light moves and where the shadows fall. Only those areas that get direct sunlight for a full eight hours will suit plants labeled for "full sun." "Part sun" means at least three to six hours of full sun a day. A "part shade" plant also requires three to six hours of sunlight a day but needs protection from the hot afternoon sun. "Shade" is any place that gets less than three hours of direct sun a day. Since flowering is energy intensive, the plants that best tolerate shade tend to have attractive leaves but inconspicuous blooms.

It's tempting to persuade yourself that showy full-sun plants will get by in your part-sun garden, or even part-shade. Some may survive, but they won't be very showy. In the long run, you'll have a more attractive and satisfying garden if you clearly understand your light conditions and seek out the kinds of plants that can truly thrive there.

FERTILIZING

Fertilizer is not plant food; plants make their own food through photosynthesis. Instead, fertilizing is a sort of insurance, to make sure your plants get enough of certain chemical elements that are important to their growth.

In nature, plants absorb all these nutrients from the soil, and if you regularly improve your soil with compost or other organic matter, it will supply much of what they need. But in certain situations—especially containers, lawns, and annual flower beds—we usually need to supply some extra nutrients.

It's easy to apply too much, though. Excess nitrogen, in particular, can stress plants or cause them to form too many leaves and few flowers. Nitrogen and phosphorus that plants don't need are wasted and washed off lawns into waterways, where they lead to serious pollution problems in rivers, lakes, and even the Gulf of Mexico. Toxic algae blooms in Lake Erie have been partly caused by surplus fertilizer runoff. Fast-release synthetic fertilizers also can damage the underground soil ecosystem.

In the lawn and garden, always use a slow-release fertilizer, which will gently release nutrients at a

rate at which plants can absorb them. All organic fertilizers are slow release. It's a good idea to mix up liquid fertilizers at half the rate suggested in the directions, just to be sure. (To learn more about fertilizing, see Fertilize/All, May, page 94.)

Apply fertilizer only to plants that actually need it. Don't try to use fertilizer to push plants to bloom or grow faster, and don't try to fix plant problems by fertilizing unless you know for sure the reason is a nutrient deficiency.

Many plants, including many native prairie perennials and ornamental grasses, don't need additional fertilizer at all in halfway decent soil. Even vegetable gardens may not need fertilizing if you dig in enough manure or compost every fall and when you prepare beds in spring.

WEEDING

Weeds are inevitable. There are tens of thousands of weed seeds in any square foot of garden soil, and many more seeds blow in every year from across the neighborhood. Nothing gets rid of weeds for good, not even paving a yard with concrete (they'll just grow in the cracks).

The key to keeping weeds within reasonable bounds is to start weeding early and be persistent. The more weeds you can remove in early spring, the fewer will survive to produce seeds in August.

■ *Start weeding early in the season and be persistent. Remove weeds throughout the season so they don't have a chance to produce seeds.*

For perennial weeds such as dandelions, be sure you remove the deep taproot, or it will resprout. A garden knife or forked-tongue weeder is useful for this task. Use a cultivator (sometimes called a three- or four-tined claw) or other tool to scratch up the roots of young weeds in the vegetable garden. Try to remove all weeds before they set seed. (For more information on weeding, see Care/All, June, page 104.)

In a lawn, the best weed fighter is tall, healthy grass. Tall grass will shade out many weed seeds so they don't get the sun they need to sprout. It also can out-compete many weeds.

There are pre-emergent herbicides you can apply in early spring that will reduce the number of seeds that germinate. One organic option, which also adds some nitrogen to the lawn, is corn gluten meal. (For more information on pre-emergents, see Problem-Solve/Lawns, March, page 57.)

Mulch is the other top weapon against weeds; like tall grass, it keeps weed seeds from getting enough sun to sprout.

If weeds seem overwhelming, try to cut the task down to a manageable size. Choose a defined area; it might be the span between two expansion joints in the adjacent walk, or, if you're me, a Hula-Hoop dropped on the garden. Weed that area absolutely clean. Then pause to congratulate yourself before you move on to another area.

LAWN CARE

Lawns are important to many homeowners, but there are some better ways to manage a lawn now than in the past. Keeping your grass tall enough is the single most important step you can take to have a healthy lawn; most lawns are mowed far too short. Set the lawnmower blade as high as it will go (usually 3 inches, but higher is even better) and leave it there.

Two other practices will also make a huge difference: Core-aerating once or twice a year to let air and water into the root zones (see Care/Lawn, March, page 54) and leaving the grass clippings on the lawn to break down and return their nutrients

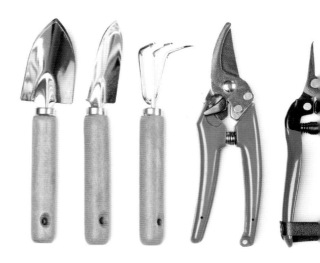

■ *Among useful gardening tools are a wide trowel and a narrow trowel for planting; a cultivator or three-prong claw for weeding; bypass pruners; and snips for deadheading and trimming.*

■ *Healthy grass will come from mowing high, core-aerating at least once a year, and leaving clippings on the lawn.*

■ *To top-dress a lawn to improve the soil, use sifted compost (with big chunks screened out).*

■ *Distribute the compost over the lawn.*

■ *Spread it with a spring rake so it falls between the grass blades. It will disappear in a few days.*

to the soil. A mulching mower, which chops the clippings finely, is your best buy. If you don't have one, run the lawnmower over clumps of clippings to chop them up and then rake them out to spread them evenly. They'll disappear in a day or two.

One application of slow-release fertilizer, or one in spring and one in fall, is better for the lawn

than a five-times-a-year fertilizer regime. (See Fertilize/Lawns, May, page 96.) Even though you fertilize, it's still a good idea to top-dress with compost once a year. Just sprinkle compost lavishly over the lawn, rake it so it falls between the grass, and water. I don't use any herbicides on my smallish lawn. Every spring I core-aerate, overseed to fill in any bare patches, and top-dress with compost. I dig up all the weeds I can find and sprinkle a little grass seed in the holes they leave behind. Once the grass grows in tall and lush, I usually have only a few weeds to dig from time to time through the summer. See more about lawn care in the Lawn Problems section of the book, on page 169.

SOLVING PROBLEMS

Every variation in the garden is not a problem. Plants naturally have great years and not-so-great years, depending largely on the weather. By August, most plants will start to look a little tattered. Not every insect is a problem, either; in fact, the overwhelming majority of insects in a garden are harmless or beneficial.

Be watchful but not fearful. If you see something that worries you, identify the problem for certain and decide whether it's just a short-term cosmetic issue or whether it really threatens the health of the plant before you decide whether to use any control measures, even organic ones.

Don't guess at the cause of the damage; that can lead you to apply insecticides, fungicides, or herbicides that won't solve your problem and can do a lot of collateral damage. Applying the wrong insecticide, or applying it at the wrong time of year, can be completely ineffective, since many insects are only vulnerable to certain chemicals and only at certain times. Seek expert guidance to make sure you use the right tactics and timing. (For more information on getting help, see Problem-Solve/All, May, page 97).

I'm fortunate to live in the Chicago area, where there are multiple botanical gardens and well-organized plant clinics run by Master Gardener volunteers, as well as top-notch garden centers that I can turn to for expert help. Even if you don't have such resources handy, there are ways you can get a plant, pest, or disease identification online. See Resources, page 189.

In my garden, I generally use organic methods, though I'm not an absolutist. I concentrate on keeping my plants healthy so they can handle most pest and disease issues without my intervention. I plant plenty of flowers to invite beneficial insects, such as ladybugs on the hunt for aphids, and I make sure my garden is safe for them by avoiding insecticides.

I use pesticides only in extreme cases, and even then I use the least-toxic product I can and in the smallest dose that will take care of the problem. For example, I may spray an indoor houseplant with a commercial insecticidal soap to beat back a serious attack of spider mites, but I would never hose down my rose garden with a general insect killer such as imidacloprid or acetamiprid to kill Japanese beetles.

When, on occasion, I've removed invasive shrubs and vines, I've painted the stumps with a herbicide containing glyphosate to kill the roots. But I have

■ *For spring color combinations, choose bulbs that will bloom at the same time, such as these late-blooming red* 'Ile de France' *tulips, pink* 'May Wonder' *peony tulips, and grape hyacinths.*

never used a weed-and-feed product on my lawn, because the herbicide included with the fertilizer would threaten the microorganisms that make my soil healthy. See more about pests on page 189 in the Resources section.

CHOOSING PLANTS

Every gardener can be seduced by plants: Bright colors and ruffly petals waylay us at the garden center. The adjective *new* in a plant catalog snaps us to attention. We plant a vegetable garden for a family of ten when there are only four of us. We convince ourselves we absolutely must have one more variety of hosta, one more heirloom tomato, or one more native plant to entice native butterflies.

But every garden has its limits—and not just space. Short of tearing down the house, you probably can't change the way the sun falls on your yard. You can (and should) add organic matter every year, but clay soil will still be clay soil. To escape the clay, you can raise the vegetables in raised beds filled with a better growing mix. But if you only have part sun, that's what you have. Your area's frost dates and its hardiness zone are beyond your control.

Fortunately, there are plants that will thrive in your yard, and you can find them if you do your homework. Different plants need different conditions, because somewhere in the world, they all have a native place where they evolved to fill a particular set of conditions. Trying to grow a plant in a place it simply doesn't have the genes for is a recipe for extra work: pruning, training, watering, weeding out aggressive seedlings, or watching the spring garden in vain for perennials that failed to survive the winter.

For a garden that doesn't make you work so hard, be realistic about what your yard is like. Watch the sun. Test the soil. Then choose plants that are genetically programmed to do well in conditions like yours. If your yard is in shade, you can't grow tomatoes, but you can grow lettuce, spinach, and cilantro. If your soil is sticky clay, dahlias won't do well but New England asters probably will be fine.

■ *One of the most important things to do in your garden is to take time to sit and enjoy it.*

By resisting seduction, doing your homework, and picking species and varieties that have been proven to fit your conditions, you'll have a more successful garden with less work. See page 173 for my lists of the best plants for special situations.

TAKING IT EASY

The whole point of this book is to help you stay on track in your garden. It will help you plan when to do the tasks you need to do or choose to do: when to dig manure into the vegetable garden, when to start the tomato seeds, when to plant a tree, when to let the lawn go dormant, when to plant the fall crop of spinach.

But it's not a set of marching orders. Nobody needs to do every task described in this book. Some of us enjoy starting seeds indoors in the depths of winter, and others would just as soon outsource that job and buy transplants at home-improvement and garden centers in May. Some people like to dig up every dahlia tuber and keep it through the winter, and others will just buy more tubers the next spring. For some, a vegetable garden is a series of 40-foot-long rows or six raised beds; for others it's three pots of tomatoes. Choose the tasks that apply to you in your garden.

You'll quickly discover that although the sequence of tasks doesn't shift much, the timing does. In a cold spring, you may need to wait until May to

■ *A garden of annuals is bright and colorful but requires lots of labor. Choose your garden style according to your taste, as well as the time and maintenance you are willing to invest.*

plant things that last year you planted in April or that a friend farther south usually plants in March. But to garden successfully, we need to accept that nature calls the shots. The weather, the plants, and the soil will tell you when to do what.

For me, listening to nature is one of the joys of gardening. There's no space in my head for worries or hassles when I'm focused on the sight of snowdrops pushing up from the leaf litter; the texture of soil that's wet from just-melted snow; how quickly that soil is losing moisture in a hot June; the first chill breeze of September that warns me to take the houseplants back indoors; the coming frost that will make the Brussels sprouts sweet. If I just pay attention, the garden pulls me through the year. And it always inspires me to look ahead to the future: Planting daffodils in October is an act of faith.

So, are you ready? Let's start gardening!

INTRODUCTION

HOW TO USE THIS BOOK

This book is divided into chapters, one for each month. Each monthly chapter lists tasks that are typically done at that time in much of Illinois, Indiana, and Ohio. But because there's so much regional variation and so much change in weather from year to year, you may find you need to do many of these tasks earlier or later.

Each chapter has an introduction that sets the stage. Then it's divided into the main topics of Plan, Plant, Care, Water, Fertilize, and Problem-Solve. These topics are further subdivided by types of plants—annuals, perennials, lawns, and container plants, for example.

It's a good idea to read through the whole book once to get a feel for the progression and the rhythm of the gardening year. After that, use it as a reference with the help of the index.

If lawn care is your assigned task in the household, you may want to focus on the Lawn sections. If you have a small urban garden consisting of containers, look for the sections on Containers. But it's still a good idea to read the introduction and scan the whole book at least once to absorb the big picture.

Most tasks are described in detail the first time they're mentioned; after that, the text usually will refer you back to that first explanation rather than repeating it. If you run across an unfamiliar term, consult the glossary.

You will find many articles of general advice with titles such as "Here's How to Plant a Tree or Shrub" and "Here's How to Solve Common Tomato Troubles." But this is more of a when-to-do-it book than a how-to-do-it book, so it won't cover every possible outcome or every kind of gardening.

Each garden is unique and all gardeners have their own ways of doing things. You will surely find that your experience differs in some ways from what is described in this book, so make a note; this is a working book, and that's what margins are for.

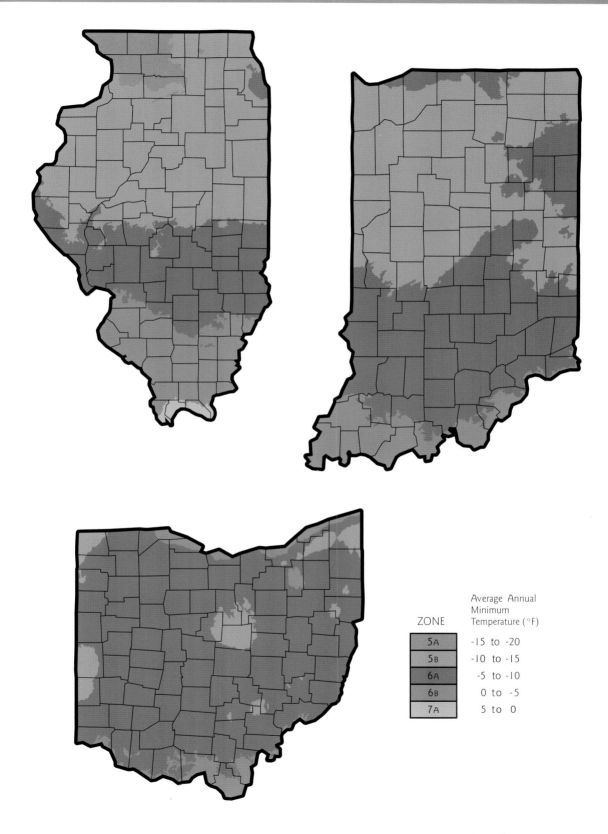

ZONE	Average Annual Minimum Temperature (°F)
5A	-15 to -20
5B	-10 to -15
6A	-5 to -10
6B	0 to -5
7A	5 to 0

January

In January, the garden is always perfect. There have been no severe storms, no infestations, no droughts, no plants that fail to thrive or that spread where they're not wanted. The garden is still perfect because it's still a dream.

Start making the dream real with a plan. In winter, you have time to think things through so you don't waste time, effort, and money once the growing season starts. And make a vow that this season, you will let the real garden be less than perfect so you can spend more time enjoying it.

Dreams can be powerful, and it's easy to get swept away by the colorful catalogs in January and spend too much or plan a vegetable garden that is too large to keep up with. Try to be realistic about what you will have time to do, allowing for vacations and other interruptions.

At the same time, promise yourself you'll try something new this year. If you've never started plants from seed, try starting just a few. If you've always grown vegetables in the ground, try growing some in pots. If you don't have a compost pile, plan to start one. And buy yourself at least one gorgeous new flower you've never grown or tomato variety you've never tasted.

Set up some sort of record-keeping system for the garden. Good notes on what you do and when you do it, what you plant, and how your garden fares can help you in years to come. You can use an old-fashioned spiral-bound notebook, a fancy garden journal, or one of many online gardening apps. It's a great idea to take lots of pictures of garden views, plants, and problems, but set up folders or some other organization system so you can find the pictures and refer to them later on.

A smartphone can be a very handy tool for record-keeping, picture-taking, and getting garden advice. But if you plan to take your smartphone into the garden to take pictures or keep notes this year, buy it a protective case. Snowdrifts, mud puddles, and compost piles attract smartphones.

PLAN

ALL

Take a walk through your neighborhood and look for touches that make yards interesting in winter: Plants with evergreen needles or leaves, bright berries, striking branching or bark, attractive dried flower heads—even colorful artwork or a trellis that catches snow in a cool way. Take pictures and make notes. Then look over your own yard to see where you might have room for a change that could make next winter less dreary.

As you browse catalogs and websites, make it a point to add a few native plants to your yard this year to provide habitat for birds and other wildlife. See Resources (page 189) for how to find information on plants that are native to your area.

Save catalogs that provide good, detailed information about plants, such as advice on when to start seeds or which perennials tolerate shade. Even if you don't order from them, they can be valuable references.

Take a class at your local botanical garden or community college so you go into spring with a new skill or more knowledge. It's also a good way to meet other local gardeners.

Check your USDA plant hardiness zone; you can find the map on page 19 and on their website at www.planthardiness.ars.usda.gov. Illinois, Indiana, and Ohio fall mainly within Zones 5, 6, and 7.

Also, learn the key dates for timing your garden: The average date of the last frost in spring and the average date of the first frost in autumn. These can vary from place to place, even within a USDA hardiness zone or a single metropolitan area. They can be affected by altitude, wind patterns, and the nearness of large bodies of water such as Lake Michigan and Lake Erie. The dates also have been shifting in recent years, as the growing season gets longer, on average.

The best source for reliable local information on these dates is your local state university Extension office or Master Gardener program (see Resources, page 189). You can also check for your ZIP code at www.plantmaps.com.

Always bear in mind that these dates are averages, and that in any actual year the frosts can occur earlier or later.

Plan and build a light setup for starting plants from seed indoors.

ANNUALS

Plan the annual flowers you will grow this season and decide whether you will start them indoors from seed, sow the seed directly in the garden, or buy transplants. Some seeds, such as cosmos, marigolds, and nasturtiums, can be simply scattered in the garden after your average last frost date. Others, such as pansies, petunias, and snapdragons, need weeks or months of growing

Choose your tool, but set up some kind of record-keeping system. Good notes can help you in the garden for years to come.

Plan your garden and order seeds early for the best selection.

HERE'S HOW

TO SET UP LIGHTS FOR SEED STARTING

For under about $100, you can create a simple light setup that will allow you to start several dozen plants.

Buy one or two simple shop lights that hold florescent tubes or LED lights. If you buy two 24-inch fixtures, you can accommodate different heights of plants.

Get one cool white and one warm white tube for each fixture to provide a broad spectrum of light. There's no need for special grow lights.

Place your light setup near an electrical outlet and out of the path of traffic (the plants will be growing for two to three months). Hang the light fixtures from the ceiling, using sturdy hooks screwed into the ceiling joists, or from well-secured basement pipes. Or build a frame of 2×4 lumber.

Hang the lights using chain with large links and S-hooks, or use rope with cleats to tie it off. Make the chain long enough so the lights are suspended just a few inches from the table or workbench where you will place the plants. The S-hooks will allow you to gradually raise the lights, link by link, so they stay just above the growing plants. You can use ropes and pulleys to accomplish the same thing.

Plug the fixtures into a surge suppresser with a circuit breaker. Use a timer to turn the light on and off; the plants need about 16 hours of light a day.

This setup involves using electricity near water, so in case of accidents, it's best to use a surge suppressor power strip with a circuit breaker. Even so, secure the surge suppressor, extension cord, and timer up away from the plant trays. You also can buy kits for ready-made light setups that can cost from $150 to several hundred dollars.

under lights before they can be transplanted outdoors. Consult catalog descriptions and the seed packet to determine exactly how to stage your seed sowing. To estimate how many seedlings to start, see Here's How to Estimate How Many Plants To Buy, page 77. Always sow some extra seeds to provide a cushion.

Order seeds from catalogs and websites early for best selection.

EDIBLES

Plan the crops you will raise this season and decide whether you will start them indoors from seed, such as tomatoes and peppers; sow the seed directly in the garden, such as lettuce and corn; or buy transplants. Your choice may depend on how much space you have; when the seeds would need to be started and whether you will be available to tend them; and how much you are willing to spend.

Starting plants from seed is usually less expensive, once you have your light setup, and you will have a wider choice of varieties.

Some plants, such as pumpkins, melons, tomatoes, peppers, and cucumbers, need such a long growing season that there isn't time to sow the seed in the ground and still have a harvest. You must start them indoors several weeks *before* the soil will be warm enough to plant them outside, or else buy transplants.

For general timing of many vegetables, see the Spring Vegetable Timing Chart on page 165. However, different varieties of any plant take different lengths of time to reach maturity. To know exactly when to plant each set of seeds, use the days to maturity listed on the seed packet and count back from your area's average last frost date. Order seeds from catalogs and websites early for best selection.

HERE'S HOW

TO PLAN A RAISED BED

Many plans, garden designs, and kits are available for raised beds, but here are some rules of thumb:

- Make the beds no more than 4 feet wide so you can reach the whole way in from one side or the other.

- Make sturdy corners. Use crosspieces to prevent long sides from bowing out when soil swells with water.

- Place raised beds where they will get at least eight hours of sun a day.

- Space the beds at least 2 feet apart to allow for a wheelbarrow.

- If you build from wood, use untreated lumber. Newer treated lumber uses copper, not arsenic, but still is best not used for food crops.

- Make the beds at least 8 to 18 inches deep. Deeper beds will allow you to grow crops with deeper roots, but also will require more soil.

- Fill beds for the first time with a mixture of one-third topsoil and two-thirds compost, or the mixture your landscape supplier recommends (see Here's How to Decide How Much Material to Buy, page 41). In later years, you can just add more compost to the top.

Plan and build raised beds for vegetables and herbs. Soil in raised beds will drain better and will warm up sooner in spring. You can continually enrich the soil in them without the need for tilling. You can plant more intensively than you can in the ground, so you can raise more vegetables in less space.

PLANT

EDIBLE

Start seeds of long-day onions and shallots. The alternative is to wait for spring and buy onion sets (baby onion transplants).

HOUSEPLANTS

Plant fragrant paperwhite narcissus bulbs in soilless potting mix or in a shallow dish filled with pebbles and water just to the bottoms of the bulbs. If you plant them in soil, make sure the container has a drainage hole.

Plant an amaryllis bulb if you received one as a gift. See Plant/Bulbs, October, page 145.

CARE

ALL

Prepare your tools for the gardening season (if you didn't do that last fall when you put them away).

- Clean and sharpen cutting and digging tools. Sharp pruners make clean cuts and are easier on the hands. Sharp digging tools such as shovels and hoes make the soil easier to work and do less damage to plant roots.

- Wash pruning shears and loppers, dry them thoroughly, and oil the joints before sharpening.

- To sharpen pruners, use a small diamond file, available at hardware stores. To sharpen shovels and hoes, use a bastard mill file.

- Hold the tool securely; use a bench vise if you have one. Draw the file away from you along the edge of the tool, keeping the surface of the file at the same angle as the original bevel on the tool.

- Note that new shovels and hoes are dull when sold and must be sharpened before use.

- If you need new tools, purchase bypass pruners and loppers, not the anvil style. Bypass pruners have blades that slide past each other, like scissors; anvil pruners have one sharp blade that strikes a flat surface, crushing the branches.

- A small pruning saw is also useful (get one that cuts on both the push and pull strokes).

- It always is worth it to buy better-quality, long-lasting tools, even if they are more expensive.

When you clear snow, try to avoid using salt or other ice melters. Salt-laden water from sidewalks and driveways often runs into the soil around trees, shrubs, perennials, and grass, where it causes roots to dry out. See Problem-Solve/All, December, page 163. Where possible, avoid using salt near planting areas and avoid shoveling snow from salted walks onto grass, trees, shrubs, or planting beds. Sand can provide traction instead.

Snow without salt is a fine insulator and source of spring moisture for plants. If you have places where snow doesn't fall—such as under roof overhangs or at the base of shrubs—shovel salt-free snow there when you clear the walks.

HOUSEPLANTS

Try to provide houseplants with extra humidity to counteract dry air from central heating. Keep houseplants away from heating vents, radiators, and other sources of heat.

If possible, group them together and use a humidifier nearby. You also can place plants on trays filled with pebbles and keep the trays full of water. The water will evaporate up around the leaves of the plants, while the pebbles hold the pots above the level of the water. Never allow the water level to rise to the bottom of the pots; roots that sit in water will rot.

Misting plants with water from a spray bottle once or twice a day is less effective, but better than nothing.

Keep plants' leaves clean of dust, which cuts off light from reaching them. Wipe the leaves with plain water using a soft cloth or give the plant a bath. Set the pot inside a plastic bag and gather the bag around the stem. Set the plant in the bathtub and turn on the shower with tepid water until the plant is clean.

Keep houseplants a foot away from cold windowpanes.

PERENNIALS

As winter goes on, cut back any standing stalks from last year's perennials if they get beaten down by snow and you find them unattractive. Or wait for one big spring cleanup.

SHRUBS

Don't rush to brush fallen snow off evergreen shrubs. In cold weather, the branches are brittle and easily damaged. You can do more harm by brushing snow off than by leaving it to melt.

If shrubs' branches are bent by heavy, wet snow that weighs them down, they usually will straighten up by themselves when the snow melts.

However, a few shrubs that have upward-pointing branches, such as tall, narrow junipers and arborvitaes, may have their branches splayed out or broken by heavy snow. Take action to prevent this *before* the snow falls: Gently tie the entire plant together with strips of soft cloth or bungee cords. Once the snow is falling, leave the plant alone.

■ *To raise humidity around a houseplant, place it on a tray or saucer filled with gravel and water. The gravel will keep the roots above the level of the water as it evaporates around foliage.*

■ *Dusty houseplants can take a shower. Place the pot inside a plastic bag to protect the tub.*

TREES

Winter is a good time to have a professional arborist assess the condition of trees or do any necessary pruning. The structure and any problems are easier to see with the leaves gone.

Maples, in particular, should be pruned in deep winter, before the sap starts running, or else not until early summer.

You can prune small trees yourself if you can reach to do it with your feet on the ground. See Here's How to Prune a Dormant Shrub, page 36.

January is a good month to have trees removed, because the ground is frozen and the risk of damage to soil or other plants is reduced.

WATER

HOUSEPLANTS

Water as plants need water—not on a set schedule. Most houseplants need less water in winter, when they are growing slowly or not at all. Water when the potting mix is no longer moist 1 to 2 inches under the surface. Soak the potting mix thoroughly, but never let houseplants sit in water; empty the saucer after 20 minutes.

Water paperwhite narcissus only as needed. In soil, water when the top inch or so of the soil is dry. In a bowl of pebbles, water so that only the roots, not the bulbs, are in water.

Water a Christmas cactus or Thanksgiving cactus when the top inch of soil feels dry. After it has finished blooming, set it in indirect light and let it dry out for a month while it is dormant. Then resume watering moderately as the growing season begins. These houseplants can live for years or even *decades* with proper care.

SHRUBS

Anytime there is a warm spell and the top layer of soil is not frozen, water both evergreen and deciduous shrubs planted within the last two years. Their undeveloped root systems probably did not store much water in fall.

This is especially crucial for evergreens, which lose water all winter long. Without extra watering, evergreen leaves and needles are more likely to dry out and die. Evergreens in exposed locations need all the watering they can get.

Do the same for any shrubs that are overwintering in containers outdoors. For potted shrubs that are overwintering in an unheated garage or other sheltered place, water once a month but not so much that you bring the plant out of dormancy.

FERTILIZE

HOUSEPLANTS

Don't fertilize most houseplants in the depth of winter; they are resting.

Wait until amaryllis is done flowering to fertilize lightly. Fertilize Christmas cactus every three weeks with fertilizer at one-half strength until its flowering is over. Then let it go dormant.

PROBLEM-SOLVE

BULBS & PERENNIALS

Winter warm spells may cause spring bulbs such as daffodils and crocus to sprout. They will survive. The plants will stop growing when the weather turns cold again and wait for better conditions. If a deep freeze hits, the edges of the leaves may be damaged, but the flower bud is still below ground and won't be affected.

Some perennials, especially non-natives, may also sprout in warm spells. The best defense is mulch. In winter, mulch insulates soil to keep it steadily frozen so temperature fluctuations don't affect plants. Evergreen boughs left over from holiday decorations can provide good protection; just lay them over beds or around shrubs. They will block the sun and keep it from warming the soil.

HOUSEPLANTS

If houseplants seem to wilt, check the soil to see if it is too dry or too wet. Many houseplants are overwatered, which keeps the soil saturated so roots can't get air and causes roots to rot. The soil should feel moist, but not wet, an inch below the surface.

Plants also can suffer if their roots stand in water. This can happen if the plant pot is inserted in a decorative pot so you don't see that surplus water has accumulated above the drainage holes in the inner pot. Empty saucers and cachepots after 20 minutes each time you water.

Check houseplants for signs of fertilizer buildup. If you see a crust of white or yellowish crystals or powder around the holes of the pot, put it in the kitchen sink and flush it with plain water. Repot the plant if necessary. See Here's How to Repot a Houseplant, page 88.

Fluoride in water may cause brown leaf tips on palms, spider plants, dracaenas, and other plants with long, narrow leaves. Using distilled water for these plants will prevent the problem. Or try flushing them out with it every couple of months.

TREES, SHRUBS & GROUNDCOVERS

Evergreen groundcovers and shrubs along sidewalks and pathways may develop brown, dried-out foliage. This is usually evidence of salt damage. See December, Problem-Solve, page 163.

Check trees and shrubs, especially those that are newly planted or young and tender, for animal damage. Deer are likely to leave shredded edges on twigs or branches, while rabbits make clean 45-degree bite marks. Voles and other small rodents tend to chew bark near the ground.

For protection methods, see Problem-Solve/Trees & Shrubs, October, page 151.

Many ash trees have died in Illinois, Indiana, and Ohio because of the emerald ash borer, the destructive larva of a beetle from China. If your

■ *Snow is a great insulator because it's mostly air. It protects plants from bitter cold and keeps soil safely frozen during winter thaws.*

ash or other trees have died, have them removed promptly before they dry out and become brittle and dangerous. Make sure you hire a licensed, trained professional arborist, and check the firm's liability insurance certificate. See Resources, page 189.

HERE'S HOW

TO DEAL WITH COMMON HOUSEPLANT PESTS

Look out for common houseplant pests, such as mealybugs, spider mites, scale insects, and fungus gnats.

Mealybugs are cottony white blobs that may appear where a leaf joins a stem or along leaf veins. They are sap-sucking insects covered with waxy secretions. Pick them off with tweezers or a cotton swab. Check to see if they are growing on the roots, and remove those too.

Spider mites are small arachnids that appear as tiny black specks on the underside of leaves. Often the first sign is their fine white webbing. Spider mites thrive in warm, dry indoor air, so the best preventive is supplying extra humidity (see Care, Houseplants). If you have an infested plant, take it into the shower, set it on a rag, and spray it with a hard blast of tepid water from a spray bottle to dislodge most of the bugs. For a heavy infestation, try a commercially made insecticidal soap, available at garden and home-improvement centers. Spider mites spread readily to other plants, so if you have a seriously infested one, it might be best to get rid of it and start over.

Scale insects are small sap-suckers that appear as small, round, waxy disks on stems or leaves of plants including schefflera, ficus, and ferns. They exude a clear, sticky goo. Wipe them off with an old washcloth and insecticidal soap. Then rinse with tepid water.

Fungus gnats live and breed in soil that is too wet. They fly up in a cloud when the plant is disturbed. Let the soil dry out between waterings to interrupt the creatures' life cycle, and make sure the bottom of the pot never stands in water.

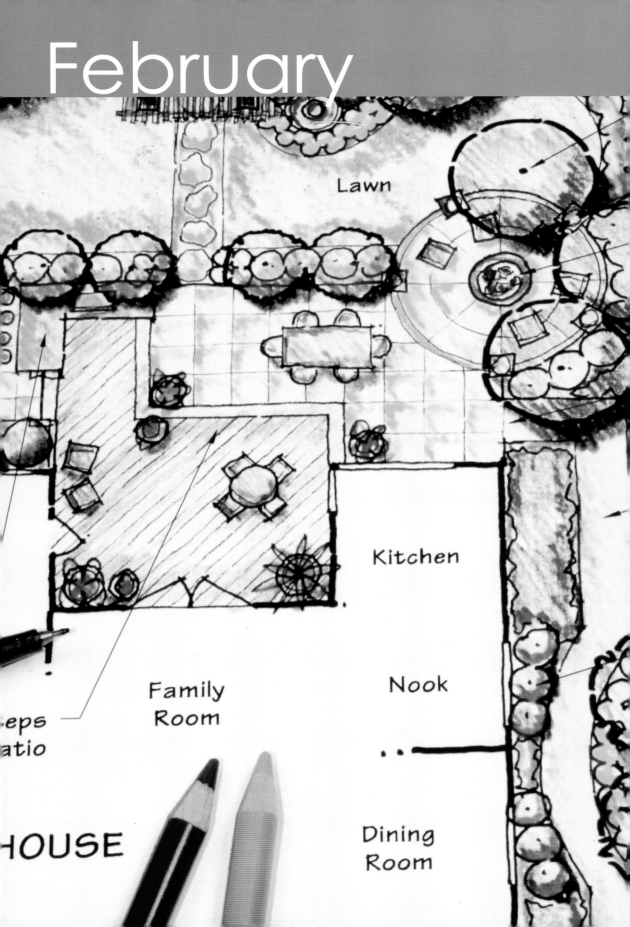

February

Lawn

Kitchen

Nook

Family
Room

eps
atio

Dining
Room

HOUSE

February is the ragged end of winter. Bone-chilling cold and big snows often alternate with warm spells that tempt bulb foliage out of the ground. Another freeze is inevitable, but every cycle of freeze and thaw brings spring a little closer.

Before you start picking out plants from all the catalogs that have flooded the mailbox, take stock of your garden. Make at least a rough sketch of the layout (it's easier to measure in the winter without all the leaves in the way). Graph paper will help, although you also can find online tools to help you draw a plan. Include large fixed objects such as the house and garage, the driveway and walks, trees, and water features. Mark the house's windows and doors, so you can plan for views from inside, and the location of outdoor faucets. Sketch out the lines of your beds, with dimensions. Consult your notes and photos from last year and write down the direction the sun comes from, how many hours of light reach different parts of your garden, the quality of the soil, and any special conditions, such as low, wet spots or dry areas.

This sketch doesn't need to be neat; it's just to help you remember clearly and stay on track as you plan. Make several photocopies of this sketch and use them to try out new possibilities.

The vegetable garden should get a more detailed plan, laying out what goes where, how you will rotate your crops, and which spaces you will refill with fall vegetables. Planning ahead will help you avoid starting more tomato varieties than you could ever possibly fit or not allowing enough space for succession plantings of lettuce.

As you read magazines and books, flip through catalogs, and browse other people's blogs, Pinterest, and Facebook pages for inspiration, remember that what you see in someone else's yard—even in the same state or city—won't necessarily grow in your conditions. As dazzling as a plant might be, don't order it before you do the homework to make sure it's the right plant for your place.

PLAN

ALL

Good soil is the basis of a successful garden. A few rare gardeners are blessed with naturally rich, fluffy loam, but most of us in the Midwest have some variation on clay. Before you plan to *plant* anything, plan to *amend* the soil.

The best amendment is compost, whether store-bought or homemade, but shredded leaves, mushroom compost, and even fine, well-rotted mulch can help. Adding organic matter will make the soil lighter, creating spaces for air and water to flow; add nutrients; create habitat and food for valuable microscopic life; and improve drainage.

HERE'S HOW

TO MAKE COMPOST

Composting is simply an accelerated way of making humus, the layer of decomposed organic matter that naturally forms from leaves, stems, and whatever else falls to the ground, enriching the soil and making it hospitable for plants. Worms, bacteria, fungi, and other microbes and invertebrates do the actual work of digesting the raw materials into compost.

If you don't have a compost pile, now or later in spring is a good time to start one. Check with your municipality to see if you are required to use a compost bin with a lid to deter animals. Otherwise, start with a simple pile:

1. Combine a majority of carbon-rich brown materials such as dried leaves with a smaller amount of nitrogen-rich green materials such as grass clippings, trimmings from annuals, or vegetable and fruit scraps from the kitchen. Precise proportions are not important, but over time, decomposition will be most efficient if you add more brown materials than green ones.

2. Add a shovel full of garden soil to provide the microbes to start the process. Moisten the pile and mix it up. Other organisms will get wind of the party and move in.

3. Every few weeks, turn over the pile with a garden fork to let in more air.

Depending on the weather, moisture, ingredients, and how often you turn it, you should have compost in the center of the pile in three to four months. It should be dark, with a clean, earthy smell. Dig out the finished compost and toss back whatever hasn't broken down to decay some more.

A cold frame allows you to move plants out sooner in spring and keep them out later in fall. It also can be used for seedlings or to grow cold-hardy winter greens. It should have a transparent lid that slopes toward the south to gather as much winter sun as possible. The lid must be easy to open for ventilation so that heat does not build up and cook the plants. This version is small enough to be moveable.

It's not difficult to make compost yourself from fallen leaves, garden debris, and fruit and vegetable scraps from the kitchen.

To get an early start on the growing season and extend it into fall, buy or build a cold frame.

It's simply a low box with a transparent lid that protects plants from wind and captures the sun's warmth. You can start some seeds in a cold frame or use it to harden off seedlings. In fall, a cold frame can keep a cold-hardy crop such as spinach going into winter.

Ideally, a cold frame's lid will slope toward the south to gather as much sunlight as possible. The lid must be easy to lift and prop open for ventilation.

The box should be small enough that you can reach into it easily, no more than 4 feet wide. The sides should be angled so the front is lower than the back, creating the slope of the lid. A box 8 to 10 inches high on the low side and 18 to 24 inches on the high side works well.

You can buy a kit for a cold frame or make one out of straw bales, old bricks, or lumber with old storm windows for a lid. Be careful to make it sturdy so that it won't blow apart in a spring storm. A lightweight cold frame should be staked securely to the ground.

ANNUALS
Plan your seed-starting if you didn't do it in January. See Plan/Annuals, January, page 22.

EDIBLES
Also plan your seed-starting if you didn't do it before. See Plan/Edibles, January, page 23.

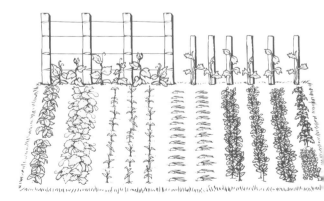

As you plan your spring garden, be realistic about how many plants of corn, beans, carrots, greens, and other edibles you need and can care for.

■ *Allow plenty of room for squash, pumpkins, and melons, which tend to sprawl.*

In planning, be realistic about how many vegetables your family can actually eat. Don't take on too much, especially if you are new to edible gardening; start small. A few tomato plants, a bed of lettuce, and some herbs will give you a sense of the gardening year and what you can expect. As your knowledge and skills grow, expand your garden.

Sketch out how you will use space in the vegetable garden. Plan where you will plant different crops, allowing for sun, support, and space to use tools or drive a tiller if you use one.

Most edible plants will need at least eight hours of full sun each day, although root crops such as beets, radishes, and turnips can handle six to eight hours. Crops that produce only leaves, such as lettuce, spinach, bok choy, and collards, need only four or five hours.

Some tall crops, such as corn or pyramids or trellises of pole beans, may cast shade on others as they grow. If you have space for row crops, place the tallest vegetables along the north end and place other crops, in decreasing order of size, toward the south. That way none will shade another.

If you grew vegetables last year, be careful to rotate the positions of this year's crops to minimize the risk of soilborne diseases this year.

Allow plenty of room in the garden for space hogs such as pumpkins and squash, following the spacing recommended on the seed packets. For example, full-sized pumpkins usually need about 5 feet of space in a row.

When you shop for tomato seeds or plants, look for varieties bred to resist diseases such as early blight and verticillium wilt. If you have other summer plans, try to avoid planting crops that will ripen when you're on vacation.

Order seeds as well as bare-root raspberry and blackberry shrubs.

HERE'S HOW

TO ROTATE CROPS

Plants that are closely related genetically tend to be vulnerable to the same diseases, so ideally, don't plant vegetables in the same soil where a plant in the same family grew last year. That way, fungus spores and other disease pathogens have time to die off. In fact, it's best to avoid planting the same family in the same place within three years. The families are:

- Cabbages (brassicas), including broccoli, Brussels sprouts, cabbage, rutabaga, turnips, kohlrabi, cauliflower, kale, mizuna, pak choi, radish, and arugula

- Nightshade relatives, including tomatoes, eggplants, potatoes, and peppers

- Squashes and cucumbers (cucurbits), including summer and winter squash, cucumber, melons, and pumpkins

- Beans and peas (legumes), including bush, pole, lima, fava, and dry beans and peas

- Onions (alliums), including onions, garlic, shallots, chives, and leeks

- Carrots and roots, including carrots, celery, celeriac, cilantro, fennel, parsnips, parsley, and dill

- Beets, including beets, Swiss chard, and spinach

LAWNS

If you want someone else to mow and edge your lawn this year, locate a contractor now. Look for a company that will mow your lawn high, at least 3 inches, for healthy grass. If possible, sign up for organic lawn care, not for a standard weed-killer-and-fertilizer regime. Healthier grass, treated with compost or compost tea and mowed high, will out-compete most weeds.

PERENNIALS

Clean up stalks and foliage from last year's perennial garden while the ground is still frozen. Leave mulch in place. I use fallen leaves to mulch in fall, and in late winter I rake lightly to fluff them up so bulb foliage can get through and I redistribute them to cover bare spots. If there's a thick layer, I remove some and stash the surplus leaves for later use. But I never allow bare soil in my garden.

Start watching garden club newsletters and local newspapers and websites for notices of native plant sales. These are a great way to start adding plants to the garden that are native to your area. Native plant sales often require you to order in February or March and pick up your plants at an event in April or May.

ROSES

Order bare-root roses. Check catalog descriptions carefully for terms such as "disease resistant," "cold hardy," and "carefree." Roses recommended for USDA climate Zones 5, 4, or 3 will likely survive winters in the northern and colder parts of Illinois, Indiana, and Ohio without protection.

TREES

If you have a construction project coming up this year, plan to protect your trees. A tree can suffer major, long-term damage if its roots are cut or if heavy materials and equipment pack down the soil around its roots. When it dies several years later, you may not realize why.

Plan to fence off trees to keep equipment away, allowing 1 foot of space beyond the tree trunk for every inch of trunk diameter. Instruct contractors to store equipment, bricks, concrete, and other heavy objects on a paved surface such as the driveway.

■ 'Graham Thomas' *is a hardy climbing rose. Prune out diseased, dead, or damaged wood on climbing roses in February.*

PLANT

ANNUALS

Start annuals that need a lot of time under lights, such as pansies, calendula, violas, petunias, snapdragons, and lobelia. To determine the exact timing of seeds, consult the seed packet for the days to maturity and count back from your area's average last frost date.

Keep the soil and seeds gently warm until the seedlings germinate. This can be anything from a special seed-starting mat to a heating pad to the top of the clothes dryer or refrigerator. Once the seedlings germinate, move them under lights for about 16 hours a day and water from the bottom. For lights, see Here's How to Set Up Lights for Seed Starting, page 23.

EDIBLES

If you garden in the southern regions of Indiana or Illinois, start seedlings of cabbage, cauliflower, eggplant, and leeks in February. If you live farther north or in most of Ohio, you may want to wait until March. Check your average last frost date and consult the seed packet to be sure.

HERE'S HOW

TO USE SEED-STARTING DISCS

■ *Peat or coir discs combine pot and growing medium. To use them: 1. Soak the discs until they expand into moist blocks of growing medium. 2. Place the blocks in a shallow, waterproof container. Use a pencil or chopstick to make holes. 3. Plant seeds at the depth recommended on the seed packet. Water from the bottom.*

CARE

ALL

Sharpen garden tools such as pruners, loppers, shovels, and hoes if you haven't done it already. See Care/January, page 24.

Inflate the tire of the wheelbarrow and the garden cart.

Inspect structures such as compost bins, trellises, cold frames, and sheds to determine if they need repair or replacement.

Stock up on floating row covers or other tools for getting an early start on the season.

Get a tetanus booster if you haven't had one for a while; in a few weeks you'll be digging around in dirt.

Birds are starting to arrive and scout for nesting sites. Clean out birdhouses and hang them up again.

BULBS

Watch for the first blooming snowdrops.

If you planted hardy bulbs such as narcissus or crocuses in containers for forcing (see Plant/Bulbs, October, page 145) and they have chilled for at least 12 to 14 weeks, move them into a sunny window in a cool room indoors and start watering

■ *Snowdrops may bloom in February or March, depending on the weather.*

■ *Service your lawnmower to prepare for the mowing season. Change the air filter (top) and replace the oil (bottom).*

them. For outdoor display, move them out into a sheltered spot in the sunshine toward the end of the month and start watering.

LAWNS

Sharpen the lawnmower blade or have it done by a hardware store or repair shop. Tune up the engine of a gas mower: Install a new air filter and a new spark plug. Drain the oil from the crankcase and replace it with fresh oil.

Check the tires and replace them if they are worn. Check the entire machine for loose parts.

Your owner's manual should have complete instructions for maintaining your lawnmower. If you have any doubt, take the machine to a repair shop.

PERENNIALS

Cut back clumps of ornamental grasses to within 1 inch of the ground. Use a hand pruner for small clumps and a power hedge trimmer for larger clumps. As you cut, note if the clump has gotten thin in the middle and will need to be divided in March.

Late winter weather in the Midwest can be erratic, with many cycles of freezing and thawing that can heave plants out of the ground. Check garden beds for pop-ups and gently press them back into the ground. Spread mulch to prevent further heaving. Soil that has recently thawed can be soggy and easily compacted, so avoid walking on it if you can.

ROSES

Cut out diseased, dead, or damaged wood on ramblers and climbing roses.

SHRUBS

February, while much of the winter is over but trees and shrubs still are dormant, is prime time for pruning.

VINES

Prune wisteria heavily now to keep it under control and encourage blooming. Trim the side branches back to two or three buds, and prune as needed to form a good structure that is well supported by the arbor or pergola. Plan to prune this vine again in fall.

Prune back summer- and fall-blooming clematis vines. Leave a few stems on the trellis and cut the rest back to 12 inches. These types of clematis bloom on new wood that they will produce this year. It's especially important to cut sweet autumn clematis (*Clematis terniflora*) back *hard*, because it can be rampant. Remove all the old growth from the trellis.

HERE'S HOW

TO PRUNE A DORMANT SHRUB

Pruning dormant shrubs in winter, roughly between Thanksgiving and the first of March, will steer their growth in the coming year. This is the time for selective pruning, using hand pruners rather than power hedge clippers. With the leaves gone, it's easier to see the structure of a shrub and make better decisions. The cold means there's less risk of spreading diseases or insect eggs. You still need to use sharp pruners and disinfect them between plants with a disinfectant spray that has benzalkonium chloride as an active ingredient or with alcohol wipes. Avoid using a bleach solution; it's less effective.

If you prune spring-blooming plants such as lilacs, viburnums, and forsythia in winter, you'll be pruning out branches that already have flower buds, so you will reduce this spring's display. It won't hurt the shrub, but to maximize flowering, wait to prune those shrubs until just after they bloom.

You can prune most shrubs that flower in midsummer or autumn because they have not yet formed their flower buds. Start by pruning out all dead wood. Dead wood is often dark and brittle. If you scratch a small branch with your thumbnail, live wood will show a layer of green just under the bark. Dead wood won't.

Now consider which major branches you want to keep and which you ought to remove. If two branches are rubbing or crossing, remove one. Take out branches that are broken, kinky, or going in the wrong direction. Remove more of the larger, old branches than young ones, while keeping an attractive, symmetrical scaffolding of older branches. Younger growth is more vigorous and usually produces more blooms. Cut side branches back to just above the attachment to the main branch. Cut large, old stems 1 or 2 inches above the ground.

To reduce the overall size of a shrub without marring its natural shape, look for the longest branches. Follow a long branch back to where a shorter stem branches off and cut the large stem just above the short one. Some shrubs, such as forsythia, spirea, and smooth hydrangea, are mostly long canes with few side branches. Remove the oldest, thickest, longest canes right down to the ground.

Step back often and assess your progress. When the shrub is shaped up, stop. Usually, take out only one-third of a shrub's growth in any one year.

Some severely overgrown and tangled shrubs such as spirea can be renewed by cutting all the stems back to 1 to 2 above the ground. Prune out any dead or broken branches on small trees. However, only prune trees if you can do so from the ground. For larger branches or larger trees, call in a professional arborist who is trained and insured against the risk of working above the ground. To find a certified professional arborist, visit the International Society of Arboriculture at www.treesaregood.org.

■ *To renew a shrub and promote new, vigorous growth, selectively remove no more than one-third of the oldest stems each season. Keep an attractive, symmetrical form. To rejuvenate a severely overgrown, tangled shrub, try cutting back all the stems near the ground.*

Prune repeat-blooming clematis lightly, just to remove dead wood and open the plant a bit. Many of these vines bloom on both old and new wood, so pruning hard now will remove too many flower buds.

Wait to prune a spring-blooming clematis vine until June or July, after it finishes flowering.

Prune a grapevine back really hard, removing 80 to 90 percent of its growth but leaving some new shoots. This will expose the fruit-bearing stems to sunlight so the grapes can ripen (if the vine is in full sun). A grapevine grows fast, gets very heavy, and, like a wisteria, needs an *extremely sturdy* support.

Check the trellis or arbor that supports a clematis, climbing hydrangea, or other perennial vine. Make any necessary repairs before the new growth begins.

TREES
Have a professional arborist prune trees that need it. Don't prune trees that already have running sap, such as dogwood, maple, walnut, and river birch. Wait to prune them until June, after their spring burst of growth.

■ *Prune* Clematis jackmanii *and other summer- and fall-blooming varieties of clematis in late winter. Leave a few stems on the trellis and cut the rest back to 12 inches.*

WATER

HOUSEPLANTS
Begin watering houseplants a little more frequently toward the end of the month as they begin their active season of growth.

TREES & SHRUBS
Keep watering any evergreens that are planted in outside containers.

FERTILIZE

HOUSEPLANTS
Toward the end of February, start fertilizing houseplants each time you water with a balanced fertilizer at *half* the strength recommended on the label. Plants need more nutrients as they grow more actively.

PROBLEM-SOLVE

PERENNIALS & GROUNDCOVERS
Evergreen groundcovers along sidewalks or the driveway may show dried-out foliage from salt damage. Consider replacing them with relatively salt-tolerant plants such as creeping juniper, ornamental grasses, daylilies, or sedum.

SHRUBS
If you have a shrub that was infested last year with insects whose eggs might be overwintering, apply dormant oil to smother the eggs. Apply it when the temperature is predicted to stay above 40 degrees Fahrenheit for a day or more so that the oil will dry on the bark without freezing. As with any control, use dormant oil only if you have first identified the problem for certain.

March

In March, the growing season arrives, but it doesn't step in sweetly. March is the adolescence of the year, the stormy transition between winter and spring, swinging tempestuously between balmy and freezing. Crocuses are blooming, but blizzards are still in play.

The difference in climate between the southern and northern parts of Illinois, Indiana, and Ohio is especially stark in March. The growing season ranges from 160 days long in some suburbs of Chicago to 200 days long at the southern tip of Illinois. Since the length of the season is influenced by wind patterns, altitude, lake-effect snow, and other factors, it's crucial to learn the average last frost date in your own area. But bear in mind that those dates are averages—meaning that in some years the last frost comes weeks later.

Warm spells that bring magnolias into bloom have hazards. The first days of stooping and lugging can be hard on muscles you may not have used much since November, so start small and pause often to enjoy the new birdsong.

Early warm days also can push trees and shrubs to leaf out early, quickly using up the reserves of water and food stored in fall. If a warm spell doesn't also bring rain, be prepared to water.

All too often, the warmth is followed by a snowstorm or a serious freeze. Those early-blooming magnolias may lose all their blossoms to a freeze overnight.

Some gardening tasks need to be finished early in March, before plants have come fully out of their winter dormancy. Others need to wait until the soil is thawed and dry enough to work. It's important not to rush, because digging in wet soil or even walking on it can pack it down, squeezing out the vital air spaces between soil particles.

Before you get too busy, finish up your planning. And resolve to keep records of plants, projects, and weather this year in a notebook or even online where you easily can include photos. Having a record of your garden all through the season will help you improve it year by year.

PLAN

ALL

Keep an eye on forecasts for temperature, rain, and snowfall through this volatile month to time your garden tasks.

As you prepare to start working the garden, decide whether to buy soil amendments and landscape materials such as topsoil, compost, and mulch in bags or in bulk. For small projects, these materials are easiest to handle in bags. If you need a large quantity, though, it will be cheaper to buy in bulk from a landscape supply company or through a good garden center. The material will be delivered by trunk, and you must have a place to dump it.

Most companies have a variety of products to fill raised beds or improve soil, including compost, mushroom compost, composted cow manure, and mixtures that also include topsoil. Explain your purpose and ask which product is best for that use.

BULBS

Snowdrops and crocuses will be among the first bulbs to bloom, with many more to follow. Take lots of photos and notes of the spring bulb garden to remind yourself of bare spots or gaps in the succession of boom. They will be useful in August or September, when you are ordering bulbs for fall planting.

Don't worry if a late freeze comes after bulbs have sprouted. Usually, a freeze only damages the leaves of tulips and daffodils and will not keep them from blooming.

CONTAINERS

Plan containers. Think about how many pots you can keep watered and how much potting mix they will require. Choose pots that harmonize or contrast with your deck furniture or architecture. Think about which houseplants can become part of your container plantings and how many plants you will need to buy.

GROUNDCOVERS

Research groundcovers carefully to avoid planting any that are too aggressive for your situation. Groundcovers get that name because many will

■ *Pachysandra is a well-behaved groundcover that will not swiftly spread out of bounds. Avoid too-aggressive groundcovers.*

quickly cover the ground. In shade, English ivy, myrtle, and *Aegopodium podagraria* (known as bishop's weed, goutweed, or snow-on-the-mountain) will out-compete most other plants. Better-behaved groundcovers include ferns, wild ginger, pachysandra, and epimedium.

To estimate the number of plants you will need, see Plan/Annuals in May, page 76.

EDIBLES

If you have an established vegetable garden, consider not tilling it this year. Instead, clean up the top growth of last year's plants, topdress with compost, and then go ahead and plant. By not tilling, you avoid bringing buried weed seeds to the surface where they can germinate and you don't

HERE'S HOW

TO DECIDE HOW MUCH MATERIAL TO BUY

A little arithmetic will help you determine how much compost, topsoil, or mulch you need and whether you should buy it in bags or in bulk. Most bags contain 2 cubic feet. Bulk goods are sold by the cubic yard. To compare, you will need to convert measurements between inches, feet, and yards.

It isn't necessary to be accurate to the inch when taking measurements, and when buying soil amendments, it's always best to round up to the nearest bag or cubic yard.

Start by calculating the area of your bed or lawn in square inches (for formulas, see Here's How to Calculate Area, p. 164). To convert square feet to square inches, multiply by 144.

To get the volume, multiply the area in inches by the planned depth in inches. For perennial beds, mulch should be about 1 inch deep. In shrub beds and around trees, plan on 2 to 3 inches. For compost to dig into the soil of vegetable or perennial beds, plan on a layer 2 to 3 inches deep. To top-dress lawns by raking in a layer of compost, figure 1 inch.

For example, suppose you plan to spread compost 2 inches deep on a bed that is 10 feet × 15 feet. Multiply 10 feet by 15 feet to get an area of 150 feet. Multiply by 144 to convert to an area of 21,600 square inches.

Multiply that area by the depth of 2 inches to get a volume of 43,200 cubic inches.

There are 1,728 cubic inches in a cubic foot. So to convert the volume in cubic inches to cubic feet, divide 43,200 by 1,728. The volume is 25 cubic feet. Since bagged compost usually comes in 2-cubic-foot bags, divide by 2 to determine how many bags are necessary. For this project, the result is 12.5; round up and buy 13 bags.

If you have a large project, it will be cheaper to order in bulk by the cubic yard. Suppose, for example, that you have three beds, each 10 × 15 feet. Their total area will be 64,800 square inches, and a 2-inch-deep layer of compost will have a volume of 129,600 cubic inches.

There are 46,656 cubic inches in a cubic yard. Divide the total volume in cubic inches, 129,600, by 46,656 to get 2.8 cubic yards. Round up and order 3 cubic yards.

Suppliers can help you determine how much to order, as long as you have your garden's measurements.

disturb the structure of the soil. You'll have less weeding to do, and over time, each year's mulch and plant roots and the compost you spread will break down and enrich the soil.

Get a soil test if you didn't do it in autumn. It's especially important to test for lead and other heavy metals in areas where you plan to grow food. (See Here's How to Get a Soil Test, page 143.)

Plan for support for climbing or vining crops such as tomatoes and beans. Make sure the trellises, stakes, cages, pyramids, or other supports you buy or build are sturdy.

In a small garden, think about where you could grow some crops by training them up against fences or trellises. (Don't try it with heavy fruits such as pumpkins or Hubbard squash.) Remember that even if tomatoes, squash, or herbs are trained vertically or grown in wall pots, they still need full sun.

Check out the frames of raised beds and repair them if necessary. The corners are the weakest points. They may need reinforcing if the freezing and thawing of winter has worked them loose. (See Edibles/January, page 24, for details on raised beds.)

■ *In a small garden, explore possibilities for growing vegetables and annuals vertically, either in wall planters or by training them up a trellis. The heavier the fruit, the stronger the trellis or cage needs to be. Really heavy fruits, such as watermelons and squash, are best grown on the ground.*

■ *Some vegetable varieties, such as 'Basket Boy' tomato, are bred to be compact for growing in containers.*

If you don't have raised beds within frames, you can get many of their benefits by creating simple mounded rectangles of topsoil and compost. You will need enough soil and compost so that your mounds can be 6 inches high in the center. Make them no more than 4 feet wide so you can reach crops without walking on the beds, and leave paths in between that are wide enough for a wheelbarrow.

Containers can make vegetable gardening possible in city gardens. Growing vegetables takes good-sized pots; for a full-sized tomato plant, choose a container at least as large as a 5-gallon bucket. Make sure any container you use has holes in the bottom for drainage. Plan for support for vining plants such as tomatoes, beans, and cucumbers. See Plant/Containers in May, page 81.

Sub-irrigated containers, which have a reservoir of water that is wicked up into the soil, can be convenient for urban gardeners who have little space or don't plan to grow many plants. They require less frequent watering than regular pots and can produce higher yields. Several brands are commercially available, or you can find many plans on the Internet for making your own.

It's crucial for the plants' roots in soil to sit above, not in, the water reservoir, and for the reservoir to have an overflow opening that will drain away surplus water. I use sub-irrigated containers—both commercially made and do-it-yourself—to grow tomatoes, peppers, herbs, and other crops on a third-floor balcony.

LAWNS

In shady places where grass was thin last year, consider replacing it. No kind of grass will ever thrive in deep shade. Under trees and shrubs, spread a wide circle of wood-chip mulch, or plant shade-tolerant groundcovers such as ferns or wild ginger.

Shopping for a new mower? Make sure it is a mulching model that will chop up grass clippings to nourish the lawn. For smaller lawns, consider an electric or rechargeable model to reduce emissions.

PERENNIALS

Browse catalogs and websites and consider new possibilities for perennial beds. Make sure the plants will fit your soil, light, and weather conditions and will suit your purposes in the garden. See Best Plants for Special Situations, page 173.

In shade, I like monkshood, goatsbeard, wild geraniums, and columbine, especially the native salmon-and-yellow *Aquilegia canadensis*. Coral bells, or heuchera, have mounds of interesting leaves all season and delicate flowers in late spring. My shady garden is full of hostas of all sizes as well as lungwort, brunnera, bergenia, lamium, and Canadian wild ginger, several kinds of ferns, and native sedges, including *Carex pensylvanica*.

I use many native plants because I like to provide plenty of bounty for native bees, birds, and other wildlife, but I'm not a purist.

ROSES

If you order dormant grafted bare-root roses, store them in a cool, dark, moist location until it is warm enough to plant them outdoors. Or store them outdoors, buried in mulch. Check them often, and if the buds begin to swell, pot them up and place them in a cool, well-lit area indoors. Wait to plant frost-tender roses outdoors until all danger of frost is past.

SHRUBS

Choose shrubs carefully to avoid creating future maintenance headaches. It's easy to be deceived by the small size of young shrubs sold in 2- or 3-gallon containers, but they will get bigger. The wrong shrub can become a pruning burden in just three or four years if it grows to impede a sidewalk or block a window. Check the plant tag for the mature size. Some varieties of the same species will grow two or three times as large as others.

Shrubs can live for a long time in the right place, so take care to invest in the right one. Your Extension office or a local botanical garden or arboretum may suggest suitable possibilities (see Resources, page 189).

HERE'S HOW

TO CHOOSE A POTTING MIX

Good potting mix should be lightweight and fluffy. It usually contains no actual dirt, which is why it is often called "soilless potting mix." Instead, it is a combination of compost; other organic matter such as sphagnum peat moss, coconut fiber (called "coir"), or leaf mold (decomposed leaves); and perlite, lightweight white pellets that store water but also improve drainage. Perlite is actually a volcanic glass that has been heated until it pops like popcorn and becomes full of air pockets.

Cheap potting soil is usually dense, heavy, and poor in quality.

Some potting mixes contain slow-release fertilizer. Avoid mixes that contain water-holding synthetic gels; research has shown they do not deliver more water to plants.

Potting mix doesn't need to be sterile, and in fact good mixes contain compost, full of beneficial microorganisms. But seed-starting mix (which usually has a finer texture) should always be sterile to deter fungus diseases that can kill tender seedlings.

You can reuse part of the potting mix in a container for one year if you mix it half-and-half with fresh mix. After the second year, discard it all and start fresh. Plants will have used up all its nutrients, and its texture will have broken down.

If you have had any disease problems with plants in a container, discard all the potting mix, wash and disinfect the container, and refill it with fresh potting mix.

To dispose of old potting mix, simply scatter it in the garden, where it will decompose, or use it to fill in divots or low places in the lawn. The white pellets of perlite will eventually break down too.

■ *Shade gardens often emphasize interesting leaves, such as those of Siberian bugloss* (brunnera), *left, coral bells* (heuchera), *middle, and lungwort* (pulmonaria), *right.*

■ *Yarrow, such as this* Achillea *'Coronation Gold', is an easy-to grow, drought-tolerant perennial for full sun.*

■ *Coneflowers* (Echinacea) *offer nectar to butterflies and seed to birds. The native species is a tall prairie plant, but more compact cultivars have been selected for gardens.*

■ *New England aster* (Symphyotrichum novae-angliae) *is a Midwest native that blooms in late summer to early fall.*

Consider planting native shrubs such as winterberry or chokeberry that have fruit to feed birds and other wildlife. To find out which shrubs are native to your area, see Resources, page 189.

As you shop for shrubs, look beyond blooms and think about interest in all four seasons. Seek out shrubs that flower in spring or summer but also have good fall color, such as black chokeberry, dwarf fothergilla, arrowwood viburnum, and ninebark, or interesting bark, such as oakleaf hydrangea and Virginia sweetspire.

TREES
If you had a tree removed over the winter—perhaps an ash that was killed by emerald ash borer—replant with a tree that is suitable for your site and conditions and will grow to be long-lived and resilient as the climate changes.

A tree is a long-term investment, so choosing the right one deserves some care and forethought. Make sure you get a species and cultivar that suits your conditions and needs and will not be too large when it is fully mature. Extension offices, a local botanical garden or arboretum, or a professional arborist can help. See Resources, page 189.

It's nearly always best to plant a tree when it is younger and therefore smaller, rather than going for the instant gratification of a larger tree. A younger tree will suffer less shock when

To determine whether the soil is dry enough to work, squeeze a handful in your fist and then open your hand. If the soil holds together in a sticky mass, it's still too wet. If it cracks and begins to crumble, it's dry enough to work.

ANNUALS

Toward the end of March in the southern regions or early to mid-April in the north, once the ground has thawed and drained, harden off the transplants of cool-season annuals you started indoors such as pansies, pot marigolds *(Calendula)*, snapdragons, and alyssum before planting them outdoors in sunny spots.

Pansies can handle a mild frost but not a hard freeze. Buy cool-season annuals such as pansies and snapdragons in flower, not bud; buds won't open quickly in cool weather.

Continue to sow seeds for annuals under lights according to the timing suggested for each variety on the seed packet.

In early March, depending on your local frost date, sow seeds that need about six weeks growing under lights before the last risk of frost, such as coleus, cleome, dusty miller, nicotiana, pinks, ageratum, verbena, salvia, statice, and petunias.

■ *Shrubs can be bought three ways: bare root (left), container grown (center), and balled and burlapped (right). Larger trees are sold balled and burlapped, although smaller specimens may come in large pots. Balled-and-burlapped trees and shrubs can be very heavy and hard to handle. Roses and shrubs are often sold bare-root by mail order because they are cheap to ship; keep the roots moist and plant them promptly.*

it is transplanted, especially if it was grown in a container. Research has shown that a smaller tree will become established faster and will catch up to a larger, more stressed tree within a few years. It's also much cheaper, and you likely will be able to plant it yourself.

Before you dig to plant a tree—or for any other major project—call your local utility company to have underground utility lines located and marked. Don't risk accidentally damaging a hidden electrical, water, sewer, or gas line.

PLANT

ALL

Wait to dig, till, plant, or work the ground until the soil has thawed and thoroughly drained from melting snow. Digging, tilling, or even walking on wet soil can ruin its structure and texture, packing it down and squeezing shut the air spaces that are vital to plants' roots.

■ *Buy pansies that are already in bloom, because the flowers won't develop much in cool spring weather. Later in the season, buy flowering plants in bud.*

TO HARDEN OFF

Young plants that you have started from seed or bought from a garden center need to be gradually accustomed to the elements before you plant them outside in spring.

Harden plants off by placing them outdoors for a few hours each day and bringing them into shelter, such as an unheated garage, during the night. Over the course of a week, gradually leave them outside a little longer each day so they become accustomed to outdoor wind and sun.

If you have a cold frame, place the transplants inside it for a few days, with the lid open during the day and closed at night or during cold snaps.

■ *Use a cold frame to grow seedlings or to harden off transplants before planting them outside. Be sure to open the cold frame during the day so too much heat doesn't build up inside.*

The second or third week of March is a good time to start seeds indoors for annual vines, such as morning glories, moonflower, and annual sweet peas. If you start them too early, they will climb all over before it's time to plant them outdoors.

Toward the end of the month, prepare the soil for cold-tolerant annual flowers that you will direct-sow in their places in the garden in late March or early April, such as sweet alyssum, larkspur, and snapdragons.

Wait until after your last frost date to direct-sow most other annuals.

BULBS

If you have sunny window space or a light setup indoors, you can give a head start to tender bulbs, tubers, and corms such as cannas, elephant ears, dahlias, tuberous begonias, caladiums, crocosmia, and agapanthus.

Four to six weeks before your last frost date, pot them up in well-drained potting mix. Water them and place them under lights or in a sunny south-facing window. Keep the soil moist until you move them to the garden once the soil is warm and all danger of frost is past.

EDIBLES

Once the soil in the garden is dry enough to work, prepare the vegetable garden. Remove old mulch and any remaining plants from last year and put them in the compost, except for any plants that showed signs of disease. If you planted a cover crop of "green manure," such as rye or clover, in fall, mow it before it sets seed and till it in.

In existing beds whose soil was well-amended to begin with, top-dress with compost and rake it in lightly. There is no need to till it deeply into the soil. Deep tilling will bring weed seeds to the surface where they can sprout.

In new beds, spread a layer of organic matter such as compost, shredded leaves, mushroom compost, or well-rotted cow manure on the soil at least 2 to 3 inches thick and dig it in to a depth of about a foot.

In existing raised beds, spread 2 inches of organic matter such as compost on the surface and scratch it in lightly. It is not necessary to dig it in, as long as you have been adding organic matter every year.

Fill new raised beds with a mix of two-thirds topsoil and one-third compost, or order an appropriate product from a landscape supplier (see Plan/All, above).

Rake the surface smooth. In row gardens, mark out the rows.

As soon as you can work the ground and amend the soil, in mid-March to mid-April, set out

In new beds, spread a 2" to 3" layer of compost or other organic matter and dig it in to a depth of about a foot. In established beds, topdress with compost and scratch it in lightly.

After you dig compost into a new bed, rake it smooth before planting.

Lightweight, translucent row covers that buffer plants from the cold can give you a head start on the season. You can use hoops to support a cover, like the one that shields these cabbage plants. Or "float" it—lay it right over the plants.

transplants of broccoli, cabbage, leeks, and onions, as well as onion sets.

You can start sowing seed for cool-season edibles in the ground in mid-March in southern areas and toward the middle of the month or early April in the north. For general help with timing, consult the Spring Vegetable Timing Chart on page 165, but consult the seed packet to be sure.

In southern regions, you can sow seeds directly outdoors in late March or early April for endive, lettuce, spinach, turnips, chives, dill, fennel, mint, oregano, tarragon, sweet woodruff, and thyme.

Plant rhubarb and asparagus in late March or early April. These are perennial plants, so locate them where you will not be rotating crops and they can stay in place year after year. That's usually at the side of the garden, but in full sun.

Start tomato and pepper seeds toward the end of the month, depending on your local frost-free date, following the directions in Plant/Annuals. For general help in deciding when to sow seeds indoors and out, see the Spring Vegetable Timing Chart, page 165.

Tomatoes need about six to eight weeks to reach a good size before being transplanted to the garden in mid- to late May.

In late March or early April, or as soon as the soil is workable and well prepared, sow seeds of peas, lettuce, mustard, turnips, radishes, and spinach out in the garden. Plant onion transplants or sets (starter onions). For general timing help, see the Spring Vegetable Timing Chart on page 165, but check the seed packet to be sure.

Toward the end of the month, harden off broccoli, cabbage, collard, and leek plants that you started in February with a few days in the cold frame. Then plant them out in the garden.

Outdoors, begin sowing carrots, lettuce, dill, and parsley in the ground toward the end of March.

Sow seed potatoes in hills of very well-drained soil that has been amended with plenty of organic matter such as shredded leaves. Drainage is the top

TO RESEED OR RESOD A LAWN

The key to successfully establishing grass from seed or sod is preparing the soil first. Grass will grow best in soil that is not packed down, so water and air flow freely, and that contains plenty of organic matter.

To reseed a large area: Remove any dead grass from the area by pulling it up, slicing beneath it with a sharp spade, or renting a turf cutter. Break up packed-down soil. Till a 2-inch layer of compost into the top 4 to 6 inches of soil and rake it smooth.

Sprinkle seed as directed on the package. Rake lightly with a spring rake to make sure each seed is in contact with the soil.

Sprinkle compost or peat moss over the seed for mulch to hold in moisture. Compost is more nourishing than peat moss.

Water gently and keep the seed moist, watering at least once a day, until it sprouts, which can take two weeks.

To reseed a small area: Dig in compost and then rake it smooth if you can. At a minimum, use a stiff rake to rough up the soil in the bare areas. Topdress with compost. Level low areas with a mixture of compost and topsoil or with old potting mix from last year's containers. Apply seed as noted.

To resod: Prepare the soil by tilling in a 2-inch layer of compost 6 inches deep. Sod laid without this preparation is likely to fail because its roots will not be able to penetrate the earth.

Be sure to buy sod with moist roots and keep it watered until you can lay it. Stagger strips of sod like bricks in a wall so the end seams don't line up. Water again.

New sod has scarcely any roots, so it will need to be watered much more frequently than existing grass until it begins to send roots down into the soil. Water it daily for at least two weeks.

■ *When you lay sod and cut it to shape, be sure to stagger the seams. Plan to water sod often for several weeks until the plants become established; new sod has almost no roots.*

issue for potatoes. They will even grow directly in shredded leaves and do well in large containers in good potting mix.

LAWNS

Once the soil has dried out from winter, in March in southern areas or in early April toward the north, rake debris from the lawn with a spring rake and overseed, if you did not in early fall. Scatter compost liberally over the lawn and rake it so it falls between the grass blades. You also can overseed and spread compost after core-aerating (see Care/Lawn).

If you have damaged or bare areas, repair them now. First, try to determine why the grass failed: Traffic? Pet damage? Standing water? If there is an underlying problem, correct it before making repairs.

Patching with sod is fast, but reseeding with the right mix of grass species will produce a stronger and more resilient lawn. The technique is the same whether you are replacing an entire lawn or only damaged patches.

PERENNIALS & GROUNDCOVERS

Wait to do any work in perennial beds until the ground has thawed and dried out. See Plant/All.

It's better to amend the soil in an entire perennial bed than to add compost to individual planting holes; if you improve just the hole, the plant's roots will stay where the soil is especially rich and not spread wide.

You can begin planting hardy perennials, including groundcovers, in well-drained, well-prepared soil once it is workable. For suggestions, see Plan/Perennials. Space them generously to allow for their mature size; you can fill in between with annuals or containers until they grow large enough to fill the space. As you plant, be careful not to disturb other perennials that may be slow to emerge.

When the new growth of perennials is 4 to 6 inches high—often toward the end of March in southern regions of Indiana and Illinois, or in April toward the north—begin to divide and transplant summer- and fall-blooming plants, except peonies and bearded irises. Plants to divide in spring include summer-blooming perennials such as hosta, yarrow, daisies, monarda, aster, sedum, rudbeckia, and coreopsis and warm-weather grasses such as miscanthus, panicum, and pennisetum.

To divide perennials, dig all around with a sharp spade and gently lever the plant out of the ground. Be careful not to slice or step on nearby plants. Gently pull the rootball apart, or use a sharp knife or the sharp shovel to divide the rootball into two or three parts, following natural divisions if they are apparent. Keep the roots moist and transplant the divisions as soon as possible.

HERE'S HOW

TO CHOOSE LAWN GRASS

In Ohio, Indiana, and Illinois, cool-season grasses—meaning species that grow most vigorously in spring and fall and slow down in summer—are best.

Kentucky bluegrass, which has a rich green color and fine texture, is the most popular grass in the region, but it is *not* the most durable, drought tolerant, or resilient. It is better in a mix with other species that are more rugged, such as tall fescues, which have a coarser texture but are tougher, or perennial ryegrass, which greens up quickly. A good mix of grass seed includes several species, at least one of which is likely to do well in most spots.

All turfgrass needs full sun to thrive and will be thinner in shady areas. However, some species, such as fine fescues, can tolerate a bit more shade. If your yard includes both sunny and shady areas, a sun/shade mix will be most versatile. Still, don't expect any grass to thrive in deep shade, such as under trees or on the north side of buildings.

■ *When planting a bare-root rose or other shrub, make a mound of soil in the hole and spread the roots over it. The root flare should be at or above the level of the soil once you backfill the hole. When planting a grafted rose, make sure the graft union will be above soil level.*

When dividing a plant, choose the strongest-looking parts of the plant and discard the rest. Ornamental grasses or Siberian iris are often dead in the center of a clump. Discard the dead part and transplant only the vigorous newer growth from the perimeter.

Accept passalong plants from friends and neighbors warily. Gardeners often give away plants that are abundant because they are aggressive spreaders. Research a gift plant to make sure it is well behaved before you add it to your garden.

ROSES

Hardy own-root shrub roses can be planted in the ground with other shrubs once the soil is thawed, dry, and workable. Wait to plant grafted or frost-tender roses such as hybrid teas until April or May, after your last frost date. Keep the roots of all bare-root plants moist until you can plant them, and plant as soon as possible.

To plant a bare-root rose, first soak the roots in warm water for at least an hour. Dig as wide a hole as possible and amend its soil with plenty of compost. Make a mound of soil in the center of the hole and set the plant on it, spreading out the roots. The crown of the plant should sit at the level of the surrounding soil. Backfill the hole, water well, and spread mulch.

SHRUBS

Plant bare-root shrubs as you would hardy roses (see Roses, above).

Transplant a shrub from one location in your yard to another as soon as the soil is dry enough to dig, ideally while it is still dormant. Dormancy will buffer the plant from the shock of transplanting. Since it will lose most of its root system when it is dug up, transplanting stresses a tree or shrub.

Water the shrub the day before you dig it up. Select the new site and prepare a wide, shallow hole. When you dig up the shrub, keep as large a rootball as you can (the soil will be heavy) and try to hold it together while you move the plant. For a large shrub, set it on a spread-out tarp and wrap the tarp around the rootball to hold it together before you move it with a wheelbarrow. Replant the shrub in its new site as soon as possible.

If a shrub is large and overgrown, it may be easier to remove it and replace it with a vigorous new plant than to try to transplant it.

Container-grown shrubs become widely available in March and can be planted as soon as the soil is drained and workable. Since they do not lose most of their roots, they usually establish well if you care for them properly after planting.

TREES

There are two good times to plant a tree: spring and fall. Summer is too hot and stressful for young trees. Plant most trees from late March or early April—as soon as the soil is dry enough to dig—through June, or wait until September or October. It's best to plant evergreens in spring so they have the entire season to develop a good root system to get them through the next winter.

Most homeowners will plant trees or shrubs that come in containers and are small and light enough to be transported in a car.

Larger trees will be sold balled-and-burlapped (B&B), meaning that they were grown in the field and then dug up. The rootball is wrapped in burlap to hold it together during transport.

B&B trees can weigh several hundred pounds and usually are professionally planted.

VINES

Plant woody vines such as climbing hydrangea, clematis, and Japanese wisteria as soon as the ground can be worked. When you plant them, have a plan for their support. Wisteria, especially, will grow into a large, very heavy vine that needs a very strong, permanent trellis or arbor.

CARE

ALL

Step carefully in the garden to avoid compacting wet soil. Two foam kneeling pads make good temporary stepping stones.

ANNUALS

Thin out surplus seedlings that are growing under lights. In individual pots where you sowed two seeds, remove the smaller, weaker seedling.

If you sowed seeds in flats, transplant seedlings to individual pots when they have their first set of true leaves and are about 1½ to 2 inches tall. Using a plastic knife or other delicate tool, prick out the strongest-looking seedlings, those that are upright and a healthy green, and transplant them to containers with moist potting mix.

If seedlings start to stretch, pinch them back to encourage side branching in order to produce plants that are bushier and thus will have more flowers.

If you are starting seeds on a windowsill or in uneven light, regularly rotate the pots so that they do not stretch toward the light.

Water seedlings from the bottom to deter fungus diseases.

BULBS

Don't be concerned if early warm spells push daffodils and other spring-blooming bulbs to sprout. The first part of the plant to appear is the foliage, not the flower buds. A frost might nip the edges of the leaves but is unlikely to affect the blooms unless it comes very late in the season.

HERE'S HOW

TO PLANT GROUNDCOVERS

■ *When planting groundcovers, first amend the bed and rake it smooth.*

■ *Lay the plants out in their pots. A staggered arrangement will fill in more quickly.*

■ *Gently remove each plant from its pot. Rough up the roots a bit around the outside of the root mass to encourage them to branch out. Set each plant in the soil at the same level as it was in the pot. Firm the soil gently around each plant. Mulch.*

■ *Water well. Check the soil moisture daily and water regularly until the plants are well established.*

HERE'S HOW

TO PLANT A TREE OR SHRUB

The most common mistake in planting trees and shrubs is planting too deep. The hole should be wide and shallow, like a soup bowl, not a bucket. Roots grow sideways, not down.

FOR A CONTAINER-GROWN TREE OR SHRUB

1. Find the trunk flare—the place where the trunk of a tree or the stems of a shrub widen out to form roots. In some containers, the flare may have become covered with soil.

2. Measure the rootball's depth from the flare to the bottom of the pot. Measure the diameter of the pot.

3. Dig a hole that is at least two or, ideally, three times as wide as the rootball, with sloping sides. At the bottom, it should be only as deep as the rootball, so the trunk flare will sit at or slightly above the level of the surrounding soil. To check the depth, lay your shovel across the hole and measure down with a yardstick or tape measure. Dump the soil you remove on a tarp to make backfilling easier.

4. Gently remove the plant from the pot. You may need to roll the pot on the ground to loosen the rootball or cut the pot. Rough up the roots around the rootball with your fingers or trim 1 inch of soil and roots from the sides and bottom to encourage the roots to branch out.

5. Mound some soil in the bottom of the hole and set the plant on the mound. Check to make sure the trunk flare is at least an inch higher than the surrounding soil (the plant will settle and end up a little lower).

6. Check from all angles to make sure the plant is straight. Refill the hole halfway with the same soil you removed. Gently press the soil in place without stomping on it, making sure the plant stays straight. Finish filling the hole but do not cover the trunk flare. If you have soil left over, spread it evenly over the area around the plant rather than mounding it against the tree's trunk.

7. Water thoroughly. A tree will need several gallons, distributed around the rootball.

8. Spread wood-chip or shredded-wood mulch in a wide, even layer covering the entire hole and farther out if possible. The mulch should be 3 to 4 inches deep. Pull the mulch an inch or two away from the bark of the trunk or stems; piling mulch against the bark invites animal damage and disease.

FOR A BALLED-AND-BURLAPPED TREE

1. Enlist at least one other person to help.

2. Handle the tree carefully, lifting it by the wire basket around the rootball and never by the trunk. Work together while lifting. Once the tree is out of the truck, move it to the planting site with a cart or wheelbarrow rather than dragging it.

3. Loosen the burlap around the trunk to find the trunk flare, which may be buried in burlap and soil. Measure the rootball and dig a wide, shallow hole as described above.

4. Working together, gently rock the burlapped tree into the hole and move the rootball into position. Check to see that the tree is straight from all angles. Make sure the trunk flare is at or above soil level. Pack a few shovels full of soil around the bottom of the rootball to hold it steady.

5. Using wire cutters, cut away as much of the wire basket as you can reach and remove it from the hole. Using a knife or old scissors, cut away and remove as much of the burlap as you can reach, as well as any string or rope.

6. Double-check that the tree is straight, and then backfill, water, and mulch.

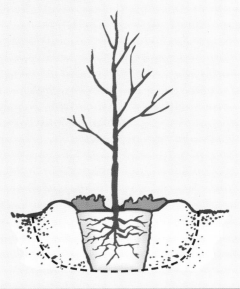

Check tender bulbs, corms, and tubers such as dahlias, cannas, and tuberous begonias that you have stored over winter. Discard any soft or moldy ones. Divide tubers so each has one eye and a piece of stem. If you plan to plant them in the ground after the soil has warmed, store them again. To pot them up for a head start, see Plant/Bulbs, page 46.

EDIBLES

For care of vegetable seedlings, see Care/Annuals, Water/Annuals, and Fertilize/Annuals.

Pull any remaining mulch away from vegetable beds to allow the increasing sun from longer days to warm the soil. Soil will warm up faster if you cover it with black plastic (because dark colors absorb light). You can save old mulch for later or add it to the compost pile.

Think about how you will support vine plants such as pole beans, cucumbers, and tomatoes. If necessary, build trellises or pyramids. Make them sturdy; plants will be heavy by harvest time.

Prune raspberries early in March before buds swell. Remove all short, weak, dead, or damaged canes,

■ *Place tomato cages and other supports early in the season.*

leaving six to eight canes per plant. For everbearing raspberries, leave most of the first-year canes, which will bear the first crop.

Be prepared to protect plants against late freezes in March and April. Floating row cover—a lightweight permeable fabric—can be simply pinned over young crops to fend off a couple of degrees of frost. Early crops such as spinach often are started in hoop houses of row cover stretched over wire or bamboo hoops.

An ancient form of protection is the cloche, a glass bell jar placed over a single plant during a cold night. It must be removed in the day or else heat will accumulate inside and cook the plant.

You can make a simple cloche by cutting off the bottom of a plastic milk jug. Leave the lid off for ventilation. Hold it in place by pushing a stick down through the spout into the soil. The translucent plastic will filter out some light, so don't leave the cloche on too long.

GROUNDCOVERS

Mow or cut back groundcovers to remove winter-browned foliage.

Clip the edges of groundcover beds and edge the adjoining lawn with a sharp spade to keep both the grass and the groundcover in their places.

In groundcover beds, prune out all dead and damaged stems. Pull up spreading groundcovers from areas where they are not welcome.

HOUSEPLANTS

Pinch back houseplants as needed to keep their growth compact. Make more plants by rooting the cuttings: trim the stem ends just below a leaf, stick them in pots of moist potting mix, and keep them under lights. Many houseplants will even root in a jar of water on the windowsill.

You can use the rooted cuttings in the shade garden in summer, as you would annuals.

As days get longer and the sunlight gets stronger, move sensitive plants such as African violets away from a south-facing window so their leaves are not scorched. Rotate your houseplants regularly so all sides are exposed to the sun and the growth is even.

Check houseplants for signs of fertilizer buildup. If you see a crust of white or yellowish crystals or powder around the holes of the pot, put it in the kitchen sink and flush it with plain water. Repot the plant if necessary. See Here's How to Repot a Houseplant, page 88.

While you're at it, wash off the leaves with plain water to remove built-up dust. Or wipe them with a moist cloth.

LAWNS

Avoid walking on the lawn while the soil is still wet from melting snow. Once the soil has dried out, usually in mid-March, rake dead leaves and other debris off the lawn so sun can reach the grass plants.

Core-aerate in late March or April, if you did not do it in early fall. This process pulls out short plugs of earth and grass, creating openings that allow air and water deep into the root zone. Leave the plugs on the lawn and they will break down within 10 days. You can rent a core aerator, although it is a large, heavy machine, or hire a lawn-care firm to

■ *Root cuttings from many common houseplants and use them as annuals in the garden or in containers. Here, purple heart vine* (Tradescantia pallida) *fills in between perennial 'Electrocution' hosta* (Hosta *'Electrocution'*) *and 'Citronelle' coral bells* (Heuchera *'Citronelle'*).

■ *A core-aerating machine removes plugs of soil and roots to create openings that allow air and water into the root zone. Leave the plugs on the lawn; they will soon break down.*

do the job. It's best to core-aerate every year, either in spring or fall. See Here's How to Aerate Your Lawn, page 138.

It's too soon to mow; the grass is hardly growing.

PERENNIALS & ORNAMENTAL GRASSES

In March, look around the garden for perennials (and bulbs and groundcovers) that have been heaved out of the ground by the freeze-thaw cycles of winter. Gently press them back into place.

Once the soil has drained, finish cleaning up the garden. Rake surplus leaves and other debris out of the beds (but leave mulch in place). Cut back any remaining stalks of last year's perennials. It's best to cut perennials back before they begin growing in spring to avoid damaging the new growth.

Cut back ornamental grasses to within 2 inches of the ground early in the month before new growth starts, if you did not do so in February. See Care/Perennials, February, page 35. Watch out for new bulb foliage nearby.

The location of your garden and the varying weather each spring will greatly influence when your garden wakes up. Some sections may get more sun and start growing earlier than others.

When you see plants growing, pull mulch away from their crowns—the place where stems and

foliage grow of the roots. I mulch my garden with leaves every fall and I don't rake them all away in spring; they will break down and enrich the soil. However, I do rake away enough so there are not deep mats of leaves blocking the bulb and wildflower sprouts. I put the leaves I rake up in the compost pile.

Toward the end of March, if the ground is drained enough to work, it's not too soon to divide summer- and fall-blooming perennials. Divide them when

■ *Place rings or grids to support tall or bushy plants early so young plants can grow up through them.*

■ *To divide a perennial, dig up the entire rootball. Pull it apart or cut it into two or three sections, each with a good bunch of roots, and replant. Divide summer- and fall-blooming perennials, such as this catmint (Nepeta), when they first sprout in spring, because they are easy to handle and are growing actively.*

they have sprouted 3 to 4 inches high (enough so you can clearly identify them). See Plant/Perennials & Groundcovers, March, page 49.

Once soil can be worked, prepare a new perennial bed by digging in a 2- to 3-inch layer of compost or other organic matter over the entire area. It's better to amend the soil of the whole bed than to add compost to individual planting holes.

Topdress existing perennial beds by spreading a 1-inch layer of compost on the soil surface.

Install supports early, as soon as perennials emerge. Place wire grids or hoops over peony sprouts and place stakes next to lilies and other plants you know will grow tall enough to lean or flop. It's easy to forget this step until plants have already grown unwieldy, and staking them once they are tall is a more awkward chore.

You can use green-dyed bamboo poles for staking, but I usually use long branches left from pruning shrubs. They're less conspicuous and more attractive. Just make sure the stake is long enough; many lilies eventually grow 4 or 5 feet tall.

ROSES

Toward the end of March or in early April, once days are consistently above freezing, uncover roses that you protected with mulch in fall. Keep the mulch handy, and if a late freeze is predicted, re-cover the roses.

If you used plastic foam rose cones, remove them and throw them away; they trap heat and moisture and encourage disease. Under the plastic, the roses may have prematurely sprouted new growth that is especially vulnerable to late-spring freezes. Protect them from cold spells, if necessary, with leaves, mulch, or floating row cover, and next year don't use plastic rose cones.

Prune repeat-blooming roses about the time the forsythia starts to bloom, usually in late March or early April. Always use pruners with sharp blades to make clean cut.

Trim off the dead wood, which is generally gray or tan, in contrast to the green live wood on lower canes. Remove canes that are damaged, diseased, crossing, or spindly and weak down to the crown or bud union (the line or knobby place on the main stem where the rose was grafted). Make sure the center of the plant is open for air circulation. Then prune for shape, considering the plant's natural form.

On hybrid tea roses, leave three to five stout canes that are evenly spaced around the plant.

The long canes of climbers and ramblers often die back in cold winters such as those in Chicago and Cleveland. Prune out the dead wood, even if you have to cut the roses back to the ground.

Shrub roses, including hardy cultivars such as the Knock Out® and Flower Carpet® series, do not need pruning except to remove dead wood. They will bloom more, however, if you remove a couple of the largest, oldest canes each year.

Old garden roses that only bloom once a year on old wood should not be pruned now. Wait to prune them until summer, after they flower. These rose types include albas, gallicas, bourbons, damasks, hybrid musks, noisettes, and hybrid perpetuals.

TREES & SHRUBS

If you protected a young tree's bark from animals with a plastic tree guard over the winter, remove it in March. Otherwise, it can trap the growing heat of the sun and damage the bark.

Finish dormant pruning on shrubs early in the month before buds break. You can still prune later, but it will affect shrubs differently, pushing them to respond with hasty growth. Wait to prune spring-blooming shrubs such as lilacs and forsythia until after they flower.

If you have formal hedges, shear them early in March while the shrubs still are dormant.

When pruning or shearing evergreens other than yews, cut only within the leaf-bearing part of the branches toward the exterior of the shrub. Do not cut into the older, bare part of the branches toward the interior. Most evergreens can only generate new growth from wood that is actively growing and has

■ Shear formal evergreens early in March. When pruning or shearing most evergreens, cut only within the leaf-bearing branches at the outside of the shrub. If you cut into the bare interior branches, they will stay bare.

needles or leaves. If you cut the shrub back as far as the older, bare wood, it will stay bare.

Prune forsythia after it blooms. Prune out any dead wood and cut back one-third of the largest, oldest canes down to the ground. Remove any canes that are bent or crossing, leaving graceful canes that give the shrubs a fountain-like shape.

Late frosts may kill the flowers of early-blooming trees such as magnolias and cherries. The loss can be heartbreaking, but the tree will be fine. There is nothing to do but wait for next year.

Check the mulch layer around trees and shrubs. It may have decayed or settled over the winter. Add more shredded-wood or wood-chip mulch to make an even layer about 3 inches deep. You can spread new mulch right over the old.

WATER

ALL

Consider using soaker hoses in perennial beds and vegetable beds. Soaker hoses ooze water right into the soil where plants need it and waste much less water than sprinklers. Because they do not get the foliage wet, you can water at night without fear of creating conditions that foster fungus diseases.

Turn on outdoor faucets that you shut off in fall from an inside valve, or remove any wrapping that protected them from freezing over the winter.

Check the garden hoses too to make sure they have not spring any leaks. Install new hose washers.

HOUSEPLANTS

Continue watering as needed, not on a set schedule. As plants get larger and their rate of growth increases, they likely will need more frequent watering.

LAWNS

Have an in-ground sprinkler system checked to be sure it hasn't been damaged by trapped water that froze over the winter.

If the system has an automatic timer, make sure you know how to reset it. Or disconnect it so that you can water the lawn only when it needs watering.

PROBLEM-SOLVE

HOUSEPLANTS

Brown leaf tips or leaf edges on houseplants can indicate that the indoor air is too dry or can be a sign that fertilizer salts have built up in the soil. To deal with fertilizer buildup, see Care/Houseplants, page 54. To provide more humidity, see Care/Houseplants, January, page 25.

LAWNS

If you see a fuzzy white webbing on the lawn after the snow melts, it is probably a fungus called snow mold. It only affects the blades of the grass, not the roots. Rake debris off the lawn to help sun and air reach the grass, and the mold will clear up as the new growth starts. If any area of the lawn has been killed, prepare the soil and reseed (see Here's How to Reseed or Resod a Lawn, page 48).

If you had a big crabgrass problem last year, you may want to use a pre-emergent herbicide, which should be applied when the soil is still cool, before the forsythia blooms. Pre-emergent herbicides will prevent the germination of crabgrass seeds and all other seeds, including grass seed. So don't use one if you are planning to reseed or overseed.

An organic alternative is corn gluten meal, which also will deter seeds from sprouting as well as adding a little fertilizer to the lawn. You may have to apply it for more than one year to knock back a big dandelion problem.

A pre-emergent herbicide won't affect perennial weeds such as dandelions.

SHRUBS

You may see some branches with yellow or brown needles or leaves on evergreens such as yews and boxwoods. Their leaves, which need to be full of water all winter, can dry out if the plants didn't have enough water stored in their root systems or the roots couldn't absorb it from frozen soil. Cold winds and salt also can dry them out; the damage

HERE'S HOW

TO MULCH TREES & SHRUBS

A layer of mulch over its roots is good for every tree, young or old. Mulch holds moisture in the soil, suppresses weeds, and buffers the soil around a tree's roots against swings in temperature. As mulch decays, it encourages microorganisms that help trees' roots grow.

For trees and shrubs, use mulch with a coarse texture—chunks or shreds of wood or bark. Don't use cypress mulch, which often is not sustainably harvested.

Spread the mulch in a wide, even circle at least 2 to 3 feet wide around the trunk. It will keep away lawn mowers and string trimmers that can damage the bark. Ideally, the region of mulch would extend as far as a tree's branches reach, but make it as wide as you can.

Never mound mulch against the trunk of a tree; keep it a couple of inches away from the bark to avoid trapping moisture that fosters disease or harboring insects or animals.

Do not use gravel or rocks for mulch. They do nothing for the plant, and as they heat up in summer they bake roots and make water evaporate from the soil faster.

Anything you plant in the root zone of a tree competes with its roots. However, if you want to plant there, it is better to choose shade-tolerant groundcovers and bulbs than greedy turfgrass. Choose long-lived perennials so you only have to dig and slice the tree's roots once.

■ *When you spread mulch, pull it a couple of inches away from the bark of the tree or shrub.*

■ *If you want to have plants rather than mulch in the root zone of a tree, choose ferns or long-lived shade-tolerant perennial groundcovers. That way, you will only have to slice the tree's roots once when you dig to plant them.*

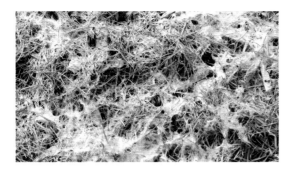

Snow mold is a fungus that can appear on grass blades, especially if the lawn was not cleared of leaves and other debris in fall. Rake debris off the lawn so air and sun can reach the grass and the fungus will clear up as new grass blades sprout.

is often most severe on the side facing a road or sidewalk where salt was used to melt snow.

If the needles are yellow but not totally dried out, water the plant and wait a few weeks to see if it recovers. If the needles or leaves are brown and crispy, check to see if there are live buds, indicating the branch is alive. If not, prune it out. Water the plant well, and over the next few months it will likely fill in with new growth. If the damage is too extensive, it may be better to just replace the plant.

Next fall, plan to water evergreens well going into winter. Consider protecting evergreen shrubs that will be exposed to winter wind or salt. See Problem-Solve/Trees & Shrubs, October, page 151.

TREES

Begin fungicide treatment for apple scab on crabapples, following the directions on the label. Consult your local Extension Service or botanical garden for advice on a control to use. Or better, remove the susceptible crabapple tree and replace it with a disease-resistant variety.

To deter scale insects on susceptible trees such as magnolias, spray with dormant oil early in March before bud break. Carefully follow the instructions on the label. You will need a day when the temperature is above 40 degrees Fahrenheit with no wind that could blow the spray onto other plants. The other possibility is to treat the tree when the insects' larvae are mobile and vulnerable in August. See Problem-Solve/Trees, July, page 125.

See Problem-Solve/Trees & Shrubs, October, page 151.

See Problem-Solve/Trees, July, page 125.

HERE'S HOW

TO USE SOAKER HOSES

Lay out soaker hoses in late March or early April, after perennials have sprouted (so you remember where they are) but before they are large enough to be in the way. Run soaker hoses in the vegetables garden once you have decided on a layout.

You can connect two 50-foot soaker hoses, but a distance longer than 50 feet will lose too much water pressure toward the end. Expect the water to soak out by capillary action about a foot on either side of the hose. Make a quick sketch of the layout so you recall which hose waters what, and where the ends are once they are all concealed by foliage.

Make sure the perennial beds' soaker hose network takes in any trees and shrubs planted within the last two years. Like perennials, they need long, slow watering if there has not been sufficient rain.

Soaker hoses may be made of spongy recycled rubber or of fabric. The rubber hoses are stiffer but usually less expensive. If you used soaker hoses last year, test them before laying them out to make sure they have not developed leaks.

Use soaker hoses with quick connectors so you can easily switch the garden hose from one soaker hose to another, and a simple mechanical timer that will turn the hose off after a certain time. That way, you can turn on a soaker hose and go off to work or to bed.

Drip irrigation systems also are available, but are more complex and finicky than soaker hoses and are difficult to alter once installed. They are most valuable to commercial growers or in arid parts of the country.

April

In April, spring is for real. Witch hazel and magnolias bloom. Daffodils, scilla, and even the first tulips are opening to the sunshine. A glow appears in the tops of maples and oaks as they bloom before their leaves unfurl. Bees and even some butterflies are busy among pansies and wildflowers.

Garden centers bloom too. Suddenly they fill with winter-weary gardeners, often stepping gingerly among puddles in high heels or fancy flats, irresistibly attracted on the way home from work or church. Sometimes they depart with arms full of tender plants that would only shiver or die in the still-cold ground.

The challenge in early April is juggling what we feel pulled to do with what the garden is actually ready for. The soil may be dried out, warmed up, and ready to go in the southern parts of Ohio, Indiana, and Illinois, while in the northern parts it may still be frozen, especially in the shade. But the arrival of spring can vary by weeks from year to year in the same place, and the fickle Midwestern climate still can deliver snow, just as it can offer up 80-degree Fahrenheit warm spells.

Every year is different. In some years, southern regions get a harsher winter, more snow, and more lingering cold than the North. In other years, there is hardly any snow and gardens go into spring too dry. And the weather is becoming more unpredictable as the climate changes.

So it's crucial not only to know which climate zone your garden falls in, but to pay attention to the actual weather and the progression of spring each year. The shade of trees or buildings can make a difference even within a garden, so always check the soil temperature and moisture right where you plan to plant.

There's plenty to do even at the start of April: preparing the soil, improving the lawn, tending to seedlings sown indoors, sowing seeds outside for early crops. By the end of the month, spring will be in full swing and gardeners all over will be rolling toward the planting frenzy of May.

PLAN

ALL

Before you buy plants, make sure you are in a position to plant them or to care for them until it's time to install them outdoors. Setting plants out into soil that is still too cold for them will *not* give them a head start; they will not start growing and their roots may rot.

If you buy bare-root plants, dampen the packing material to keep their roots moist and plant them as soon as possible. If you can't plant them outdoors for a week or two, consider potting up smaller plants in moist potting mix to hold them.

Make sure you know the pH of your soil—whether it is acid or alkaline—as you plan your garden. Soils in most of the Midwest tend to be neutral to slightly alkaline, with a pH of 7 or slightly higher. But there are many variables, including the underlying rock formations, whether your garden was once prairie, dune, or forest, and how the soil has been changed by construction. So get a soil test to be sure (see Plan in October, page 142).

Most garden plants grow best in soil that is neutral to slightly acidic, about 6 to 7, although the majority can handle a wider range. Some plants, such as river birch and pin oak, will really struggle in soil that is not acid enough. In alkaline soil, bigleaf hydrangea (*Hydrangea macrophylla*) will tend to have pink blooms rather than blue.

BULBS

Continue noting when bulbs bloom this spring and record gaps in the display. Take photos to help your recall in August, when it's time to order bulbs for fall planting.

As you admire neighbors' yards and public garden displays, make a list of new bulbs you are inspired to try planting in fall for next spring's bloom.

Watch daffodils as they bloom and note which clumps are overgrown and not flowering as much as they used to. Plan to divide them in June.

If you have crocuses or scilla planted in the lawn, don't start mowing until at least two or three weeks

■ *If you planted crocus or other bulbs in the lawn, wait to mow the grass for at least two to three weeks after blooming. The plants need their leaves to grow more bulbs for next year.*

after they are done blooming. The bulb plants need the sunlight collected by their leaves as they create flowers for next year. When you do mow, make sure the lawnmower blade is set at its highest to leave as much of the leaves as possible. (Of course, mowing high is good for your lawn grass too.)

EDIBLES

If you haven't started the vegetable garden yet, take time to plan for sun, crop rotation, and supports. See Plan/Edibles, February, page 31.

LAWNS

This year, plan to treat the power mower with respect; it's a dangerous machine. Power mowers are responsible for more than 250,000 emergency room visits each year, according to the Consumer Product Safety Commission. Riding mowers cause 20 times as many deaths as walk-behind mowers.

Read and follow your machine's instructions. Always wear long pants, sturdy shoes, safety glasses, and ear protection. Rake the lawn clean of debris before you start. Never try to unjam a machine without unplugging an electric mower or removing the spark plug of a gas mower. Do not use riding mowers on slopes. And never take children for rides; if they think of the machine as fun, they will be tempted to play with it.

PERENNIALS

April is a good time to plan and prepare a rain garden. It's a good solution for a place that is naturally low and often wet, or where there is a gutter

HERE'S HOW

TO BUY A GOOD PLANT

- Look for plants that are mature for their size. The roots are especially important. Don't buy a plant that has a large crown but puny roots. On the other hand, if you can see a mass of white roots through the holes in the bottom of the pot, or roots are growing out of the holes, the plant is potbound. Healthy plants will have a good, broad structure of (usually white) roots in plenty of soil.

- Always ask permission before gently tipping a plant out of the pot to check the roots. Be careful to avoid damaging the plant and replace it carefully.

- The plant should not look spindly or weak or have brown spots or blotches on the leaves or stems. The stems should feel firm. Plants should look well cared for, clean and tidy with no yellow leaves or dead sprigs.

- Plants should be the right color, which usually is a bright, fresh green (although some cultivars are bred to have chartreuse, yellow, splotched, or purple leaves; check the label).

- Usually, it's best to resist buying plants in full flower. You want the plant to do its blooming in your garden, not the garden center. Look for full, healthy annuals with just enough barely open buds so you can confirm the flower color.

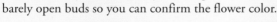

■ *Check the label to learn whether the plant prefers sun or shade, how large it will grow, and other essential information. Never buy a plant without a label.*

- The exception to buying plants in flower is cool-season annuals such as pansies and primulas that you buy in April. They will not have time to develop buds and flowers in the garden before the weather gets too warm for them, so buy them in full bloom.

- Be especially wary of perennials that are blooming at the wrong time. Since most gardeners shop in April and May, perennials are often forced into bloom at that time to catch a shopper's eye. But if a coneflower or daylily is blooming in spring, it will *not* bloom again at its normal time in midsummer; it won't get back on a normal schedule in your garden until the following year. Check the label for the plant's normal bloom time.

- When you buy a tree or shrub, ask where it was grown. Even if a species, such as redbud, is considered hardy in your climate zone, a plant grown in the south for its first two or three years may not be able to handle winters in Chicago, South Bend, or Youngstown. This is a special consideration when buying from large national chains that purchase plants in bulk and distribute them all over the country.

- Never buy a plant without a label.

downspout or a sump pump outflow. It's a bowl-shaped low area full of plants with large root systems where water is allowed to collect after rain until plants' roots absorb it or it soaks in. A rain garden can transform a mucky spot into a lovely planting that never needs watering and can help contribute to solving the problem of stormwater runoff.

ROSES

If you have a bare wall or blank fence, consider adorning it with a climbing rose in sun or a climbing hydrangea (*Hydrangea anomala* subsp. *petiolaris*) in shade. These plants will need a strong

INVASIVE PLANTS ALERT

As you shop for perennials and shrubs to plant in late April or early May, protect natural areas near you by avoiding invasive plants. These are plants that are known to spread rapidly, choking out native species so that native wildlife can't survive. Most invasive plants have escaped from gardens. For sources to find out what plants are invasive in your area, see Resources, page 189.

For example, all these common garden plants are considered invasive in Ohio, Indiana, and Illinois:

- barberry (*Berberis*)
- several species of honeysuckle (*Lonicera*)
- common orange daylilies (*Hemerocallis fulva*)
- reed canary grass (*Phalaris arundinacea*)
- yellow flag iris (*Iris pseudacorus*)
- creeping Jenny (*Lysimachia nummularia*)
- burning bush (*Euonymus alatus*)
- privet (*Ligustrum*)
- Callery pear (*Pyrus calleryana*)
- periwinkle (*Vinca minor*)

The sale of some invasive plants, such as purple loosestrife (*Lythrum salicaria*) and common buckthorn (*Rhamnus cathartica*), is illegal in most states.

■ *Purple loosestrife* (Lythrum salicaria), *top, creeping Jenny* (Lysimachia nummularia), *middle, and burning bush* (Euonymus alata), *bottom, are examples of plants that have escaped gardens to become an invasive threat to natural areas. Learn what plants are considered invasive in your area and avoid planting them so you don't add to the problem.*

support and regular pruning and training, but they should live for many years.

Climbers or ramblers are simply rose bushes selected for very long, flexible canes, so you can train them against a support. (Ramblers grow faster and farther, but usually bloom only once in June; modern

■ *Climbing roses must be tied to attach them to their support. Use soft ties that won't cut into the bark, and leave some slack so the branches can flex in the wind.*

climbers often rebloom.) Roses have no means of attachment so you will have to tie them up.

In northern regions, such as around Chicago or Rockford, South Bend, and Toledo, the long canes often die back quite far in winter so the display will never be quite as lush as it can be in Evansville or Cincinnati. Look for especially cold-hardy varieties such as 'John Davis', 'Zéphirine Drouhin', 'John Cabot', and 'Clair Matin'.

TREES & SHRUBS

Do some research and consult experts to make sure you are making the right choice before you plant a tree or even a major shrub. See Plan/Trees and Shrubs, March, pages 43–44.

PLANT

Make sure the ground is thawed and is not soggy from winter snow and rain before you dig or till.

HERE'S HOW

TO CREATE A NEW GARDEN BED

■ *To create a new bed, lay out a smooth outline with a garden hose and dig just inside (be careful not to cut the hose).*

■ *You can remove the turf with a sharp spade. Remove the clods and compost them or dispose of them in the landscape waste.*

■ *If you have time, you can smother the grass instead. In spring, spread newspaper 10 to 12 layers deep or black plastic and cover it with 6 inches of mulch or straw. Let it stand all summer or until the grass is dead.*

■ *Once the grass is gone, dig plenty of organic matter deeply into the soil.*

See Plant/March, page 45. Working wet ground can destroy its soil structure. Sunny parts of your yard may be ready to work before shady ones are.

Harden plants off before you plant them in the garden. See Here's How to Harden Off, page 46. A few hours before you plant them, water them well so they are in top shape and will slide easily out of the pot.

ANNUALS

Shortly before your last frost date, you can sow seeds outdoors for cool-season annuals including bachelor's button (*Centaurea cyanus*), pot marigold (*Calendula officinalis*), and poppies. See Plant/Annuals, March, page 45.

Soak large seeds overnight before planting them to help soften the seed coat. Sow the seeds into soil that has been well amended with compost and raked smooth. Follow the packet directions for planting depth.

Wait until after your last frost date to sow most other annuals. This may occur in April toward the south or in May in northern regions. See Plant/Annuals, May, page 80.

HERE'S HOW

TO SOW SEEDS OUTDOORS

■ *Smooth the surface of the soil. Depending on the required seed depth, you may scratch a shallow furrow.*

■ *Follow the directions on the seed packet for planting depth and spacing when you direct-sow seeds.*

■ *You can use seed-starting mix, which has a fine texture, to cover seeds you have sown outdoors. Be careful not to cover them more deeply than the package specifies.*

■ *Label the planting spot so you remember what you planted where.*

Transplant sweet pea seedlings outdoors around your average last frost date.

BULBS
If you get a potted Easter lily as a gift, keep it watered and try planting it in the garden once all danger of frost is past. See Plant/Bulbs, May, page 80.

CONTAINERS
Empty any containers left over from fall and use the potting mix to fill depressions in the lawn or scatter it over garden beds. Inspect the pots for cracks or other damage. Wash them with soapy water before replanting with fresh potting mix.

EDIBLES
Once the ground is thawed and drained enough to be workable, sow seeds of cold-season vegetables if you didn't do it in March. See Plant/Edibles, March, page 46. Peas germinate faster if you soak them in water overnight before sowing.

Plant rhubarb and asparagus if you didn't do it in March. See Plant/Edibles, March, page 46.

Radishes, which germinate quickly, are a handy marker plant for plants that are slower to sprout, such as lettuce. Sow alternate rows of radishes and lettuce. Thin the young radishes (and put the peppery baby greens in salads), and they will be ready to harvest in three or four weeks, leaving the later crop space to mature.

You can sow successive batches of radish seed until early to mid-May and they usually have time to mature before the soil gets too warm. Do the same for other root crops such as turnips and beets, as well as greens such as lettuce and spinach. If the last batches of lettuce you sow are slow-to-bolt varieties, you can extend your harvest of greens well into summer.

Sow seeds in containers for lettuce or mesclun, snap peas, radishes, or baby carrots (if you have a deep pot). Sow several pots a week apart for a longer harvest.

Plant some pansies among the early vegetables too. Pansies are edible.

Parsley often will overwinter, but it is not as tasty during its second year. Discard old plants and plant new transplants.

Plant berry-bearing shrubs, such as raspberries and blueberries, in April in full sun in well-drained soil. Water them regularly all through their first year or two.

LAWNS
Rake debris off the lawn if you didn't in March. Core-aerate, topdress with compost, and overseed (see Care/Lawns, March, page 54).

If you have bare patches, reseed or resod (see Plant/Lawns, March, page 49).

PERENNIALS
Wait to do any work in perennial beds until the ground has thawed and dried out, which may not be until mid-April in some years. See Plant/All, March, page 45.

Divide and transplant summer- and fall-blooming perennials (see Plant/Perennials, March, page 49).

Begin planting hardy perennials (including groundcovers) in well-drained, well-prepared soil toward the middle or end of April. For suggestions, see Plan/Perennials, March, page 42.

Shortly after your location's last frost date, in mid- to late April or early May, sow seeds of most perennials in the garden. Perennial seeds are increasingly available through websites and catalogs, and growing them from seed can be *a lot* less expensive than buying them in pots. Don't expect them to bloom this season, though; most will spend their first season getting established and bloom next year.

Perennial seeds that you can sow right in the ground in spring include yarrow, monkshood, amsonia, fall-blooming anemones, butterfly weed, boltonia, campanula, columbine, coreopsis, dianthus, coneflower, meadowsweet, hardy geraniums, geum, baby's breath, helenium, ox-eye daisies, heuchera, Shasta daisy, lobelia, lupine, monarda, Oriental poppy, penstemon, obedient plant, Jacob's ladder, rudbeckia, salvia, Stokes' aster, verbena, and viola. Whew!

Grow only straight species of perennials from seed, or buy seed of named F1 hybrids. If you saved seed from cultivars of hybrid perennials, the new plants will have resorted their genes in the course of reproduction and will not have the same characteristics as their parents. See Plan/Annuals & Perennials, August, page 128.

ROSES

After your last frost date, in late April or early May, you can plant even tender varieties of bare-root or potted roses in full sun in well-amended, well-drained soil. For bare-root roses, see Plant/Roses, March, page 50.

Plant potted roses in well-prepared soil, scattering slow-release fertilizer into the planting hole according to the label directions. Make the hole wide, but not too deep; make sure that the crown of the plant is at soil level. On grafted roses, make sure the graft union (the faint line or crook in the stem where one type of rose was grafted onto the roots of another) will be above soil level. Backfill the hole and water well. Spread mulch over the roots but not against the stems.

SHRUBS & VINES

Plant shrubs and woody vines, such as clematis, in April as soon as the ground has drained enough to dig. See Here's How to Plant a Tree or Shrub, page 52.

TREES

Plant trees from now through June, or wait until fall. See Here's How to Plant a Tree or Shrub, page 52.

It usually isn't necessary to stake a newly planted tree. In fact, the young tree will grow stronger if its trunk flexes in the wind. If you do stake a tree, make sure the ties will not constrict or cut into the bark. Remove the staking within a year, once the plant has grown enough roots to securely anchor it.

CARE

ALL

Here's a simple way to check your soil for drainage: Dig a hole 12 inches deep. Fill it with water. Ideally, the water should drain away within an hour.

If there is a stretch of warm days, flowers may pop into bloom. Keep floating row cover or old sheets handy to cover especially prized blooms in case of frost. Late frost and snow still are possible, especially in the north. Most plants will be fine.

Weed early and often. Weeds are inevitable, but if you keep up, they will be easier to deal with. The other major weapon is mulch, which shades out weed seeds so fewer of them can germinate. Rake mulch occasionally to keep weed seeds from taking root in it.

Since you spread the mulch around your plants but not right up to the stems, you will know that anything growing directly through the mulch is a weed.

BULBS

As spring bulbs finish flowering, pinch off the flower stalks but leave the foliage. The plants need their leaves to collect energy to build next year's flowers. See Here's How Bulbs Work, page 144.

Divide dense clumps of snowdrops as soon as they finish flowering. Dig up the whole clump, gently tease it apart into several smaller sections, and replant each section in part shade. By next spring, the transplanted bulbs will multiply.

EDIBLES

Thin greens, root crops, and other seedlings to the spacing recommended on their seed packet. Remember that the leaves of turnips, beets, and radishes are edible (delicious, in fact).

Radishes mature quickly. If you sowed seed in late March, you may have roots big enough to eat within 21 to 28 days, depending on the weather and the variety. They are best when young; if you wait too long to harvest, the roots will grow woody.

For a tender salad, use the "cut and come again" method of harvesting small leaves of lettuce, spinach, and other greens instead of pulling up the plants. When the largest leaves are 3 to

HERE'S HOW

TO MULCH BEDS

Mulch is a layer of plant matter over the soil that holds in moisture, helps suppress weeds, insulates roots against extreme heat and cold, and improves the soil as it decays. Here's how to use it properly:

Keep the mulch an inch or so away from the crowns and stems of the plants.

1. In annual and perennial beds, use a relatively fine material. I use shredded leaves and compost, but you also can purchase fine-textured mulch at a garden or home-improvement center. In vegetable beds, you can use leaves, straw, or compost, if you have a large supply. To help shade out weeds and hold in moisture, try laying newspaper two or three pages deep and spreading mulch over it. The ink on black and white pages is perfectly safe, even in vegetable beds.

2. Spread mulch in an even layer 1 to 2 inches deep in annual and perennial beds and 2 to 3 inches deep in vegetable plots.

3. Do not use landscape fabric under mulch. It does not suppress weeds better than plain mulch, and it becomes unattractive as it tears and bunches up over time.

4. Keep the mulch an inch or so away from the crowns and stems of the plants, where it can trap moisture that may lead to disease.

5. In annual beds and vegetable gardens, pull back the mulch in early spring so the soil can warm before planting. If it's in good shape, you can reuse it. Otherwise, dig it in or compost it.

6. From time to time, refresh the mulch by raking it lightly. Add more to thin or bare spots, but don't build it up more than 1 or 2 inches deep. It looks most tidy if you use the same material as before. You can lay new mulch right over the old.

7. For trees and shrubs, see Here's How to Mulch Trees & Shrubs, page 58.

4 inches long, instead of pulling up the plant, use sharp-pointed scissors to snip out just the largest leaves. The plant will grow new leaves to useful size in a week or two. You can repeat this three or four times on most plants. If you sow batches of seed a week apart through April, you'll extend your harvest this way through June and perhaps into July.

If you want to grow full heads of lettuce, leave them alone.

GROUNDCOVERS

Tidy up groundcovers if you didn't do it in March. See Care/Groundcovers, March, page 54.

LAWNS

Start mowing the grass in April when it is about 3 inches tall. Set the mower blade as high as it will go, 2 to 3 inches high (or higher, if possible). Taller grass is healthier, with longer, stronger roots. For more on mowing, see Care/Lawns, May, page 88.

TO PLANT A SALAD BOWL

■ *Baby greens for salads are easy to grow in containers. You can use a shallow bowl, but make sure it has holes for drainage. Fill it with good-quality potting mix and either direct-sow with lettuce or mesclun seed or plant transplants. Water and keep the soil moist. On especially hot days, move the bowl to the shade. Sow several containers, each one week apart, to keep the harvest going. To harvest, use the cut-and-come-again method: snip off the largest leaves rather than pulling up the whole plant. Smaller leaves will still grow.*

■ *Thin seedlings to the spacing recommended on the seed packet. These radish seedlings have edible leaves; add them to salads.*

clump back higher than you normally would, safely above the level of any new growth.

Try to avoid working in beds when the soil is wet. And be careful not to step on spring bulb plants or sprouting perennials, including those that haven't yet broken through the mulch.

Continue to divide and transplant summer- and fall-blooming perennials. See Plant/Perennials & Groundcovers, March, page 49. Wait to divide spring bloomers until after they finish flowering.

SHRUBS

Start treating soil with sulfur if you want to shift it from alkaline to acid for a special plant. You may decide to do this to make some mophead or lacecap hydrangeas have blue blooms. In alkaline soil, they will be lavender or pink. A soil test can confirm your soil's pH (See Here's How to Get a Soil Test, page 143).

Topdress the soil with an aluminum sulfate preparation, usually sold in garden centers. It's a good idea to split the amount and apply half in spring and half in fall. Follow the directions on the package, and wear gloves and eye protection.

You can avoid this chemical manipulation by embracing pink, or by planting other hydrangea species such as smooth hydrangea or panicle hydrangea. They mostly bloom in white but there are also cultivars with blooms tinged in pink.

Prune shrubs that bloom in early spring, such as forsythia and flowering quince, within two weeks after they finish flowering. If you wait too long, you'll remove the flowers the plants are setting for next year's bloom.

Core-aerate if you did not do it in March (see Care/Lawns, March, page 54). Or wait until fall. Core-aerate at least once a year.

PERENNIALS & ORNAMENTAL GRASSES

If you didn't cut back the stalks of grasses and perennials in February or March because of a late snow or freeze, it's not too late. Cut them back as early in April as you can.

Be careful not to harm the new green growth that will likely have sprouted. The new shoots can be hard to see, so separate the old stalks carefully and cut them back one by one. Use sharp pruners or scissors. That can be impossible to do on dense clumps of ornamental grasses. So cut the whole

TREES

If spring storms crack branches, cut them off cleanly just outside the branch collar if you can easily reach them. If you would have to climb a ladder to deal with tree damage, hire a professional arborist. See Resources, page 189. *Never* touch a branch that is near a fallen power line; stay away and call your local power company immediately.

WATER

ALL

If the weather gets especially warm in early April, be prepared to water a bit more, especially if it hasn't rained or snowed much. Plants pushed to grow by the warmth will quickly use up the water stored last fall in their roots and the surrounding soil.

All newly installed plants will need regular watering to keep their soil moist. Check the soil right next to the plant, not just the surrounding bed. Plants are grown in a potting mix that drains better than most garden soil so the rootball will dry out faster. These plants will need watering more often until their roots grow out into the soil of the bed.

Lay out soaker hoses to position them in your beds if you didn't do it in March (see Water/All in March, page 57).

ANNUALS

Keep newly sown seeds moist, sprinkling gently to avoid washing them away. Keep watering seedlings from the bottom of their tray if they are under lights.

BULBS

It's almost never necessary to water spring-blooming bulbs, except in containers. In fact, most prefer it on the dry side.

EDIBLES

Continue checking the moisture in the soil to determine when your vegetables need watering. Don't depend on rain, but don't water if the soil is already moist.

Keep newly sown seeds moist, sprinkling them gently.

CONTAINERS

Check the soil in containers and water as often as necessary to keep it moist an inch under the soil. You are more likely to need to water containers than plants in the ground.

LAWNS

Keep newly sown grass seed constantly moist, which may require sprinkling gently twice a day. Once the grass sprouts, reduce watering to every three days, or when the soil dries out on the surface.

Water new sod often. See Water/Lawns, May, page 92.

Don't get in the habit of watering on a set schedule; as with all plants, water an established lawn only as needed. Watering too often will keep the grass from developing long, strong roots and make it less drought tolerant.

PERENNIALS & GROUNDCOVERS

Water newly planted perennials enough to keep the soil moist. Most established perennials need little or no watering, and in spring they should usually be able to rely on rain.

ROSES

Water newly planted roses every couple of days, until they grow enough roots to collect more water from the soil. Water a wide area to encourage new roots to grow outward.

Established plants need less frequent watering. Check the soil to make sure it is moist an inch or two below the surface, but don't keep it wet. Overwatering, especially in cool weather, can encourage disease.

TREES, SHRUBS & VINES

Water newly planted trees, shrubs, and woody vines slowly once a week with a dribble from the hose or a soaker hose, so the water soaks in at a rate at which the plant's roots can absorb it. Try to spread the watering around the rootball so roots grow out in all directions.

Trees that were planted balled and burlapped are especially vulnerable to drought because most of their root system was cut off in transplanting. Even

■ *Side-dress plants with fertilizer pellets or compost by sprinkling it around them and scratching it into the surface of the soil.*

if it rains, they don't have many roots to absorb water with. Be very careful not to let the rootball dry out.

FERTILIZE

ANNUALS & CONTAINERS
If you sprinkle slow-release fertilizer when you plant, annuals in the ground and containers should not need more nutrients for several weeks.

BULBS
The time to fertilize bulbs is after they flower, when they are building next year's blooms. You can sprinkle slow-release fertilizer around early bulbs, such as crocus, snowdrops, and scilla, in late April once they are done blooming.

EDIBLES
If you planted into compost-rich soil, there is no need to add supplemental nutrients in spring.

LAWNS
Avoid applying "starter fertilizer" to force the grass to green up quicker. It tends to stress the plants. The lawn will be green once the grass plants have put on a couple of inches of new growth. You can rake the lawn to get rid of most of the brown grass leaves from winter.

Wait until late April or May, when the grass is vigorously growing, to apply a slow-release fertilizer that should carry the grass into its dormant period in July.

PERENNIALS & GROUNDCOVERS
Most established perennials need little or no fertilizing. See Fertilize/Perennials, May, page 96.

TREES & SHRUBS
Most trees and shrubs will do well on the nutrients they obtain from adequately rich soil. Don't fertilize them unless you know that a nutrient deficiency, confirmed by a soil test, is causing a problem.

PROBLEM-SOLVE

ALL
Protect against animal damage by covering vulnerable bulb plants, annuals, greens, vegetables, and other plants with netting, securely staked down at the edges.

The best protection against rabbits is a sturdy fence of chicken wire that is at least 2 feet high and extends 18 inches underground to block burrowing. This only works if you keep the gate closed.

Many strong-smelling and nasty-tasting repellants are sold to deter animals. They can have some

■ *The best protection against rabbits and other animals is a wire mesh fence. Bury the bottom edge deep in the soil to prevent rabbits from burrowing under it.*

■ *A fence must be 8 feet high to keep out deer; they can jump a 6-foot fence.*

effect, but they will need to be reapplied each time rain washes them off.

These substances scare animals because they are unfamiliar; once the rabbits or deer get used to a taste or smell and no longer associate it with danger, they'll ignore it. That means you need to switch repellents every few weeks to keep the animals off guard. Start in early spring, when there is a new crop of rabbits.

There are other approaches: Plant enough so you can afford to share. Or plant things animals are less likely to eat. (There are *no* rabbit-proof or deer-proof plants; an animal that is hungry enough will eat what it has to.) Search the Internet for lists of these less-attractive plants. They usually have thorns, a prickly or scratchy texture, fuzzy leaves, or an unpleasant smell.

LAWNS

Dandelions will begin to appear in late April. They have a long, deep taproot that will resprout if you leave it in the ground. To remove it, stick a garden knife or fork-tipped weeder straight down next to the center of the plant and then lever it sideways to pop the taproot out of the soil.

Attack creeping Charlie (*Glechoma hederacea*) as soon as you spot its new rosettes of round, scallop-edged leaves in April. It will be much harder

to remove after the plants send out their long, slender stems, which insinuate themselves between perennials, groundcovers, and grass blades and which can take root all along their lengths. And once the plants bloom with their purple flowers in late May, they can set seed and spread still farther.

Patrol shady areas in beds and the lawn and use a garden knife or trowel to dig up the whole plant, with the roots. Try not to leave any piece of creeping Charlie root or stem behind or it may take root. I put creeping Charlie in the landscape waste, not the compost heap, for fear that some scrap may survive.

If you find that a lawn has been completely taken over by creeping Charlie, you may need to kill it with a systemic herbicide, such as one that contains glyphosate, and start over. See Here's How to Reseed or Resod a Lawn, March, page 48.

But first, ask yourself if the lawn area isn't too shady for grass. Creeping Charlie out-competes grass in shady areas because it is more shade tolerant. You might be better off with a groundcover in that area.

I don't use weed-and-feed products or other blanket herbicides on my grass; I keep my smallish lawn mostly weed free by hand-pulling. I dig up dandelions in April and May as soon as I notice their recognizable foliage, without waiting for them to bloom. After that, I patrol the lawn every couple of weeks.

■ *To combat creeping Charlie* (Glechoma hederacea)*, hand-pull it starting in spring before the long stems creep out among grass blades or perennials. Remove the entire plant, including roots.*

May

After months of anticipation, May is here and spring is leaping toward summer. For a Midwestern gardener, it's D-Day, the Olympics, and a moon shot all rolled into one. Suddenly it seems like there are a million things to do before the summer heat—which, given the way our weather works, could be next week.

The sun is high in the sky and the air is warmer, but what really matters to many plants is that the soil has warmed up. A lot of our favorite annual plants, including vegetables such as tomatoes and peppers, are native to subtropical places. They really don't like being planted into cool soil, so don't rush.

Although seed packets and garden books talk about timing in terms of days before or after the last frost date, that's largely a proxy for soil temperature. To be really sure whether your soil is ready for planting, take its temperature. A soil thermometer costs $25 or so; if you get one with a long probe, you also can use it to check the temperature in your compost pile.

Knowing your average last frost date is crucial, but remember that it's just an average. In much of the Chicago area, the average date is May 15, but there have been frosts on Memorial Day. So pay attention to the actual weather. If it has been a cool spring, the soil may not have warmed as completely as it usually does and you might want to sow seeds or set out transplants a little later.

Mother's Day weekend is like Black Friday at garden centers, the day everyone suddenly goes shopping, but that doesn't necessarily mean all your purchases should go in the ground then.

There's a lot to do this month, so pace yourself. Take lots of breaks. And if you realize now that you don't have time to do all you dreamed of in January, let yourself off the hook. Think about what you can put off to early June and what you can put off until autumn—or next year. You'll still get enough done to have a glorious garden.

PLAN

ALL

If you need to hold annuals, perennials, vegetables, or other plants for a few days before planting, place them in a part-sun area, water them, and watch the weather forecast. If nighttime temperatures below 40 degrees Fahrenheit are predicted, cover the plants with floating row covers or old sheets to protect against frost damage. Remove the covering in the morning. Don't use plastic sheeting, which can trap moisture.

If you didn't get around to starting plants from seed, reconsider. Go over the seed collection and see what you can sow directly in the garden (even if they will bloom later) and what cool-season vegetables you might be able to use for a fall crop. Place the rest of the seeds, in their original seed packets, in a plastic zippered bag and mark it with the date. Keep all your bags of seeds sealed inside a larger zipper bag in the freezer. Every year, add a bag with this year's leftovers and toss the oldest ones. Most seeds will last for three or four years, although the germination rate will go down as they age.

ANNUALS

When you are buying annual flowers for the garden in May, consider how closely you will need to space them in the garden. Consult the tag for the recommended spacing and calculate how many it will take to fill your space (see Here's How to Estimate How Many Plants to Buy). If you want a bed to fill in faster, it may be worth the money to buy more plants and space them a little more closely.

A 48-cell flat has smaller plants than a 36- or 24-cell flat of the same size. Larger plants are usually better developed and will flower and fill in more quickly.

Make sure to buy good-quality plants. See Here's How to Buy a Good Plant, page 63.

BULBS

Many gardeners plan to "lift" tender summer-blooming bulbs such as dahlias, cannas, tuberous begonias, caladiums, and elephant ears in the fall to overwinter them. But it's not a requirement. You can just buy inexpensive ones and think of them as annuals.

If you do plan to lift them in autumn, you will find that many multiply over the summer, and you can keep a favorite variety from year to year.

If you didn't start tender bulbs early in pots (see Plant/Bulbs, March, page 46), you may be able to buy some already started in garden centers. Bare bulbs or tubers planted in the ground in mid- to late May will take longer to reach full size and bloom. See Plant/Bulbs.

EDIBLES

Plan on sowing many crops, such as corn, peas, and lettuce, in batches at one-week intervals to extend the harvest season. Allow space in the garden for the later batches.

CONTAINERS

For a handsome and lasting container landscape, choose the containers as carefully as the plants. You will find the largest selection in garden centers in May.

PERENNIALS

Save labor by planning the perennial garden so plants with similar needs are grouped together. In a place far from the hose, group drought-tolerant plants that can probably survive on rainfall. Collect the neediest plants nearer to the house, and near the faucet, where it is easier to tend them. Don't let garden center finds throw off your groupings; a single thirsty plant in a bed of drought-tolerant ones will require you to haul the hose out there, and the frequent watering will be bad for the other plants.

■ *Edit the garden to have a smaller variety of plants but more of each kind. Planting just one of many different plants can lead to a chaotic look.*

HERE'S HOW

TO ESTIMATE HOW MANY PLANTS TO BUY

Before you start seeds or go shopping for plants, you may want to estimate how many plants you'll need to fill the space you have in mind.

There are many variables. For example, if you are using smaller plants, such as those grown in 4- or 6-plant cellpacks, you will need more plants to fill a container or a bed than if you are using larger annuals grown in 4-inch pots.

The numbers also will vary depending on the habits of the plants—are they upright or spreading? Full and lush like thyme or petunias or delicate and distinct like pansies or annual salvia? Will you fill the entire container or bed with one kind of annual, or use larger perennials in the combination?

If you plant annual flowers or groundcovers at the recommended spacing shown on the plant label, they will take a few weeks to fill in. If you want a full, lush look more quickly, you will need to plant them more closely, which will require more plants. (You should always plant perennials in the ground at the recommended spacing so they will not be crowded when they are full grown; if necessary, fill between them with annuals for the first year.)

FOR BEDS:

To figure spacing, use the landscapers' term "on center," meaning the distance from the center of one plant to the center of the next.

For example, suppose you have a 3 × 5-foot bed that you want to plant with the groundcover pachysandra on 8-inch centers.

Start by calculating the area of the bed (for formulas, see Here's How to Calculate Area, page 164). In this case, multiply 3 by 5 to get 15 square feet. Multiply by 144 to get 2,160 square inches.

To figure the area each pachysandra plant will cover, multiply 8 by 8 to get 64 square inches.

Divide 2,160 square inches (the area of the bed) by 64 (the area to be covered by each plant) to get 33.75, or about 34 plants. Always buy a few extra just in case. If you are purchasing plants in flats, round up; in this case, for example, buy two 24-plant flats of pachysandra.

If you place plants in staggered rows, rather than in a square grid, they will fill in more quickly, but it takes about 15 percent more plants. In the case of our pachysandra, it would take roughly 38 plants.

FOR CONTAINERS:

These are just rough rules of thumb that assume upright annual flowers of a single variety, such as pansies. Your needs will vary depending on the plants, your container, and your design.

10- to 12-inch container: four to six small cellpack annuals or about three 4-inch annuals

14- to 16-inch container: six to ten small cellpack annuals or four to five 4-inch annuals

18- to 20-inch container: 14 to 16 small cellpack annuals or seven to nine 4-inch annuals

HERE'S HOW

TO CHOOSE A POT

Containers need to be frostproof to stay outdoors through Midwestern winters. Terra cotta containers are classic in the garden, but they must be taken indoors during the winter or they will crack. Fiberglass, high-quality plastic, lead, and stone containers can generally be left outside. Highly fired ceramic containers may be winter worthy if they are labeled as "frostproof." Inexpensive plastic containers are likely to crack in the cold.

In a windy site such as a balcony or rooftoop, a heavier container such as stone or terra cotta is less likely to blow over. Fiberglass pots are lightweight.

Any container *must* have a drainage hole in the bottom. Some plastic and fiberglass containers are sold without a hole, requiring you to drill one or pop out a plug.

■ *For a harmonious container display, choose containers that are suited to the plants. These rustic hypertufa containers fit perfectly with the sculptural succulent plants, which are native to rocky environments.*

■ *Deadheading, or removing spent flowers, can encourage more bloom in many annuals and some perennials. It also looks tidier. Remove the flower stem down to a leaf; don't leave an empty stalk.*

Edit the garden border for greater effect. Now that most perennials have emerged and you can remember what you have, decide what to remove as well as what to plant. Give the surplus plants away or compost them.

To keep the garden from looking higgledy-piggledy, plan to plant fewer kinds of plants and more of each. Instead of buying just one of any plant that catches your eye, buy plants in groups of three, five, or more and plant them in masses. Repeat the same plants in masses in different parts of the garden to draw the eye, create calm and balance, and give a cohesive effect.

Look for perennials that have interest all season long, whether because of their foliage, like hostas, ferns and lungwort; because their bloom can be extended by deadheading, such as coreopsis; or because they will rebloom if they are cut back after flowering, such as catmint, calamint, and perennial salvia.

Think about late summer and fall color when choosing perennials, even though it's easy to forget August and September when you are surrounded by the plants that bloom in May. Among the perennials to plant now for bloom in late summer and fall are New England aster; fall-blooming monkshood; goldenrod; fall-blooming anemones; toad lilies; grasses such as prairie dropseed and little bluestem; and tall sedums such as 'Autumn Joy'.

Provide nectar for butterflies with plants such as liatris, zinnia, coneflower, tithonia, ageratum, gaillardia, and asters. Feed the caterpillars of monarch butterflies by planting milkweed or butterfly weed, and for swallowtail butterfly caterpillars by planting some parsley and fennel among the flowers. Locate your butterfly garden in the sun, where butterflies are more active; a fence or windbreak will give them shelter. To give butterflies a drink, sink a shallow saucer filled with sand into the soil up to its rim and keep the sand wet. And, of course, don't use insecticides or herbicides.

GROUNDCOVERS

Now that the trees have leafed out, you can see the spots in your garden that likely will be in dry shade. Much of the rain that falls on the trees' leaves overhead evaporates and never reaches the ground. Avoid planting moisture-loving plants beneath trees and instead opt for long-lived groundcovers such as bishop's hat (*Epimedium*), ajuga, tiarella, lamium, and liriope.

SHRUBS

Consider dwarf shrubs as part of your perennial plantings, not just as background. Many compact cultivars available today grow only 2 to 3 feet tall, such as Citrus Swizzle forsythia (*Forsythia viridissima* 'McKCitrine'), dwarf fothergilla, spireas, and Bobo panicle hydrangea (*Hydrangea paniculata* 'Bobo'). Don't plant full-sized shrubs among perennials; they will shade everything else out.

VINES

Before you plant a vine, plan how you will support it. Some woody vines, such as wisteria and hops, will grow to be very large and heavy. Even annual wines such as morning glories can become very dense and surprisingly weighty over the course of a season and can pull down a flimsy trellis.

If you're planning to plant a vine against a wall, make sure that it has a structure to climb that stands an inch or two clear of the wall so water can drain behind it and air can circulate. This will make it less likely that wood siding will rot or mortar will deteriorate. It also will be good for the plant, preventing trapped moisture that can cause disease.

TREES

If you're planning to plant groundcovers or perennials around and beneath a tree, the best time to do it is when the tree is first planted, before it has spread out roots that would be damaged by digging. Choose long-lived, shade-tolerant groundcovers and bulbs so you will not have to disturb the tree's roots often.

GOING NATIVE

Planting native species of shrubs makes your garden part of the larger habitat for birds, butterflies, and other wildlife, especially if the shrubs have berries. Some native species that have evolved a relationship with the wildlife of the Midwestern states are:

- black chokeberry (*Aronia melanocarpa*)
- spicebush (*Lindera benzoin*)
- fragrant sumac (*Rhus aromatica*)
- elderberry (*Sambucus canadensis*)
- winterberry (*Ilex verticillata*)
- smooth hydrangea (*Hydrangea arborescens*)
- chokecherry (*Prunus virginiana*)
- witch hazel (*Hamamelis virginiana*)
- ninebark (*Physocarpus opulifolius*)
- American filbert (*Corylus americana*)
- summersweet (*Itea virginica*)
- buttonbush (*Cephalanthus occidentalis*)

Also consider serviceberry (*Amelanchier*), which is a small multi-stemmed tree. These plants need a variety of conditions, and not all are native to all habitats. Check with your local botanical garden or native plant society for information on shrubs that are native to your location (and therefore in sync with your local wildlife) and will do well in the conditions of your yard. (See Resources, page 189.)

PLANT

ANNUALS

Continue to harden plants off before you plant them in May (See Here's How to Harden Off, page 46). Even after the last frost date has passed, the outdoors is still a different environment than a greenhouse.

Plant annual transplants in the garden or pots. First, prepare the soil well and scatter slow-release fertilizer granules or pellets as recommended on the package (annuals need more nutrients than perennials).

Check to see if the plants are potbound in their cellpacks or pots. If so, you'll see white roots circling the rootball in a dense netting. Gently pull the roots apart or snip the rootball with pruners to encourage more side roots to branch.

There are many annual flowers that can be direct-sown in the garden after your last frost date in May. Try cosmos and morning glories (although they won't start blooming until midsummer); marigolds (plant some in the vegetable garden to attract pollinating insects); nasturtiums (soak the big seeds for a few hours or overnight before planting to soften the hard shells and encourage germination); four o'clocks (be ready for them to reseed); hyacinth bean and castor bean (striking and tropical looking); moss roses (a good little underplanting for taller perennials in sun); and sunflowers. There are many varieties of annual sunflowers, from 3 feet tall to 12 feet tall, so make sure you are getting one that will fit your space.

Plant zinnias among your sun-loving perennials; keep the soil moist for the first few weeks, but once zinnias are established they don't need as much watering as other annuals.

Before sowing, rake the surface of the soil smooth, removing big clods. Sprinkle on slow-release fertilizer granules or pellets. Moisten the soil. Sow the seeds, following the directions on the seed packet for planting depth. I usually sow seeds a little more closely than their package suggests to make sure I get good germination, and thin the seedlings to a better spacing when they are 2 or 3 inches tall.

Water the seeds with a gentle sprinkle so you don't wash the seeds away. Check daily to keep the seeds and soil moist until the seedlings sprout.

BULBS

Late in the month, after the soil has thoroughly warmed above 60 degrees Fahrenheit, plant tender bulbs, tubers, and corms such as cannas, elephant ears, dahlias, tuberous begonias, caladiums, crocosmia, and agapanthus. These are tropical plants, so do not rush and plant them into cold soil. The way to give summer bulbs a head start so they develop and bloom earlier is to pot them up indoors in March (See Plant/Bulbs, March, page 46). You can also plant them in containers now.

Elephant ears are basically swamp plants in their native Asia, so they need consistent moisture. Although they can do well in a semi-shady spot where they get consistent moisture, they may do best in the more controlled conditions of a container (see Plant/Containers).

Plant gladiolus bulbs in batches a week apart to extend their period of summer bloom.

If you got a potted Easter lily (*Lilium longiflorum*) as a gift, try planting it in the garden once the danger of frost is past. The plant may have been too stressed by forcing to survive, but what have you got to lose?

Remove the spent bloom but leave the stalk and leaves. Plant it, like any lily, in full to part sun in well-drained soil with plenty of organic matter where you have space for a tall plant. Water it well. It won't bloom again the first year, but it may come back and bloom the second.

CONTAINERS

Plant containers in early May. Frosts in May are not unheard of in the northern regions, so be prepared to cover containers or move them indoors if frost is predicted.

There's no need to place a layer of gravel, pot shards, or other material at the bottom of the pot; contrary to folklore, it does *not* improve drainage. However, you must make sure the pot has a hole. Some containers are sold without a hole and you have to drill one. Or there may be a plug you must remove.

HERE'S HOW

TO PLANT TRANSPLANTS

■ *To plant transplants, remove them gently from their pots or cellpacks. You can plant annuals a bit closer together than the label suggests to fill in the space faster. But when planting perennials, don't cheat; allow them plenty of space for the size they will reach in future years.*

■ *When plants come in peat or paper pots, tear off the top of the pot so that when you plant it no part is above the soil. An absorbent pot sticking above the soil can wick moisture out of the ground.*

■ *Pinch back most annuals a bit when you plant them to encourage fuller, bushier growth.*

To make sure potting mix does not wash out, place one piece of broken pot or a scrap of window screen or landscape fabric over the hole.

Apart from the hole, the most important thing you can do to ensure drainage and safeguard plants' health is to choose a high-quality potting mix (see Here's How to Choose a Potting Mix, page 43).

In May, after your last frost date, plant tuberoses and other summer bulbs, such as cannas, elephant ears, dahlias, tuberous begonias, caladiums, crocosmia, and agapanthus.

Plant elephant ears in large, heavy pots so they do not blow over when they grow to be huge plants with sail-like leaves. Because they evolved in low, wet places in Asia, elephant ears need consistent moisture. One way to help them is to violate the general rule that container plants should never sit in water: Plant an elephant ear in a large container and set it in a saucer. When you water, don't empty the saucer, as you would with other plants; let the elephant ear plant absorb the excess water through the soil.

You can plant small shrubs or roses in containers, but be prepared to water them often over the summer. If you plan to move them out into the garden in early fall, simply plant them in good potting mix. But if you hope to keep them alive in the container through the winter, you'll need to plan ahead, because plant roots are much more vulnerable to winter's cold in a pot than planted in the ground. Use as large a container as possible so there is more soil to insulate the roots, but not so large that you can't move it; you will need to shift the pot to a sheltered place for the winter.

You can plant cascading annuals or herbs around the outside of a container with a shrub in the middle, as long as you don't disturb the shrub's roots.

Plant edibles in containers if you have a sunny deck, patio, or balcony. Use a large pot or a sub-irrigated container (see Plan/Edibles, March, page 40). For all large vegetable crops such as tomatoes, beans, and peppers, place the pot where it will get at least eight hours of sun a day. If you have part

HERE'S HOW

TO PLANT CONTAINER PLANTS

■ *Fill your pot three-quarters full with good-quality potting mix (there's no need for gravel or broken pots at the bottom; it will not improve drainage). Add slow-release fertilizer according to the package directions.*

■ *Try out your arrangement with the plants still in their pots.*

■ *Place the plants in the container. Fill in around them with more potting mix so they are at the same level as in their old pots and gently firm them in place. Make sure the soil level is 1 inch below the rim so water has room to pool and soak in.*

sun, you still can grow some crops such as lettuce, chard, and peas.

Provide a tomato cage or a pyramid of bamboo poles to support vining plants such as beans, tomatoes, or peas. Look in garden centers for compact or patio-sized varieties. Determinate varieties of tomatoes—those that will grow to a certain size and then stop—are best.

After you've planted transplants, or after your seeds have sprouted, spread mulch over the soil in containers just as you would in the ground. Use a fine-textured mulch such as shredded leaves or compost.

EDIBLES

Continue to sow seeds for carrots, chard, lettuce, and radishes.

Wait until after your last average frost date to plant warm-season vegetables such as tomatoes, peppers, cucumbers, and eggplant, as well as basil. In fact, it's usually best to wait until the end of May or even early June, when the soil is thoroughly warm and nighttime temperatures are consistently in the 50s. These are subtropical plants that hate cold soil. Tomatoes, for example, will not grow well at soil temperatures below 60 degrees Fahrenheit. Peppers, eggplant, and basil like it even warmer, at about 65 degrees Fahrenheit.

Cage or stake tomato plants when you plant them. It's a lot easier than trying to corral a sprawling tomato vine later.

A week or two after your last frost date, plant pumpkin, squash, and melon seedlings.

Sow beans one to two weeks after your average last frost date. Set up a pyramid, trellis, or other support at the same time. Try sowing lettuce seed inside a bean pyramid; the lettuce will grow quickly to start, and then the bean plants will grow to shade it from the summer sun, extending the salad harvest.

Sow corn from seed a week or two after your last frost date; it needs warm soil, about 65 degrees Fahrenheit, to germinate quickly. You can extend

HERE'S HOW

TO PLANT TOMATOES

■ *You can space plants a bit closer in raised beds than in the ground, but make sure they have enough room so air can circulate freely to prevent disease.*

■ *Pinch off the bottom set of leaves on a tomato transplant and plant it deeply. Roots will develop from the buried lower part of the stem.*

■ *Place tomato cages or set up other supports when you plant the tomatoes; don't wait until they are too large to handle. Water tomatoes or other transplants thoroughly at planting.*

the harvest by sowing more than one variety, including those labeled "early" that will mature relatively quickly. To ensure that corn plants pollinate each other, you will need at least 12 plants that bloom at the same time.

To extend the harvest, sow new batches of corn, beans, carrots, radishes, beets, and cucumbers every two weeks until late June.

Cilantro is sensitive to cold, so wait to sow the seed after your last frost date. Sow a new batch every couple of weeks through June to keep the herb harvest coming.

Buy oregano, thyme, sage, and rosemary as transplants. Plant these rather woody, drought-tolerant plants separately from basil, parsley, cilantro, and other herbs that like more moisture.

Grow herbs in the garden or in pots that you can keep handy on the deck or the kitchen steps. Mix in some flowers for color, and remember, some flowers are edible. Try some edible marigolds with curly parsley, or trailing nasturtiums in hanging baskets.

Plant some extra herb plants just for their flowers. Many herbs, such as coriander, basil, and chives, will bloom if you leave some plants uncut. However, blooming will change the flavor of the herbs, so don't plan to harvest herbs from the plant you grow for the blooms.

If you have a sunny patio, deck, or balcony, plant edibles in containers. See Plant/Containers.

LAWNS

You still can overseed a lawn or lay sod in early May, unless the weather is hot and dry (see Plant/Lawns, March, page 49). *But don't do it any later.* The new grass needs time to develop enough roots to survive during the hot months of July and August.

GROUNDCOVERS

Plant groundcovers to replace lawn in shady areas or under trees. Groundcovers are usually less work to maintain than grass in small areas such as small front or side yards. The more closely you space the plants, the more quickly they will fill in the area.

Many groundcover plants spread aggressively (that's why they cover the ground). Think ahead and avoid planting aggressive spreaders where they will compete with nearby perennials. Some groundcovers, such as English ivy and myrtle, will choke out other plants. But others, such as lamium and sweet woodruff, can twine agreeably between other perennials.

PERENNIALS

When you plant potted perennials into an existing bed, add some compost to the planting hole and also topdress the soil with compost in a wide area around the new plant. You may add a little slow-release fertilizer to the planting hole when you transplant perennials to help them get established, but in the long term, few perennials need added fertilizer if they are growing in good soil. See Fertilize/Perennials.

Make sure the plant is not potbound. If there are white circling roots, make some cuts in the outside of the rootball with pruners or a soil knife to encourage the roots to branch out into the soil and not stay in the planting hole.

Space perennials far enough apart to allow for their mature size (check the label). Many transplanted perennials won't bloom or look full during their first summer because the plants concentrate at first on establishing roots. But they will fill in during the next year. For a lush-looking garden this year, plant annuals or place containers between the perennials.

■ *Spring is the time to plant fall-blooming perennials, such as shade-loving toad lilies* (Tricyrtis), *left, and monkshood* (Aconitum), *middle, as well as sun-lovers such as 'Autumn Joy' sedum* (Hylotelephium spectabile), *right.*

■ *Provide nectar for butterflies with native plants such as blazing star* (Liatris). *There are several Midwestern species that prefer different conditions.*

■ *Monarch butterflies feed on the nectar of coneflowers* (Echinacea). *But to support monarchs on their journey from Mexico to Canada each year, also plant milkweed for their caterpillars to feast on.*

■ *Mexican sunflower* (Tithonia) *is attractive to many kinds of butterflies that feed on its nectar, including monarchs and swallowtails.*

HERE'S HOW

TO GROW PERENNIALS FROM CUTTINGS

Take the cuttings from new growth in spring, usually in May. Snip about 6 inches from the end of a stem, with about two sets of leaves (the new roots will sprout from the leaf nodes, the places where the leaves are attached). Keep the cuttings moist.

Prepare small pots or a flat filled with moist potting mix. Use a chopstick, pencil, or stick to make a hole in the potting mix. On each cutting, cut just below the lowest set of leaves. Snip off the lower leaves. Dip the bare stem end in rooting hormone powder and place it in the hole in the potting mix. Gently snug the potting mix around the stem.

Place the cuttings in part sun, if they are sun-loving perennials, or part shade, if they are shade lovers. Keep them watered, being especially careful during dry spells, until they develop a strong set of roots, which typically takes six to eight weeks. You can tell the cuttings have roots when you feel resistance while gently tugging on the stem.

Plant them out in the garden before the end of June, or keep them in pots during the hot summer. Wait until the weather cools in September rather than planting them during the hot, dry months of July and August.

If you interplant annuals with perennials, make sure they have similar needs. Most perennials need less water and fertilizer than most annuals, so planting needy annuals among them means doing more work on the bed than the perennials really need. The best annuals to use as companions for sun-loving perennials are relatively drought-tolerant species such as cosmos, moss rose, zinnias, and marigolds. In the shade, use begonias, or place houseplants among the perennials.

Shortly after your last frost date, sow seeds of most perennials in the garden. See Plant/Perennials, April, page 67.

Grow only straight species of perennials from seed, or buy seed of named F1 hybrids. If you saved seed from cultivars of hybrid perennials, the new plants will have resorted their genes in the course of reproduction and will not have the same characteristics as their parents. See Plan/Annuals & Perennials, August, page 128.

To expand your supply of perennials, start new plants from cuttings of your own or your friends' perennials.

Continue to divide summer- and fall-blooming perennials such as coneflowers, asters, catmint, and toad lilies until the middle of May. But wait to divide peonies until fall.

After your last frost date, plant bulbs of hardy lilies. They need full sun and well-drained soil.

ROSES
Continue to plant roses until early June. See Plant/Roses, April, page 68.

TREES & SHRUBS
Continue planting shrubs, woody vines, and small trees (see Here's How to Plant a Tree or Shrub, page 52). It's best to get this done before early June; once the hot weather sets in, young trees and shrubs will be stressed and will have a harder time establishing their roots, even if you water them faithfully.

VINES
Toward the end of the month, once the soil is warm, sow seeds of annual vines such as black-eyed Susan

vine, thunbergia, hyacinth bean, morning glory, and moonflower. Be wary of morning glory; it often reseeds and can become a nuisance in future years.

CARE

ALL

Improve the soil of established perennial beds and shrub plantings by scattering compost about ½ inch deep. You can scatter compost directly over the mulch. It's not necessary to distribute compost perfectly evenly or rake it in; I just fling handfuls of it.

Once compost is ready to use, it's not doing your garden any good if it stays in the pile. Use up all the mature compost now, either by digging it into the soil of new plantings or by topdressing existing plantings. Then turn over whatever is not fully broken down to aerate it and start a new batch of compost. It will develop over the summer and be available for fall plantings or for topdressing when you put the garden to bed.

■ *Mulch holds in moisture, deters weeds, and breaks down to enrich the soil. Some gardeners like the tidy look of exposed mulch; others plant so lushly that mulch is scarcely seen.*

Beef up the mulch layer where it has decayed or been scattered. You can spread new mulch directly over the old. Around trees and shrubs, it looks best to use the same kind of wood chips or shredded wood as before; rake it around a bit to blend it in. Around perennials, use a material with a finer texture, such as shredded leaves. It will break down fairly quickly, so matching usually is not an issue. In any case, the foliage of mature perennials should cover most of the mulch as they open up.

Weeds sprout lustily in May, and they will outrun you if you don't keep up. In a vegetable garden with rows, you can use a hoe or cultivator to uproot small weeds as they sprout (be careful, though, around plants with fine roots such as corn and beans). Bear in mind that you also will be exposing more weed seeds to sunlight, where they can germinate. Mulch will help shade them out.

It's best to hand-pull weeds as you see them, preferably when the soil is moist so the roots slip out easily.

ANNUALS

A few weeks after you plant them, pinch back annuals to encourage them to send out more side branches for a fuller shape and more flowers. All through the season, tidy them up by removing yellowed leaves and dead flowers.

■ *Any kind of vine needs a sturdy trellis to climb, including annuals such as this black-eyed Susan vine* (Thunbergia alata).

Place stakes in May for very tall annuals such as sunflowers and dahlias that may need them later. For staking techniques, see Care/Perennials.

BULBS

Leave the foliage of spring-blooming bulbs such as daffodils alone after flowering. The bulb plants need all their leaves to collect the sun's energy to produce food and flowers for next year. You can remove them after they start to turn yellow, indicating that the plant has gone dormant, which may take several weeks.

Don't tie the leaves up or braid the leaves, either; that will reduce the area of the leaves exposed to the sun. To draw attention away from the leaves, plant spring bulbs among perennials that will take over the spotlight, or place a showboat container among them to draw the eye.

If you planted hybrid tulips as annuals, remove them, bulb and all, and compost them after they flower. Tulips often don't rebloom in our region; they will sprout and put out leaves, but not flowers. Remove them before the broad leaves detract from your other plantings.

If a large clump of daffodils failed to bloom this year, it may be crowded and need dividing. Just after other daffodils have bloomed, carefully dig up the entire clump. Gently pull the crowded bulbs apart. Plant some of them back in their original spot and plant the rest in groups in new locations

■ *Pinching back annuals, such as coleus, two or three times during the growing season will encourage them to branch and keep them looking full.*

■ *Mulching around strawberry plants with straw or leaves will keep the fruit off the ground.*

with slow-release fertilizer, following the directions on the label. Water well.

EDIBLES

Mulch strawberries to keep them off the ground (as well as providing all the other benefits of mulch). Straw is traditional (that's why they're called "strawberries"), but you also can use pesticide-free grass clippings, dried leaves, or other clean materials.

GROUNDCOVERS

Weed groundcover areas before they put on their full, dense growth. Weeds will be easier to spot.

HOUSEPLANTS

After your last frost date, once nighttime temperatures are consistently in the 50s, start bringing houseplants out into the shady parts of the garden. Slip a lightweight plastic pot into a larger, heavier container (with a hole) to prevent it from blowing over.

Remember that most houseplants come from tropical rainforests; if you have any doubt about whether it is too cold for them, wait a couple of weeks or until June. Help them acclimate to the outdoors by placing them in a shady, protected site for a week or so.

Most houseplants need a part-shade to shade location, although cacti and succulents need full sun.

Repot houseplants that need it.

HERE'S HOW

TO REPOT A HOUSEPLANT

A houseplant can eventually grow so many roots that they crowd the pot and water flows right past them. You can tell that a plant may be potbound if it stops growing. Water may flow too quickly out of the drainage holes and you may see roots on the soil surface or growing out of the holes. The crowded roots may even crack or stretch the pot.

■ *A plant, such as this spider plant, that has filled its pot with roots is rootbound. It needs to be repotted into a larger pot.*

Here's how to repot a houseplant that needs it:

- First, confirm the need by gently pulling it from the pot. If roots fill the pot or are circling the rootball, it is rootbound.

- Choose a new pot 1 or 2 inches larger in diameter than the old one. Use the appropriate potting mix, such as cactus mix for cacti or a good all-purpose potting mix for most houseplants (see Here's How to Choose a Potting Mix, page 43).

- If the plant is too crowded, gently pull or cut the roots apart to make two or more divisions and replant them separately.

- To keep the potting mix from washing out of a pot, cover the hole with a shard of broken crockery, a small piece of window screen, or a bottle cap. Cover multiple drainage holes with fiberglass window screening. Don't add a layer of gravel or pot shards; it does not improve drainage.

- Place a handful of potting mix in the pot. Gently tease apart the roots of the plant to stimulate them to grow out. Fleshy or tough roots, like those of a spider plant, can be cut with a clean, sharp knife.

- Fill the pot with potting mix so the crown (where the plant meets the roots) is at soil level, about 1 inch below the rim of the pot. This will allow space for the water to pool and soak in when you water.

Plants that will stay indoors can use a good bath to wash off dust, cobwebs, and spider mites. Take them out to the porch or the balcony and spray them with the hose or douse them with a couple of buckets of water, or wash them off in the shower. Let them drain thoroughly and pinch them back to shape them up before you take them back indoors.

LAWNS

Mow the lawn as often as needed. The grass will be growing faster in May than any other time of year, so you probably will need to mow once a week.

Use a mulching mower to recycle the nutrients in the clippings back to your grass plants. Rake out any wet clumps of grass that remain on the lawn to distribute the clippings.

Mow when the lawn is dry; mulching mowers, especially, don't work well in tall, wet grass.

For healthy grass, set the lawnmower blade as high as it will go, at least 2 to 3 inches (or higher, if possible). Most lawns are cut too short. Taller grass will shade out most weeds and keep them from sprouting. The added height also will allow it to develop longer, stronger roots that will make it more drought tolerant. Even though I hardly ever water my lawn, my 3-inch-tall grass usually stays green longer than

■ *Set the mower height at 3 inches, if possible, or as high as your mower will go. Taller grass is healthier grass.*

■ *If you edge the lawn carefully, tall grass will still look neat.*

my fussier neighbors' does in July because I never mow as low as they do.

Don't ever cut more than one-third of the grass blades' height; the plants need plenty of leaf surface to collect sunlight. If the lawn has become overgrown, cut it at 4 inches one week and then down to 3 inches the next.

Edge when you mow. A lawn that is neatly edged along the sidewalk will seem tidy even if your grass is taller than the lawn next door.

After your annual and perennial beds are planted this month, neaten up the edge of the lawn along the beds. Using a sharp square-edged spade, go along the edge, slicing straight down. Then slice horizontally under the unwanted clumps of grass to remove them.

Use the grass clumps to patch bare spaces in your lawn. (You will have to water them diligently, like sod, until they are established.)

Keep the blades on your mower sharpened for a cleaner cut. A rule of thumb is to sharpen the blade after every eight hours of use.

Be careful to keep the lawnmower and string trimmer away from trees. They can do serious damage to the bark. Protect a tree by surrounding it with a wide circle of mulch so you will never need to bring power tools near.

PERENNIALS

Set a wire hoop or grid to support peonies early in May, just after they sprout. The plants will grow

up through the grid or hoop so it can hold the stems up when the heavy flowers open.

Stake tall perennials such as lilies early, when the plants are small.

Use a stake that will be tall enough for the plant's full height. The taller the plant will be, the stronger the stake needs to be, because the plant will pull on it when the wind blows. Green-dyed bamboo stakes are common, but I use straight, smooth branches I save from pruning.

Tie the plant to the stake gently. I use green jute twine. Cut a 6-inch piece of twine and make a figure eight: Wrap the twine around the stake, cross it, then wrap it around the plant's stem and tie it in a double knot. Leave plenty of slack so the plant can flex in the wind without the twine rubbing on the stem. Trim the ends of the twine neatly and it will be much less noticeable. As the plant grows, come back and tie the newer, taller parts of the stem to the stake at intervals of 8 to 12 inches.

Pinch back chrysanthemums when they are 6 inches high to encourage them to send out side branches and delay flowering. Without this treatment, most chrysanthemums will bloom in July or August, not in September.

You can fence in floppy plants with green twine and bamboo poles or branches. When tying a single stem to a stake, make a figure eight, crossing the twine between the stake and the stem. Allow some slack in the twine when you tie it. This will keep the stake and the stem apart and allow them both to flex in the wind.

Pinch back chrysanthemums in May and a time or two more before mid-July. This will keep them bushy and delay their bloom until late summer or early fall.

You can cut back many other perennials, such as phlox, when they are 4 to 6 inches tall to keep them more compact. It delays flowering but reduces the need for staking.

If you cut back one-third of the stems on most perennials each time two times a week apart, it will extend the flowering period because the cut-back stems will flower later.

Finish dividing perennials before June, when it can get hot. See Plant/Perennials & Groundcovers, March, page 49.

ROSES
In mid- to late May, after growth has started on climbing and rambling roses but before they get

HERE'S HOW

TO DIVIDE PERENNIALS

Divide summer- and fall-blooming perennials in spring. Start by digging all around the plant with a sharp spade.

Gently pull or cut the rootball apart, following natural divisions if they are apparent.

out of hand, train the new, flexible growth to its support. Check first that the trellis still is sturdy and strongly anchored.

A climbing rose plant should have a framework of stems, with new twigs growing from side stems. Ramblers grow boisterously and need lots of space.

Growing horizontally encourages the plants to bloom more, so bend the canes sideways as much as you can. Tie them to the support with something strong but flexible, such as green jute twine or strips of old black pantyhose. Leave some slack so the branches can grow and flex in the wind.

SHRUBS

Prune spring-flowering shrubs and trees such as lilacs, honeysuckle, magnolia, flowering cherry, and crabapple within three weeks after they finish flowering. These shrubs will form next year's flower buds on this year's new growth, so if you wait too long to prune you will be removing the buds of next year's bloom. It won't hurt the plant, but it will reduce flowering.

VINES

Check climbing hydrangea and other woody vines to make sure they are still well-secured to their support. Prune out any dead wood and prune as needed to direct any new growth in a direction that will make it easy to attach it to the trellis.

WATER

ALL

All your new plants, in the ground and in containers, will need attentive watering until they settle into their new soil and send out the fine roots they need to anchor themselves, to collect and store water, and to absorb nutrients.

ANNUALS

Gently sprinkle newly planted seeds to keep the soil moist until they germinate.

Water newly planted annuals and houseplants once a day. After ten days or two weeks, back off to watering every other day or whenever the finger test tells you the soil is not moist enough.

Annuals generally need more watering than perennials all season because they are blooming constantly. However, some drought-tolerant species may prefer the soil a little drier, such as cosmos, moss rose, zinnias, and marigolds.

BULBS

Keep soil evenly moist, but not saturated, for summer-blooming bulbs such as cannas, tuberous begonias, and elephant ears. As elephant ears' leaves get larger, they will need a lot more water.

CONTAINERS & HOUSEPLANTS

Check the potting mix in containers daily and water as needed. Containers dry out much faster than soil in the ground, so you may need to water small ones every other day.

■ *To save work, try to position plants that need to be watered with a watering can closest to the water source.*

■ *If you water by hand, soak the soil, not the plants. It's the roots that need water.*

When you do water, water thoroughly. Wait a few seconds to make sure water flows out through the drainage hole. If you use a saucer, empty it; never let the container stand in a saucer of water. That can cut off oxygen to the roots and cause them to rot.

Be especially careful about checking containers and hanging baskets on the porch or under the roof overhang. Rain may not reach them. Containers under trees also will not get much of the rain.

EDIBLES

Sprinkle newly planted seeds gently to keep the soil moist.

Water newly planted transplants once a day. After ten days or two weeks, back off to watering every other day or as needed.

Water established vegetable plants as often as needed to keep the soil evenly moist.

LAWNS

Water a newly seeded lawn every few days, using a sprinkler. (See Here's How to Reseed or Resod a Lawn, page 48.)

Sprinkle recently planted sod daily for at least two weeks for about 20 minutes. After that, water it every other day for another two weeks. Then plan to water at least once a week, and more frequently in July and August.

■ *You can use an electronic meter to measure soil moisture, or you can simply dig down 6 inches with a trowel and see if the soil is moist. Or stick your finger into loose soil or potting mix and feel if it is moist 1 or 2 inches down.*

Checking the soil moisture won't help you tell whether sod needs water, since it has few roots that extend down into the soil. Assume that it needs regular watering throughout its first season.

An established lawn of appropriate cool-season grasses should not need watering in spring, unless the weather is unusually hot and dry.

PERENNIALS & GROUNDCOVERS

If you sowed seeds for perennials, gently sprinkle them to keep the soil evenly moist until they germinate. Once they sprout, keep the soil evenly moist through the summer.

Water transplanted perennials and groundcovers daily during the first few days after planting and two or three times a week after that, depending on conditions. Even plants that are described as "low maintenance" or "drought tolerant" need this help when they are new. Water the area around the plant so the roots will spread out.

Water established perennials only when they need it. Many perennials—especially prairie species such as coneflower and black-eyed Susan—can get by on rainfall except in hot, dry weather. You probably won't need to water them in May.

■ *It's best to use a sprinkler in the morning so turf or leaves have plenty of time to dry off before nightfall, reducing the risk of disease. If you use a sprinkler at mid-day in summer, much of the water will be lost to evaporation.*

HERE'S HOW

TO WATER TO KEEP PLANTS HEALTHY

Most of the plants in our gardens, from tiny seedlings to trees, need some watering sometimes. But it's important not to overwater. Sopping-wet soil can cut off oxygen to the plants' roots and cause rot.

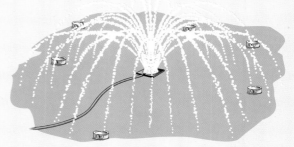

Your soil type makes a difference. Water will quickly drain through sandy soil near Lake Erie or Lake Michigan, so plants there may need more frequent watering. Clay soil, on the other hand, easily becomes saturated, which can lead to root rot. A good loam, the happy medium, with plenty of organic matter, will hold enough water for plants' roots but let the excess drain away.

Most plants in our climate need about 1 inch of water a week, from rainfall or supplemental watering. You can check rainfall with a rain gauge. To figure out how much you are supplying with a sprinkler, place a straight-sided container—a tuna can is classic—under the sprinkler. When it has filled 1 inch deep, turn the sprinkler off. Note how long it took so you will know next time how long you should leave the sprinkler on.

What really matters, though, is how much moisture is in the soil. Don't guess; a long, light rainfall may not actually deliver much water to plants. A rain gauge—or two in different parts of the garden—can be a useful reality check. But it's easy to lose track of the last time it rained or to overestimate how much water you deliver by hand-sprinkling.

Check often to see whether the soil actually needs more water. Stick your finger in down to the second knuckle in several places. If you don't feel moisture, water. Or use a trowel to dig down 5 or 6 inches and feel for moisture.

For all established plants, including lawns, the general rule is to water slowly, deeply, and not too often. Light, frequent watering is counterproductive. If the top layer of soil stays moist, plant roots never have to grow down to reach water; the plant will only have short, feeble roots that are dependent on your daily sprinkles.

If, instead, you water deeply and then give the moisture a few days to ebb down into the soil, plants' roots will grow down to reach for it. The longer roots will make the plant stronger, more self-reliant, and more resistant to drought.

As the summer goes on, plants will need more water because they are larger and because they lose more water to evaporation when it's hot.

Water the soil where the roots are, not the leaves. Overhead watering wastes water and wet foliage can encourage fungus diseases. A watering wand or soaker hoses can help. See Here's How to Use Soaker Hoses, page 59.

If you water with a sprinkler, try to do it in the morning so the leaves have time to dry off. Avoid watering in the evening; the leaves will stay wet all night. In-ground sprinkler systems are great water wasters. If you have one, learn to adjust the timer and to turn it on or off as needed; don't just leave it on the installed settings regardless of the weather. That not only wastes water but leads to overwatering, which can result in problems such as disease and lawn grubs.

Perennials that prefer drier soil include yarrow, artemisia, coneflower, black-eyed Susan, Russian sage, lamb's ear, veronica, daylilies, coreopsis, butterfly weed, blanket flower, and sedum.

Among the perennials that prefer more moist soil are lobelia, ligularia, delphinium, astilbe, bellflower, hosta, and fern.

ROSES

Water newly planted roses daily for a week or so, and then back off to every two or three days. After a month, water just as you do your other roses.

Sturdy shrub roses may be able to get by mostly on rainfall once they are established, but most roses do need regular watering. Check the soil around established roses for moisture and follow the same rule with them as you do for other plants: Water slowly, deeply, and not too often. In springtime, you may need to water only once a week.

Use a watering wand or soaker hoses to put the water right at the soil; getting rose leaves wet is an invitation to fungus diseases.

TREES, SHRUBS & VINES

Newly planted trees, shrubs, and woody vines need daily watering. After a week or two, depending on the weather, water only every few days. Keep watering new shrubs regularly until they are two years old.

The best way to water trees and shrubs is with a slow trickle from the hose that deeply soaks the rootball. Leave it on top of the plant's rootball for 20 minutes or so and then move it to another place on the rootball. After an hour or so, turn the water off. You also can buy or make a short length of soaker hose, capped at the end, to distribute water slowly all around the plant.

Watering at soil level is especially important for evergreens. Their needles can shed rain or water from a sprinkler like an umbrella away from the rootball, where it is really needed.

Established trees and shrubs should generally be able to get by on rainfall in a normal spring.

FERTILIZE

ALL

Fertilize only those plants that need it. Depending on the plant and the chemical makeup of your soil, a plant may be able to absorb what it needs without supplemental fertilizer. Your soil test (see Here's How to Get a Soil Test, page 143) will tell you about the nutrients in your soil.

Too much fertilizer, or fertilizer a plant doesn't need, can be harmful. And chemicals from surplus fertilizer, especially nitrogen and phosphorus, will run off into waterways or

Organic fertilizers are all slow release. Slow-release fertilizers are best for most plants.

seep into groundwater and cause pollution in rivers and lakes. Always err on the side of less fertilizer rather than more.

The best source of nutrients for plants is organic matter in the soil. Incorporating compost in the soil of new plantings and top-dressing existing beds with compost will go a long way toward supplying plants with the nutrients they need.

ANNUALS

If you incorporated slow-release fertilizer when planting, it should generally provide enough nutrients until July. If plants seem feeble a few weeks after planting or their youngest leaves are yellowish, fertilize no more than once a week with a liquid fertilizer at half the strength recommended on the label.

BULBS

Sprinkle a little slow-release fertilizer around the plants of spring-blooming bulbs when they are done flowering. May and June, when they are developing new flowers for next year, is the time they can use some extra nutrients.

HERE'S HOW

TO READ A FERTILIZER LABEL

Every fertilizer is required by law to have a "guaranteed analysis" that lists all the nutrients it supplies and the ratio of the three primary nutrients: nitrogen, phosphorus, and potassium.

Nitrogen (abbreviated N) supports the growth of green parts—stems and leaves. Since lawns are nearly all leaf, they need ample nitrogen. But too much nitrogen can make plants stressed and weak or push them to make leaves at the expense of flowers.

Phosphorus (P) helps develop roots and seedlings. Most Midwestern soils have ample phosphorus; don't add it unless a soil test shows your soil is deficient in it. Phosphorus is a serious water pollution problem in waterways such as Lake Erie.

Potassium (K) affects the way plants use water and the chemicals in their systems. It is important for overall health. Many Midwestern soils have plenty of potassium.

The package will have a three-number ratio showing the percentages the fertilizer contains of N, P, and K, in that order. For example, 6-0-2 means the product contains 6 percent nitrogen, 0 percent phosphorus, and 2 percent potassium.

Single-digit percentages in the N-P-K ratio indicate that the fertilizer is likely slow release. Slow-release fertilizers are formulated to release the chemical elements at a rate at which plants can absorb them. All organic fertilizers are slow release.

In lawn fertilizer, look for a slow-release formula with a higher nitrogen number and a phosphorus number of 0, such as 6-0-2.

A double-digit nitrogen number in the N-P-K ratio, such as 26-3-4, indicates the fertilizer is fast release. If you use fast-release lawn fertilizer, there's an added danger of harming the plants. Most of the nitrogen and phosphorus will be wasted and will wash away to cause pollution.

For annuals, containers, and houseplants, use an organic formula or a synthetic slow-release formula with a balanced ratio such as 8-8-8 or 6-6-6.

Beyond the big three nutrients, 14 other elements also are important to plants in varying amounts. Look for "micronutrients" on the package, or check the "guaranteed analysis" section to be sure it lists a wide array of elements.

Synthetic slow-release fertilizers come in the form of pellets or granules that you scatter or mix into the soil. An organic fertilizer will be made of some combination of plant and animal products that contain the essential nutrients. There are granular products to spread on the soil and liquid fertilizers to mix with water.

Fast-release water-soluble fertilizers, often in the form of blue crystals, will deliver the primary nutrients to annuals and containers quickly. With any soluble fertilizer, never exceed the concentration that's recommended in the directions. In fact, it's safest to use these fertilizers at half their recommended rate.

CONTAINERS & HOUSEPLANTS

Fertilize annuals and edibles in containers every other week with a liquid fertilizer at half the strength recommended on the label. Fertilize foliage plants, such as most houseplants, every three weeks or once a month. For edibles, use only organic fertilizer. Plants in containers need regular fertilizer because they're watered so often, washing nutrients away.

EDIBLES

Compost-rich soil should provide greens and vegetables with most of their nutrients. If you want to give them a little help, scatter slow-release organic fertilizer around them once in May, following the directions on the label.

LAWNS

If you didn't yet topdress the lawn with compost, do it now. Spread about ½ inch of compost over the grass and rake it so it falls between the leaf blades. Do this when rain is predicted or water the lawn to encourage microorganisms to work on the compost.

In mid- to late May, fertilize the lawn with a slow-release fertilizer, following the instructions on the label. One application in May, when the grass is most actively growing, and one in fall should be sufficient, especially if you plan to let the grass go dormant in July and August.

Organic lawn fertilizers are available; I use them.

Avoid developing a five-times-a-year fertilizer habit. Too many applications during the season

■ *Whether a fertilizer is organic or synthetic, measure it carefully and never use more than the directions state. Many gardeners use liquid fertilizers at half strength to be sure they will not burn plants.*

■ *Most established perennials need no supplemental fertilizer. They can get all the nutrients they need from good soil.*

will make the grass weak and dependent on fertilizer and will damage the healthy community of microorganisms in the soil of your lawn.

PERENNIALS

Scatter a granular slow-release fertilizer, preferably organic, over the soil around those perennials that can use extra nutrients, such as chrysanthemums, daylilies, hibiscus, garden phlox, lilies, and astilbe. It should be enough for the season.

However, most perennials don't need much, if any, fertilizer. If you enriched the soil with compost when you planted and if you topdress your perennial beds from time to time with compost and other organic matter, such as shredded leaves, the plants will normally be able to get their nutrients from the soil.

Many perennials do best with no fertilizer, including ornamental grasses, sedums, and native prairie plants like coneflowers, liatris, black-eyed Susans, butterfly weed, and coreopsis. Overfed perennials will grow too tall and floppy.

Even newly planted perennials will generally get the nutrients they need from the potting mix they came in.

TREES & SHRUBS

Fertilize an established tree or shrub only if a soil test has revealed a deficiency that is causing a problem in the plant.

PROBLEM-SOLVE

ALL

Avoid using home remedies such as chewing tobacco tea or soap sprays made from detergent to kill pests. They are likely to do more harm than good, killing beneficial insects and damaging plants. Commercial insecticidal soaps are formulated not to harm plants if used as directed.

Always identify a problem for certain before deciding whether you need to take any measures to control it. Most insects are harmless or beneficial, and many disease breakouts do little damage to the plant. The best course may be to relax and do nothing.

If you decide to take action, try non-chemical methods, such as hand-picking, first. If you resort to spraying, always use the least toxic alternative in the smallest amount that will be effective.

Using the wrong chemical or using it at the wrong time in the pest's life cycle can be futile. At worst, it can harm the plant.

ANNUALS

If an annual plant's younger leaves are yellow, they may need a little more nitrogen. See Fertilize/Annuals.

EDIBLES

Place 3-inch lengths of paper towel tubes over small new seedlings and transplants to keep out cutworms. Remove them in a couple of weeks when the stems get sturdier.

Once a week, spend a few minutes patrolling your vegetable garden for problems. For example, watch potato plants for potato beetle larvae that can eat the leaves. Inspect the undersides of the leaves for the bright orange eggs or the tiny red-brown larvae. Pluck off the infested leaves and dispose of them in the trash or landscape waste, not the compost pile.

LAWNS

Look out for creeping bentgrass, which is sometimes planted on golf course putting greens but is a common weed in lawns. It spreads vigorously in spring but quickly turns brown in summer and is very prone to disease.

■ *Use only commercial insecticidal soaps to manage insects. Home-brewed mixtures, including household detergents, can damage plants.*

■ *Animal repellants must be reapplied every time it rains. They work by frightening animals with an unfamiliar smell or taste. Switch repellants often so animals don't get used to any of them.*

■ *To discourage slugs, scatter diatomaceous earth on the soil around the vulnerable plants. It is made of shards of seashells that are too sharp for slugs and snails to cross.*

■ *Horticultural oil can coat some kinds of insect eggs and smother them. As with any pest control, use it only if you have identified the problem and confirmed that an oil spray is likely to be effective.*

The best way to handle a bentgrass infestation is to kill the whole patch with a herbicide containing glyphosate. Apply it very carefully on a still day to avoid getting any of the spray on nearby plants; it will kill them too. Remove all the dead bentgrass. After a week or so, improve the soil of the bare patch with compost and reseed with a drought-tolerant, hardy grass mix before the weather gets too hot. (See Here's How to Reseed or Resod a Lawn, page 48.)

PERENNIALS

If leaves of hostas or daylilies have brown edges from a late frost, snip them off. The plants will grow new ones.

ROSES

When your grafted roses start putting on new growth, be alert for suckers growing from beneath the graft union at the base of the stem. They are growing from the rootstock and will not have the same characteristics as the rest of the plant. Prune them out at the base.

Sometimes the scion—the top plant that is grafted onto the rootstock—dies from harsh winter weather, and only the rootstock sprouts. You may not notice until it blooms with unfamiliar flowers.

Occasionally, a grafted rose may start to put on new growth and then quickly shrivel and die. Most likely it is because the rootstock died, and the scion could not draw water from the dead roots.

You can avoid the problems associated with grafted roses by buying roses that are grown on their own roots.

If the spring is cool and wet, watch roses carefully for signs of fungus diseases such as blackspot and rust. Make sure roses are pruned to allow good air circulation (see Care/Roses, March, page 56).

Before you use any fungicides, be sure that you have properly identified the problem. If in doubt, take some leaves to a good garden center or to your local state university Extension office or botanical garden for identification and suggested controls.

HERE'S HOW

TO GET HELP WITH PLANT PROBLEMS

You can get advice from state university Extension offices, Master Gardener plant clinics, many botanical gardens and arboreta, and good garden centers with knowledgeable staff. See Resources, page 189.

To get the best response, provide plenty of information, including the name of the plant if you know it. Identifying a plant problem usually requires identifying the plant, since many insect pests and diseases are host specific. Take pictures not only of the pest or problem but of the entire branch and the whole plant, to show its habit. Think about its growing conditions and recent events: Is it in sun or shade? Is the soil moist? When did you last fertilize? Have you or a neighbor sprayed herbicides or insecticides lately?

Bring in or e-mail photos with your question. It's harder for experts to give good answers in a phone call, when they can't see the evidence.

If you bring in samples, place them in a sealed zipper bag to avoid spreading the problem. To confirm the identification, include a branch with several leaves as well as the bug or the damaged leaf. Consider bringing a sample of the soil too. Some university Extension plant clinics charge $15 or $20 to analyze a sample and confirm a diagnosis.

■ *Inspect potato plants, including the undersides of leaves, for the bright orange eggs or the black-dotted red-brown larvae of potato beetles. Pluck off infested leaves and stems and dispose of them in the trash or landscape waste, not the compost pile.*

Make sure you are buying the right product and follow the label directions precisely.

Some rose gardeners use a homemade solution of baking soda and water with good results.

Using a fungicide is a commitment: most fungicides are only effective if applied starting early in the season, before the symptoms appear, and once a week all season.

Clean up diseased foliage carefully to avoid spreading the problem and discourage infections next year. You also may want to consider replacing disease-prone roses with more disease-resistant varieties.

Once a week or so, on a sunny day in the morning, hit rose bushes with a stiff spray of water to remove aphids, dust, and spider mites.

SHRUBS

If the spring has been cool and wet, you may see fungus diseases such as powdery mildew, downy mildew, and apple scab in shrubs. The leaves may show yellowing, black spots, or a pale, cloudy film.

Remove any infected leaves and clean up fallen ones. Put them in the landscape waste or the trash. Disinfect your pruners after you work on a diseased plant.

Before you consider using a fungicide, identify the problem for certain and get advice on the best product to use. See Resources, page 189. Follow the directions precisely.

Fungicides will not eliminate any problem forever. The spores that cause most fungal diseases are always present, although they only multiply when the conditions are right. If the weather is drier next spring, you may have no problem.

Some plants are more susceptible to disease than others. If a plant has the same problem year after year—such as an old lilac that always gets powdery mildew or a crabapple tree that always gets apple scab—consider removing it and replacing it with a newer, more disease-resistant variety, or a different plant altogether.

If all the leaves on an azalea or rhododendron seem to disappear overnight after flowering, the problem may be azalea sawflies. They hatch in May and the tiny green caterpillars feed into June, feeding on leaves and flowers. If you detect the problem early, you can pick off the small caterpillar-like larvae and drown them in a bucket of soapy water.

If there are too many to remove by hand, spray each caterpillar with a commercial insecticidal soap. There are insecticides that are effective against sawflies, but they also will kill beneficial insects such as bees. Get expert advice before using any insecticide and follow the package directions precisely.

■ *Powdery mildew thrives in humid air. Discourage this fungus disease by spacing and pruning plants for good air circulation.*

June

In June, the garden is entering its full glory. Annuals planted in May are lush in their pots, and perennials have asserted themselves to fill the garden beds. The scent of lilacs is gone, but many other shrubs are in bloom, and trees have unfolded their green glory to shade the streets. It's time to take a walk.

Garden walks sprout all over in June and July, and they are splendid opportunities to learn, to dream, and to get inspiration and information. Take plenty of notes and photos (where photography is permitted). Ask for names of plants that intrigue you and note how they are arranged.

You'll often find the most spectacular inspiration in gardens in affluent neighborhoods. But the gardens in more modest areas often offer more accessible ideas.

Even a stroll around your own neighborhood can yield inspiration. And if you strike up a conversation with the gardener—compliments are great icebreakers—you may start a relationship that yields advice, seeds, and plants.

Now that your own garden is mostly planted, start keeping notes on what is working and what isn't as the months go by. Note spots and times of year that didn't have enough color or seemed bare or boring, so you can try something different next year. Take pictures often.

Meanwhile, it's time to settle into sensible summer routines: watching the rain; checking soil moisture before you water; mowing the grass, but not too short; wearing long pants, sturdy shoes, and eye and ear protection whenever you use power tools; keeping up with the weeding. There's one more habit that's worthwhile: every day, sit for a minute or take a short stroll to admire your own efforts.

It's hard to believe, but although the hottest days are yet to come, by the end of this month the days will be growing shorter again and it will be time to plan for the fall vegetable garden. So spend plenty of time in the garden enjoying the balmy joys of June while they last.

PLAN

ANNUALS

As cool-season spring annuals such as larkspur, nigella, pot marigolds, and pansies start to fade in June, plan to replace them with more heat-tolerant annuals such as petunias, calibrachoa, or lantana that will bloom through the summer.

BULBS

Admire lilies as they bloom in other gardens and decide which ones you will plant in fall. Easy-care Asiatic lilies bloom in June, followed by LA hybrids, a cross between Asiatic and Longiflorum types. Through the summer, look for martagon lilies, trumpet lilies, tiger lilies, and finally Oriental lilies in late summer.

If you already have lilies, pay attention to your lilies as they bloom and make a note of which ones you will need to divide in fall. Clumps that seem crowded or aren't blooming as much as they used to are good candidates.

Also note if your lilies are leaning toward the light. That probably means they aren't in a site with enough sun, and you should plan to move them.

■ *If cool-season annuals have faded or become scraggly, pull them up and replace them with summer bloomers.*

EDIBLES

Keep notes on the vegetable varieties you especially like or that perform well to guide your ordering for next year.

Store any leftover seeds you are saving for next year. See May/Plan, page 76.

LAWNS

Toward the end of June, decide whether you plan to let your lawn go dormant during the dry months of July and August. If you don't water during that time, the grass will get a brownish color as many leaf blades die back. But the plants' crowns and roots will remain alive, waiting for cooler weather. Summer dormancy is normal and won't hurt the lawn. A good rain, or a good watering, once or twice a month is enough to keep dormant grass alive.

Either let the lawn go dormant or don't, but don't change your mind and try to revive a brown lawn. Swinging in and out of dormancy will stress the grass.

PERENNIALS

Keep an eagle eye out for the first sales at garden centers toward the end of the month. You may spot a great buy! But if you buy plants in the summer, be careful to avoid those that are stressed because they have been neglected. Plants at some retailers don't get as much attention after the spring rush.

Choose plants that still have healthy, full foliage with normal color for the season and a number of green buds. Avoid plants with dry soil, excessive browning along the edges of the leaves, yellowing leaves, or stems that have died back.

Check for circling roots that indicate the plant is potbound. Densely matted roots will dry out quickly in the summer, so water the plant well and gently break up the mass of roots before you plant.

ROSES

As the roses bloom in your garden, your neighborhood, and your local public garden, stroll among them to consider those you might want to plant for next year. This is a good time to look for hardy, disease-resistant shrub or species roses that might replace higher-maintenance varieties.

■ *In early June, once the soil is warm, plant gladiolus corms and other summer bulbs.*

PLANT

ANNUALS

Plant annual flower seedlings to fill in where spring bulbs' flowers have faded. (Don't cut back the bulb plants' foliage until it yellows, though, if you want flowers next year; see Care/Bulbs, page 104.)

Now that the soil is warm even in the north, there are many seeds for annual flowers that you can still sow directly in the ground early in the month. Try marigolds, cosmos, sunflowers, morning glories, four o'clocks, evening primrose, and nasturtium.

BULBS

Plant a last batch of dahlias and gladioli before the middle of the month. They will bloom at the end of summer.

EDIBLES

In the north, plant out transplants of heat-loving vegetables such as pumpkins, peppers, and tomatoes early in the month if you didn't plant them in May.

For a longer harvest of sweet corn and cucumbers, sow a new batch of seeds every two weeks until mid-June.

LAWNS

It's too late to overseed a lawn in June, but you *can* still plant sod if you are willing to water it often

all summer. See Here's How to Reseed or Resod a Lawn, page 48.

PERENNIALS

You can continue planting trees, shrubs, and perennials through June, as long as you care for them attentively through the summer. They will need more watering because they do not have as much time to establish a good root system as those planted earlier.

Watch for ripening seeds on columbine, corydalis, celandine poppy, and Virginia bluebells. These

■ *Sow cucumber seeds every two weeks until mid-June. The harvest of many crops can be extended by sowing seed in batches over several weeks.*

■ *Look for ripening seed pods on plants you'd like to spread, such as these on columbine, as well as Virginia bluebells and celandine poppies. Collect the pods and scatter them where you'd like the plants to go.*

plants will self-sow readily in their immediate vicinity, but if you want to sow the seeds elsewhere, collect the seedpods in summer as soon as they are ripe and the pods start to open, and scatter them where you want them.

ROSES

Roses are plentiful in garden centers in June when they are in bloom, although the ideal time to plant roses is earlier, in the spring. To plant roses, see Plant/Roses, April, page 68.

TREES & SHRUBS

You can still plant trees, shrubs, and woody vines, if you mulch them well and water them regularly and deeply through the summer. If you don't plant by the end of June, it's wiser to wait until fall. See Here's How to Plant a Tree or Shrub, page 52.

Any balled-and-burlapped tree or shrub you buy in June will have been dug in late winter and held since them. It's crucial to buy one that has been cared for well, and whose roots have never been allowed to dry out. Choose a plant that is fully leafed out, with leaves that are a normal green. Usually, yellowed or undersized leaves are a sign of stress.

CARE

ALL

Bring summer into your house by cutting flowers from the garden all through summer. Snip flowers early in the morning or late in the evening when they are filled with water, not in the heat of the day. Place them *immediately* in water. Cut some herbs, shrub branches, or large leaves from plants such as hostas to fill out the arrangement.

Indoors, recut each stem at an angle as you place it in your arrangement and remove any foliage that would be underwater in the vase. Change the water every other day to make your bouquet last longer.

Keep patrolling for weeds. It's much easier to keep them under control all along than to try to fight back a horde in August. Try to remove weeds before they flower and set seed to make more weeds.

ANNUALS

Pinch back annuals such as petunias that cascade from pots to encourage more side stems for a fuller appearance. Pinch long stalks off about halfway, above a good set of leaves. The new growth will flower again in a couple of weeks. If you pinch back a few of the longest stalks every couple of weeks, you keep encouraging new growth without ever having to cut back the whole plant.

Many annual flowers, such as marigolds, geraniums, nemesia, and diascia, will bloom more if you deadhead, or remove old blooms that are wilting and browning before they have a chance to turn into seeds. Generally you can just snip or pinch off the bloom itself. But if there is a long stalk that would be left naked, remove that too.

When you deadhead petunias, remove the entire flower, including the green base that encloses its seed-building organs.

Maintain a 1-inch-deep layer of mulch over the surface of the soil for annuals, including in containers. Mulch will hold moisture in the soil and insulate against the heat of summer.

Remove seedlings of self-sowing annuals such as love-in-a-mist. You can consider them weeds and compost them, or use them as filler to refresh containers.

Stake tall annuals such as flowering tobacco (*Nicotiana sylvestris*) as they grow. See Care/Perennials in May, page 89.

BULBS

Resist the impulse to remove the leaves of spring-flowering bulbs before they turn yellow. Some daffodil foliage may not go dormant until July 4. You can remove the leaves when they start to turn yellow.

Once the foliage has yellowed, divide clumps of daffodils whose flowering slowed down this year. Before you dig, decide on the full-sun sites where you will replant the divisions and amend their soil with plenty of compost.

Dig up the daffodil clump, gently tease the cluster of bulbs and roots apart, and replant promptly while the roots still are moist. Dig a hole and

HERE'S HOW

TO WEED

Don't just pull off the top leaves and stems of weeds; be sure you remove their roots. If you weed when the soil is moist, the roots of shallow-rooted weeds will slip out more easily.

A hand weeder (1), trowel (2), or soil knife (3) is helpful. There are many different weeder designs, so try several to see which is most comfortable for you. A forked-tongued weeder is especially effective for some weeds such as dandelions with deep roots that will resprout if left behind.

To remove a dandelion—roots and all—stick a weeder straight down next to the center of the plant and then lever it sideways to pop the taproot out of the soil.

Quack grass is a special agony, because it spreads by slender, delicate underground stems. If you pull too hard on the stems, they'll break, and the weed can sprout from the broken parts. Use a soil knife or other slim weeder and your fingers to stems underground from clump to clump. Dig the clumps up from below with your weeder and try to remove as much stem as you can. As with all weeding, persistence is key.

Creeping Charlie is another particularly difficult weed, because it sends slender stems twining through grass and between other plants. Carefully follow a stem with your fingers back to the crown of the plant. Dig up the plant, roots and all, and pull on it gently to try and extract all the fragile stems without breaking them. Do *not* put creeping Charlie in the compost heap, because it can take root from any stem.

If you pull weeds that have set seed, don't put them in the compost heap either. Put them in the trash or the landscape waste. Home compost piles rarely get hot enough to kill weed seeds.

Mulch in vegetable gardens and beds can help keep weed seeds from sprouting.

position the daffodils so the bottom of the bulbs lies about two to three times as deep as each bulb is wide. Backfill the hole and water well.

EDIBLES

To keep herbs going all summer long, use them. The more you pinch back herbs, the more leaves they will produce. Pinch off any flower buds of basil, parsley, cilantro, and chives plants and they will produce many more leaves.

If you find yourself overwhelmed with chives, divide them and transplant some to the perennial garden. They are winter hardy and have lovely purple balls of bloom in late spring.

Where you direct-sowed seeds, thin the seedlings until the plants have enough room to mature properly (consult the seed packet for spacing). Thinned greens of lettuce and kale, as well as beets, turnips, and kale, are edible too.

Be careful when using a weeder or hoe around corn and bean plants. They have delicate roots, just under the surface of the soil, that can be easily damaged.

CONTAINERS & HOUSEPLANTS

If some annuals, such as nasturtiums, start crowding others in a mixed container, thin them by cutting some of the bullies' stems back close to the soil. A new stem will sprout.

■ *Snip off developing flowers on basil, mint, and other herbs before they bloom. Blooming will alter the flavor of the plants' leaves.*

By early June, it should be safe to move all houseplants out into the yard. Most cacti and succulents can go in full sun, but other houseplants should usually be in shade or filtered light, such as under a tree.

Throughout the summer, move containers around in the garden to fill in "black holes" that develop where bulb foliage has faded or other plants didn't work out. Just make sure you keep containers in the right conditions (most houseplants can't take full sun, and petunias can't handle shade).

LAWNS

Throughout the summer, watch out for lawn grass spreading into adjacent garden beds. Some lawn grasses, such as fescues, spread by rhizomes; others spread by seed. You can dig out clumps from beds and use them to patch bare places or divots in the lawn, but you will need to water them attentively until established, as you would sod.

Keep mowing as often as needed. The grass will gradually slow its growth as the weather gets hotter and dryer.

PERENNIALS

If you didn't do it in May, pinch back chrysanthemums when they are 6 inches high in early June to encourage them to send out side branches and delay flowering.

After early-blooming perennials flower, deadhead them for tidiness' sake, unless you want plants such as columbine to reseed.

Bleeding heart will rebloom sporadically through the summer if you cut back old stalks to the next branch. The tiny sprout in the crotch will grow and eventually flower.

Pinching back perennials in early summer will make them branch more to keep them compact and manageable, although it will make them bloom a week or so later. Try this for asters, salvia, columbine, scabiosa, coreopsis, and catmint.

Cut back many perennials in June after their first bloom and they will rebloom later in summer. Plants that respond well to this treatment include perennial salvia, catmint, calamint, lavender, coreopsis, yarrow, and bellflower.

Even if some perennials start to look overcrowded, wait to divide them until September when the weather is cooler. It would be hard for divided plants to reestablish themselves during the hot summer.

If you didn't stake lilies in spring, stake them now. See Care/Perennials, May, page 89.

Groom your beds and borders to keep them attractive. Remove yellow or tattered leaves on hostas and other foliage plants.

ROSES

Deadhead roses to keep June-blooming roses flowering longer and encourage reblooming roses to flower more through the summer. Snip off each faded bloom back to the next set of leaves.

Prune shrub roses and roses classified as old garden roses (which bloom only once in June) through the summer as you would any shrub. Cut off suckers and remove any dead or diseased canes at the base whenever you spot them. After once-blooming roses are done flowering, give them an overall shaping.

Prune roses to keep an open form that allows air to circulate freely to deter fungus diseases. Hot, humid summers encourage these diseases on susceptible roses. Fungicides are preventatives: Once a fungus disease has attacked a rose, it is too late for a fungicide to do much good.

Check climbing roses as they grow and tie them to their support as needed. Prune out new growth that is unwanted, such as stems that stick out into a walkway from an arbor.

VINES
Prune spring-blooming clematis soon after it flowers.

SHRUBS
Check to make sure shrubs have a good layer of mulch before the weather gets hot.

Shear formal hedges after the first flush of growth has come in. Make sure to shear a hedge with slanting sides so it is wider at the bottom than at the top, allowing sunlight to reach the lower branches and leaves. Without sun, those lower braches will become bare.

On deciduous shrubs, cut off no more than half the length of the new green growth. On evergreen hedges, be careful not to cut back into bare wood, which likely will not resprout.

■ *Deadhead roses to keep June bloomers flowering longer and encourage re-bloomers to continue the show. Snip faded flowers off to just above any leaf.*

■ *To control the growth of pines, pinch off the "candles" of new growth at the ends of branches.*

On formal boxwood hedges, wait until the springtime flush of growth is over and growth has slowed. Shear them overall but also prune some of the oldest stems on an established boxwood hedge down to the ground to let more air and light into the interior of the shrubs.

Plan on shearing again in late July.

A hedge doesn't necessarily need to be smoothly sheared. Try using hand pruners to create a more natural look by making individual cuts at different heights throughout a shrub. Prune right above a leaf or set of leaves to help hide the cuts. This will control the size and shape of the hedge with a less rigid look.

VINES
As vines grow, check them regularly and tie them up as needed.

Remove annual sweet pea vines and compost them when the leaves start to yellow.

TREES
Prune pine trees, if necessary, by cutting off the puffs of new growth, called "candles," at the end of stems. This will help keep small pine trees compact.

Now is the time to prune trees that are not pruned during the late-winter dormant season because of running sap, including dogwood, maple, walnut, and river birch.

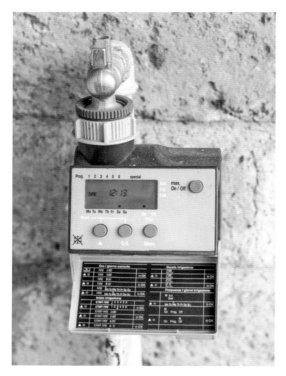

An automatic sprinkler system can be an enormous water waster and lead to lawn problems caused by overwatering. Don't set it and forget it; turn it on only when there has not been enough rain to keep the lawn healthy.

Safety First: If you would need to climb a ladder to prune a tree, it's best to hire a professional for the job. See Resources, page 189.

WATER

ALL

Water as needed, depending on the weather and the soil moisture. See Here's How to Water to Keep Plants Healthy, page 93.

As you make plans for summer getaways, also make a plan for vacation watering. A reliable neighbor may be willing to take on the chore in return for tomatoes or cut flowers. Be sure to leave explicit written instructions that call attention to containers.

There are a number of devices that can help if you are only going to be away for a few days. For example, to water a single tomato or pepper plant

slowly, make a tiny pinhole in the bottom of an empty milk jug, fill it with water, and set it on the plant's root zone.

For larger areas, investigate a digital timer to turn your soaker hoses on for half an hour in the middle of the night. Bear in mind, however, that a digital timer isn't reliable unless it is set correctly and the batteries are fresh.

Just before you leave, water everything *thoroughly*. This may take a couple of days for a large garden.

ANNUALS

Keep the soil of annual flower beds evenly moist in June. Check the soil moisture with your finger. But don't overwater. Soggy soil can lead to root rot, and wet foliage can encourage fungus diseases such as powdery mildew or downy mildew on such plants as zinnias, impatiens, geraniums, and phlox.

BULBS

Water elephant ears more as they get larger and their leaves grow huge. Most summer bulbs such as agapanthus and caladiums come from the tropics and also appreciate steadily moist soil.

CONTAINERS & HOUSEPLANTS

Check containers daily. Their potting mix dries out much more quickly than in the ground. As the summer gets hotter and plants get bigger, you will need to water more often. Terra cotta containers dry out faster than plastic ones, and pots in

Blossom end rot of tomatoes is caused by a calcium deficiency, which is usually due to an inconsistent supply of water. Check the soil often to be sure it stays steadily moist.

■ *Overwatering often contributes to grub problems in lawns. Let the lawn dry out between waterings to discourage the beetles that lay the eggs that become grubs.*

full-sun locations need watering more often than containers in shade.

EDIBLES

Give vegetables a consistent water supply as they are forming their fruits. Keep checking the soil moisture and keep mulch over the soil to reduce evaporation.

It's crucial that tomatoes have even soil moisture and not seesaw between wet and dry to avoid blossom end rot. To provide a slow, steady water supply, use soaker hoses or the milk-jug-with-pinhole trick (see Water/All, page 108).

LAWNS

Keep watering sod or newly seeded lawns. Otherwise, rainfall is usually enough for established lawns in early summer in Illinois, Indiana, and Ohio. Get in the habit of checking the soil moisture and water only if there has been no rain for a week or 10 days.

Make sure your underground sprinkling system is not set to water at frequent intervals. Overwatering leads to many turf problems. It's best to leave the timer off altogether and turn the system on manually only as needed. If you do use the timer, set it to water infrequently but deeply, no more than once a week.

One of the problems caused by overwatering is grubs. They are the larvae of beetles that prefer

to lay eggs in moist soil. If you let the lawn dry out thoroughly between waterings, it will be less attractive to beetles and less likely to harbor grubs.

PERENNIALS

Water in the morning, so leaves dry in the sun. Wet foliage at night encourages fungus diseases.

Don't water perennials that don't need it, but do water any that were planted this spring.

ROSES

Water roses deeply once a week if it hasn't rained 1 inch.

TREES & SHRUBS

Water trees and shrubs that you planted this spring about once a week, slowly and deeply. See Water/Trees, Shrubs & Vines, May, page 94.

Established trees and most established shrubs usually can get by on rainfall. But if the summer weather is especially hot and dry, give them the same slow-but-deep watering treatment. Trees and shrubs need more supplemental watering if they are sick or stressed or if they have a restricted root zone—for example, hemmed in by house, path, and driveway.

Some more sensitive shrubs, such as bigleaf hydrangeas, will need regular watering in summer even in a normal year.

HERE'S HOW

TO TELL IF YOUR LAWN NEEDS WATER

- The grass isn't as green as usual or has a grayish cast.
- When you walk on it, the grass doesn't spring back and you can see your footprints.
- The grass blades fold up vertically.

When you do water, water slowly, long enough so the water sinks 6 to 8 inches deep into the ground. Then don't water for at least a week. This will help the grass grow long roots that help it resist drought.

FERTILIZE

ALL

Fertilize only those plants that need it, and only in amounts they can handle. Too much fertilizer, or fertilizer a plant doesn't need, can be harmful.

ANNUALS

Use a water-soluble fertilizer, either an organic type such as fish emulsion or a synthetic version, at half the strength recommended on the label every other week.

BULBS

Fertilize summer bulbs, such as agapanthus, caladiums, and elephant ears, as well as amaryllis that are spending the summer outdoors, with a water-soluble fertilizer at half strength every other week.

EDIBLES

Once the first fruits on tomatoes, eggplant, and peppers are about the size of marbles, fertilize them with a water-soluble fertilizer at half strength. Otherwise, vegetables should be able to get by on

■ *Give tomatoes and peppers one boost of fertilizer at half-strength when the fruits are about the size of marbles.*

compost and the slow-release fertilizer that was applied in spring.

CONTAINERS & HOUSEPLANTS

Use a water-soluble fertilizer at half the strength recommended on the label every other week.

If the weather becomes hot and you need to water more often, you may need to fertilize more often too to make up for the nutrients washed away. But keep the fertilizer at half strength.

LAWNS

Don't fertilize the lawn in summer. Overfertilizing makes a lawn weak and thirsty and fertilizer can "burn" the grass in hot weather. Fertilizer also stimulates the growth of crabgrass and other weeds in hot weather.

PERENNIALS

Established perennials that are growing in good soil rich in compost rarely need additional fertilizer. For needier plants, a slow-release fertilizer that was added at planting should be sufficient.

ROSES

If you spread a slow-release fertilizer over their roots in spring, roses, even rebloomers, should not need more nutrients now. If you didn't, use a water-soluble fertilizer, either organic or synthetic, at half the strength recommended on the label every three weeks. Apply the solution at the base of the plant and avoid getting the foliage wet.

Roses that bloom only once in June, such as old garden roses and hybrid teas, can use a boost just after their flowering is finished. Spread a balanced slow-release fertilizer over their roots.

SHRUBS

Established shrubs in the ground need no fertilizer, except when you know of a problem that's caused by a specific nutrient deficiency.

Shrubs in containers should be fine if you mixed a slow-release fertilizer into the potting mix at planting. If you didn't, apply a liquid fertilizer at half strength once a month.

PROBLEM-SOLVE

ALL

Warmer weather brings out insects and diseases. Monitor your plants for early signs of problems:

- yellow, spotted, or stippled foliage

- stunted leaf growth

- curled or cupped leaves

- holes in flowers or foliage

If you see insects, remember *not all bugs are bad*. Most are beneficial and will help to manage the damaging ones. Never spray just because you see insects. When you use an insecticide, you kill the good insects, including bees, butterflies, and other pollinators, along with the bad ones.

Before trying to treat for any insect or disease problem, first make sure you have identified it correctly and understand it (See Here's How to Get Help with Plant Problems, page 98). Timing is also important: If you don't apply the right control at the time when pests and disease are most susceptible, it can be totally futile.

Once you have identified a problem insect, assess whether it is doing so much damage that you cannot tolerate it and must try to control it. Most insects feed for a short period of time and are then gone from the garden.

Watch all plants for signs of fungal diseases such as powdery mildew or leaf spot. Keep notes in your garden journal of all such problems, with photos, if possible. This will not only help you identify problems, but help you decide whether to keep problem plants or replace them next year with disease-resistant alternatives.

When you remove diseased plants or plant parts, always put them in the trash or the landscape waste, not in the compost heap. Home compost heaps rarely get hot enough to reliably kill fungus spores, disease bacteria, and weed seeds.

■ *Insect predators such as the praying mantis, ladybug, and hoverfly are beneficial in the garden; they eat the insects we think of as pests. Avoid spraying insecticides to keep from killing the good bugs along with the bad.*

Mosquitoes breed in still, standing water, so deprive them of places to hatch. All summer, make sure no water stands in plant saucers and birdbaths as well as less obvious places, such as water pooled in folds of tarps or in wheelbarrows. A little puddle and a week is all mosquitoes need.

■ *A dish of beer can trap and drown slugs, if it is positioned properly. Scoop a depression in the soil and set the dish with its rim at soil level so slugs don't have to climb up to fall in.*

ANNUALS

If powdery mildew or other fungus disease appears on such plants as zinnias and annual phlox, remove the infected plants. Thin the bed to allow more air circulation. Put the discarded plants in the trash or landscape waste, not the compost heap.

CONTAINERS

To deter animals from digging in containers, fill "decoy" pots with soil and set them on the perimeters of container groupings. River rocks arranged across the soil in containers also can frustrate animals.

GROUNDCOVERS

Watch out for aggressively spreading groundcovers such as lamiastrum (yellow archangel), English ivy, goutweed, lily-of-the-valley, and myrtle. Pull out any that are sprouting beyond their assigned territory; otherwise, they could out-compete other plants.

When you weed out unwanted groundcovers, remove every scrap of the plant you can. Even a small piece of the underground stems by which many groundcovers spread can resprout into a new plant.

Don't let English ivy or other woody vines climb the trunks of trees. Cut the vines off at the base and pull off any stems that have attached themselves to the tree bark.

EDIBLES

Toward the end of the month, watch out for tomato hornworms, which are green and can be up to 5 inches long. Handpick them and drown them in a solution of water and detergent. Or try applying Bt (*Bacillus thuringiensis* var. *kurstaki*), a type of bacteria that poisons the hornworms. Other insecticides also are available if you have a severe problem. Check with your local Extension for approved insecticides in your area (see Resources, page 189).

LAWNS

Toward the end of the month, check for grubs by peeling back a piece of turf to look for white C-shaped insect larvae. Grubs are beetle larvae, living in the soil and feeding on the roots of grass plants. They are most common in moist soil.

You may first notice the problem when raccoons and skunks dig for grubs in the lawn. But as the weather gets hotter and drier, grass plants whose roots have been damaged by grubs will turn brown.

Grub problems vary from year to year, and if you have only a few, there's no need to try and control them. Typically, you won't see visible damage unless there are eight to twelve grubs per square foot.

If you do decide to treat for grubs, be sure to read the label carefully to make sure you're using the right product at the right time of year. Products designed to prevent grubs are generally applied from late June to mid-July.

■ *Holes that appear in the broad leaves of hostas are often caused by slugs, which are active at night.*

■ *Pluck off the first Japanese beetles you see so they don't attract more of their own kind. Beetle traps are a bad idea because chemicals from the beetles in the trap will summon more beetles.*

There is a kind of bacteria, *Paenibacillus popilliae*, that feeds on Japanese beetle grubs, but products containing it should not be applied until late July or early August.

To prevent grub problems, let the lawn dry out between waterings and let it go dormant in July and August. Turn off an automatic sprinkler system.

Got moles? Just roll the lawn to smooth out the ridges made by their tunnels. If it's any comfort, they are probably eating the grubs of Japanese beetles.

PERENNIALS
If hosta leaves look ragged, slugs are the likely culprit. Keep slugs away from prized hostas by sprinkling the surrounding soil with diatomaceous earth, sold in garden centers. This material consists of razor-sharp particles, the pulverized shells of tiny marine animals, that will slice the tender skin of slugs.

Another popular method is to use beer to attract and drown slugs. For this to work, it's essential to sink the container up to the rim in soil so the slugs will fall in.

ROSES
Watch for Japanese beetles, which have a distinctive green-gold metallic color and a special attraction to plants in the rose family. Look for them on roses in early morning. Pick them off and drown them in a water-and-detergent solution.

Japanese beetles attract more Japanese beetles, so it's best to catch the problem early before the population builds up. For large ornamental areas with a heavy infestation, spraying with an insecticide labeled for Japanese beetles is a last resort.

Don't use Japanese beetle traps. They will attract beetles from all over the neighborhood.

Many roses are susceptible to fungus diseases such as blackspot and powdery mildew, especially in hot, humid summer weather. Prune them to an open form for good air circulation. A weekly spray of a solution of baking soda may help.

Spider mites can cause rose leaves to appear speckled or spotted. If you've identified spider mites on your roses, try spraying with insecticidal soap or light horticultural oil.

If a rose blooms with flowers completely unlike the one you expect, it probably means the rose's graft has failed. See Problem-Solve/Roses, May, page 98.

Avoid regular spraying in the rose garden. Insecticides kill far more beneficial insects than harmful ones. If you don't spray, insect predators will eat many of the pest insects.

SHRUBS & TREES
Look in hedges and at the base of shrubs for tree seedlings such as buckthorn, mulberry, and box elder. Unwanted tree seedlings are common wherever birds perch and leave seeds behind, such as under power lines and along fence lines, and often go unnoticed in hedges. Dig them out when they are small.

If these unplanned trees grow too big before you notice them, cut them off at the base and treat the stem with a herbicide containing a high concentration of glyphosate to kill the root system. You may have to cut back sprouts and reapply the herbicide several times to finally kill the tree.

July

Summer is here. Days are hot and muggy and nights may not be much cooler. And after the lavish spectacle of the June garden, it can start to feel like the fireworks are over.

Sure, it's past the ideal time to plant most perennials, annuals, shrubs, and trees. They can't establish themselves in the ground during the hot, dry summer weather, so it's best to wait until early fall brings cooler temperatures and more rain. The task now is to keep everything watered and weeded, and enjoy the harvest.

But these are glory days for the vegetable and fruit gardener. The sweet corn is ripe, and a gardener is able to enjoy it the best possible way: picked in the backyard at the last minute and briefly cooked before any of the sugar turns to starch. There's more: summer squash, green beans, blueberries, early melons, and the first tomatoes. Lucky is the gardener who has a big shade tree to relax under while savoring a sun-warmed tomato.

Summer storms may bring lightning and downpours, but overall there's less rain now. The lawn will soon develop a brownish haze as the grass goes dormant and leaf blades dry up. That's normal; the plants will revive in late August when it's rainier and cooler.

A gardener may be tempted to stay under that shade tree and watch the hydrangeas bloom, or even depart for the beach. But the weeds are not taking the summer off. Neither are the reblooming roses, or the daylilies, or the watermelons. And it's time to start on the fall vegetable garden. There's plenty to do.

Try to do it early in the morning before the heat builds up. If you work in the heat of the day, take it easy; wear a hat, sunscreen, and gloves, take lots of breaks, and drink plenty of water.

This is a good time to update the garden notes, which may have been neglected during the May and June rush. They will be invaluable next year, and it's a good task to undertake beneath a shady tree.

PLAN

ANNUALS

Watch garden centers for early sales. Even sad-looking annuals may be worth buying to fill in bare spots in containers if they are very inexpensive and have a good set of roots. Cut them back at the time you plant them and water well.

BULBS

Bulb catalogs will start coming in the mail in July. Consult your notes from last spring to make a plan for ordering spring bulbs to plant this fall. Often, ordering early will get you a substantial discount (but leave some funds in the kitty for later impulse purchases). See Plan/Bulbs, September, page 134.

EDIBLES

To determine when to plant fall crops, use your area's average first frost date and the days to harvest shown on seed packets. Add about 20 days to that number, because in fall, when days are shorter and cooler, crops will take longer to mature.

Some plants, such as broccoli, cauliflower, and cabbage, won't germinate or grow well in midsummer heat, so they will need to be started indoors under lights and transplanted to the ground in August. See the Fall Vegetable Timing Chart on page 168. Most other seeds can be sowed directly in the ground in July (or August).

Arrange your seed sowing so that bush beans and most greens will mature about two weeks *before* the last frost date. For cool-weather crops that can handle a little frost, such as broccoli, carrots, cabbage, cauliflower, collards, kale, kohlrabi, mustard, radishes, and spinach, plan your crops so they mature on or about two weeks after the frost date. Because autumn weather can be unpredictable, it's a good idea to sow seeds in two or three batches a week apart to cover eventualities.

Garden centers' seed racks may be picked over by now. Mail-order houses will have a better supply, but check how fast they can ship. Look for short-season varieties that will mature in less than 60 days, or 70 days for frost-tolerant crops.

Plan to plant fall crops in the space left as spring crops such as peas and lettuce run their course.

PERENNIALS

Perennials start going on sale in July. But keep a clear head about your conditions and the space you have available. A plant is no bargain if you can't provide the light or soil it needs, if you don't have a suitable place for it, or if it will be too large or aggressive for your garden.

PLANT

ANNUALS

Sow seeds indoors for fall-blooming annuals such as pansies, calendula, and ornamental cabbages and kale. It's too hot to sow them outdoors.

Pull up tired, leggy pansies and replace them with transplants of marigolds, petunias, geraniums, or moss roses that will last until frost.

BULBS

Plant colchicum, fall-blooming crocus, and hardy cyclamen for fall or winter bloom.

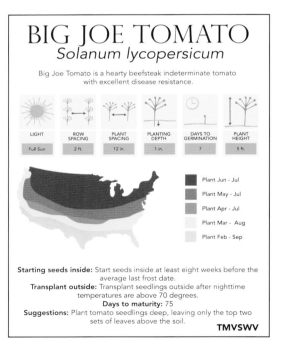

BIG JOE TOMATO
Solanum lycopersicum

Big Joe Tomato is a hearty beefsteak indeterminate tomato with excellent disease resistance.

LIGHT	ROW SPACING	PLANT SPACING	PLANTING DEPTH	DAYS TO GERMINATION	PLANT HEIGHT
Full Sun	2 ft.	12 in.	1 in.	7	5 ft.

Plant Jun - Jul
Plant May - Jul
Plant Apr - Jul
Plant Mar - Aug
Plant Feb - Sep

Starting seeds inside: Start seeds inside at least eight weeks before the average last frost date.
Transplant outside: Transplant seedlings outside after nighttime temperatures are above 70 degrees.
Days to maturity: 75
Suggestions: Plant tomato seedlings deep, leaving only the top two sets of leaves above the soil.

TMVSWV

■ *When spring or fall planting, consult the seed packet for the plant's days to harvest and compare it to your first frost date in spring or your last frost date in fall. For late-season crops, allow extra time for plants to mature before the first frost. They will grow slowly in the short days and cool weather of late summer and fall.*

HERE'S HOW

TO START SEEDS INDOORS

■ *Some late-season crops will need to be started indoors because the garden is too hot for them in summer. To start seeds indoors, use a light, fine, sterile seed-starting mix. Fill peat pots or starter trays with moist mix and sow the seeds according to the seed packet directions.*

■ *Cover the tray with plastic to keep the seed-starting mix moist. Keep the tray warm until the seeds germinate.*

■ *When you see tiny green sprouts, remove the plastic. Place the tray under lights and water from the bottom to keep the mix moist. Keep the lights on 16 hours a day.*

EDIBLES & CONTAINERS

Sow seeds of broccoli, Brussels sprouts, cabbage, and cauliflower for later transplanting into the garden. Or plan to buy transplants.

Plant root crops for fall harvest in July, such as carrots, radishes (including winter radishes, which grow larger and take longer), turnips, and beets.

You also can sow seeds for summer squash (if you plan to harvest them young). You can plant short-season snap beans, snow peas, and sugar snap peas because their pods are eaten whole without waiting for the peas to mature.

If you're gardening in containers, you can use the same potting mix for a fall crop, but enrich it with a fresh shot of slow-release fertilizer.

If you can provide shade for part of the day, plant seeds of lettuce and spinach.

PERENNIALS

If you plant perennials in the heat of midsummer, you will have to be very attentive to watering.

CARE

ALL

When the weather is especially hot and dry, a layer of mulch is particularly important to hold moisture in the soil. See Here's How to Mulch Beds, page 69.

Keep weeding. Try to put in 10 or 15 minutes in the early morning, when it's cool. Weeds are starting to go to seed, so any you can remove now will reduce your weeding chores next year. Put weeds with seeds in the landscape waste or the trash.

ANNUALS

Pinch back leggy annuals. If you pinch back one-third of the oldest stems for three weeks in a row, you will renew the plant but never be without bloom.

Deadhead plants that need it to encourage more bloom. For bushy plants with many small flowers, such as alyssum, ageratum, or lobelia, shear the

■ *Keep weeding. Weeds sprout all season, and it's easier to keep weeding steadily than to tackle a jungle of weeds all at once.*

entire plant. For large-flowered plants such as salvia, marigolds, zinnias, tuberous begonias, annual geraniums (pelargoniums), and petunias, cut the stalk of each faded flower individually. Cut back to the next pair of leaves, where new flower buds will form. Avoid leaving the old bare stalks (sometimes called "dead generals").

In severe heat, the flowers of some annuals such as ageratum may turn brown. Cut the browned flowers off and water normally. Flowering will resume when the weather cools.

CONTAINERS
Check to see if soil has shrunk in containers. If so, top-dress with compost or more potting mix and shake the pot gently to settle it around the sides.

EDIBLES
Pull up spring crops. Peas and beans will be finishing up and lettuce is probably bolting (going to seed) in hot weather. Yank out those plants and start using the space for fall crops. It's a good idea to pull back the mulch and topdress with more compost before sowing seed.

If you had a disease problem with a spring crop, don't replant in the same soil. Plan to rotate crops in the spring. In the meantime, consider planting a fall crop in large containers set in that spot, filled with fresh potting mix and slow-release fertilizer.

Harvest vegetables regularly to encourage plants to produce more. Most vegetables are most delightful when picked young and tender; leaving old zucchini or okra on the vine will slow production. Hot weather will cause leaves and fruits to mature faster, so keep up.

Summer squash is ready to pick when it's 3 to 4 inches long. The skin should still be soft enough to pierce with a fingernail. Eggplants are ready when they are glossy and plump, not hard.

Harvest bell peppers and other sweet peppers when they are green or leave them on the plant to turn red. They will have a different, usually sweeter taste.

Hot peppers, or chilis, have a very different flavor when picked green and when picked ripe. Pick at the stage you prefer. Once peppers turn red they deteriorate quickly, so pick them promptly.

Corn is ripe when the silk turns brown, and when you can press a plump kernel and get "milk." Onion tops will turn yellow and droop when the onions are mature. Potato plants will start to die back.

For fruits that aren't easily removed, such as eggplant or heavy squashes, *cut* the stalk with a sharp knife or pruning shears. Wear gloves when harvesting okra to avoid their sticky prickles, and pick the pods young before they get woody.

Remove any overripe, damaged, or mis-shapen fruits.

Harvest herbs such as basil, mint, oregano, and marjoram regularly to keep the plant bushy. Harvest parsley by cutting the whole stem back at the soil.

When you have an overabundance of vegetables, share them with a food pantry. To find one that can handle produce donations, see the website of the Plant a Row for the Hungry program of the Garden Writers Association at www.gardenwriters.org.

■ *Cut back annuals that have grown leggy. They will start flowering again in a couple of weeks.*

■ Harvest vegetables by pinching or cutting the stem, not by pulling on the fruit. For heavy vegetables such as squash or melons and those that aren't easily removed such as eggplant and peppers, cut the stem with a sharp knife.

After everbearing raspberries have their first crop, prune the old canes back to within a few inches of the ground. Leave the tender new canes that will bear the fall crop.

LAWNS

You will need to mow less often now that the grass is growing more slowly. If it goes dormant and starts to look brownish, stop mowing.

Patrol the lawn for weeds. The summer's drought is an opportunity for many weeds, especially in shorter and less vigorous lawns.

PERENNIALS

Pinch back perennials after they bloom to keep them more compact. Many will rebloom in a few weeks.

Deadheading some perennials to keep the flowers from turning to seed will help them bloom longer. See Care/Perennials, June, page 106.

Cut back bee balm to keep it tidier and remove old growth that may have mildew. It won't rebloom, but the new growth will be cleaner. Cut back the whole flower stalk when irises and once-blooming daylilies are done.

For repeat-blooming daylilies such as 'Stella d'Oro' and 'Many Happy Returns', cut back the spent flower stalks to keep seedpods from forming and encourage more flowering. It's easy to mistake the seedpods for flower buds, but a bud is long and slender and a pod is oval with three distinct sections. Cut off any stalks with pods.

Pinch back chrysanthemums one last time early in the month. Don't wait longer, or they may not have time to form flower buds for fall bloom.

Regularly patrol the garden and tidy up. Remove yellowing or tattered foliage. To restrain overgrown perennials, cut entire leaves or stems off at the base to reduce the bulk unobtrusively.

You may want to leave spent flower stalks that are interesting or have seeds for the birds, such as those of astilbe and coneflowers.

Stake tall perennials such as lilies that have flopped. Make a note so that next year you can install a support system early before the plants actually need it.

ROSES

Check climbing roses monthly to make sure they are still securely attached to their support. Don't tie them so tightly that the ties will chafe when the stems move in the wind. But make sure that summer thunderstorms can't blow them down.

SHRUBS

Wait to prune summer bloomers such as hydrangeas, rose-of-Sharon, and butterfly bush until right after they finish flowering.

Shear formal hedges one last time toward the end of the month, but definitely before the middle of August. See Care/Shrubs, June, page 107.

Cut back any branches on shrubs that have grown too long or out of scale or are in the way of paths. Cut back to the next branch or down to the ground. Remove any dead wood.

VINES

Prune wisteria now and again in fall to keep it under control and encourage blooming. Trim the side branches back to two or three buds, and prune as needed to form a good structure that is well-supported

■ Shear hedges toward the end of July. Don't shear them after mid-August, or the new growth will not have time to harden off before winter.

by the arbor or pergola. The heaviest pruning will be in late winter when the vine is dormant.

WATER

ALL

If the summer is especially hot and dry and watering is becoming burdensome, prioritize. Let the lawn go dormant (it's not dead). Give up on the neediest annual flowers. Focus watering on the vegetable garden and on trees and shrubs.

Trees, which take decades to grow, are your highest-investment plants. Lawns and perennials are easier to replace than large shade trees. So in times of drought, put trees at the top of your watering priority list.

Keep track of soil moisture by checking every day. Stick your finger into the soil to feel for moisture or dig down 3 to 5 inches. Don't wait until plants wilt to water; that means they already are stressed.

How often you will need to water depends on many factors, including the weather, your soil, and the type of plants you have. For general watering advice, see Here's How to Water to Keep Plants Healthy, page 93.

If you go on vacation, provide for your garden to be watered. See Water/All, June, page 108.

ANNUALS

Remember that you need to water more often in hot weather. Not only is water evaporating more quickly from the leaves, but the plants are now larger, with more roots and leaves to support.

BULBS

Water caladiums and elephant ears often, whether they're in pots or in the ground.

CONTAINERS & HOUSEPLANTS

Water containers often in July. The limited amount of soil in a pot doesn't hold much water. Check daily. In the hottest weather, you may need to water containers twice a day.

EDIBLES

Keep watering vegetables to keep the soil evenly moist. Your plants need water to make tomatoes, peppers, and cucumbers, and water evaporates extra fast when the weather is hot.

If tomatoes stop setting fruit when it's especially hot, the temperature may be to blame. Keep watering, and when it drops back into the 80s, you'll get more tomatoes.

Some herbs—such as rosemary and oregano—prefer drier soil. Others, such as basil, chives, and parsley, prefer evenly moist, but not wet, soil.

If you have sown seeds for fall crops, keep them constantly moist until they sprout. You probably will need to water at least two times a day to keep the seeds moist under the hot sun. Use a gentle sprinkle to avoid disturbing the seeds.

LAWNS

Either let your lawn go dormant or commit to keep watering it. See Plan/Lawns, June, page 102. Don't change your mind and try to revive a brown lawn. It stresses the grass to whipsaw in and out of dormancy.

To keep the lawn green, water only every week or 10 days, and then only enough to deliver the equivalent of 1 inch of rain.

PERENNIALS

Water to keep soil moist for the needier perennials such as astilbe, lobelia, ligularia, delphiniums, bellflower, hosta, and ferns, as well as any perennials that you planted this year. Don't wait until you see signs of stress, such as wilting.

The more drought-tolerant established perennials will most likely need little watering unless it is very hot and dry.

Avoid overhead watering, especially in the evening. Moisture clinging to leaves overnight can encourage fungal diseases.

SHRUBS & VINES

Regularly water any shrubs you planted within the last two years. Use a long, slow trickle from a hose placed near the base of the shrub.

Water clematis and bigleaf hydrangeas regularly, and water other hydrangeas in full sun.

TREES

Regularly water any tree planted within the last three years. As you do for shrubs, water slowly and deeply for a long time, using a trickle from the hose, a soaker hose, or a watering bag such as a Treegator®. In general, an 8-foot-tall young tree will need 10 to 15 gallons of water about once a week. But keep track of the soil moisture near the rootball and water more often if need be.

Even mature trees need watering during hot weather or when it hasn't rained for a while.

In times of drought, consider watering the trees on the street in front of your home, even if they aren't on your property. Imagine how much you would lose, in beauty and property values, if those trees died from drought stress. They often have little space for their roots or to collect rainwater. So help them out.

FERTILIZE

ALL

If the weather is unusually hot and dry, don't fertilize. Plants are already stressed, so don't push them to grow leaves or flowers that will just be vulnerable to wilting or drying out.

ANNUALS

If you applied a slow-release fertilizer to your beds in April, scatter a bit more now, following the package directions, and water afterward. If you are using a liquid fertilizer instead, apply it at half the strength specified in the directions about every other week.

BULBS

Continue fertilizing summer bulbs about twice a month, using an organic liquid fertilizer or a synthetic liquid labeled for flowering plants at half the strength directed on the label.

CONTAINERS & HOUSEPLANTS

Keep fertilizing regularly at half the strength recommended on the label.

If you added timed-release fertilizer to the soil when you potted the containers, scatter some more on the surface of the soil now. Water, but hold off on liquid fertilizer for a month.

EDIBLES

Except for containers, avoid fertilizing vegetables in hot weather. The good compost you added to the soil in spring will give them some nutrition without stressing them.

LAWNS

Don't fertilize the lawn in the heat of summer.

ROSES

Toward the middle or end of July, scatter a bit more slow-release fertilizer around reblooming roses and apply a water-soluble fertilizer, ideally an organic one, to the soil around their roots. Flowering constantly uses a lot of nutrients.

SHRUBS & TREES

Scatter a little slow-release fertilizer on the root zone of bigleaf hydrangeas when they have finished flowering.

If you think other shrubs are looking poorly, determine the cause for certain before trying to fix the problem with fertilizer.

If summer storms crack small trees or bring down limbs, immediately remove hazardous branches or downed trees. Prune broken branches back to the collar at the base of the branch, not flush with the trunk. But don't leave a stub.

If the damage is to a large tree and the branch is big enough to require taking a chainsaw up a ladder, call a professional. See Resources, page 189.

PROBLEM-SOLVE

ALL

If you see caterpillars or other insects, identify them before you take any action. See Here's How to Get Help with Plant Problems, page 98. Unless the bugs are doing considerable damage, the best course may be to leave them alone.

To prevent mosquitoes from hatching in your yard, don't give them any spots with still, standing water. Change birdbath water often. After a rainfall, look around for places where water may have collected, such as gutters, wheelbarrows, buckets, tires, wading pools, tarps, and the seed-catchers under

■ *A spreading yellow mass that appears on moist mulch or leaves is a totally harmless organism called a plasmodium that is digesting the woody material. It is sometimes called dog vomit slime mold or scrambled eggs slime mold.*

birdfeeders. It takes only a few days for mosquito larvae to hatch, and it's important to be vigilant since they can carry West Nile virus.

If you find an odd-looking, jellylike, beige-to-yellow mass on mulch or leaves in a bed, don't be concerned. It's probably a harmless and beneficial organism commonly called dog vomit slime mold. This is not a disease; it's a natural recycler of organic matter. Slime molds are common in warm, wet weather. Leave the mass alone and it will dry up on its own in a few days, or rake it out if it annoys you.

Watch out for aphids on annuals, perennials, and vegetable plants. The best treatment for aphids is a blast of water from the hose to wash them off. Make sure you wash the undersides of the leaves.

EDIBLES
If you had a disease problem with a spring crop, don't plant in that spot in the fall and plan to rotate crops next year.

Before blueberries and grapes ripen, surround the plants with netting to keep the birds out.

If you see black- and green-striped caterpillars on parsley, dill, and fennel, they are likely to be the larvae of black swallowtail butterflies. Don't spray them, but pick them up and try to contain them to just one plant. Some gardeners keep a dill or parsley plant in a pot to move swallowtail caterpillars to.

If rust spots appear on mint—the result of a fungus—cut it down to the ground. The new growth should come in clean. Dispose of the spotted foliage in the trash or landscape waste, not the compost pile, to avoid spreading the fungal spores.

Watch mint like a hawk. It spreads readily by underground stems. Try to gently pull out the whole underground stem and roots along with the top growth; if you leave it behind, it can resprout. You can try to contain mint by growing it in a container, but be alert for stems that grow out of the pot and root in the ground.

CONTAINERS & HOUSEPLANTS
If you see brown patches on houseplants you have moved outdoors, it is probably sunburn. Move the plant to a more shaded location.

Watch for spider mites on indoor houseplants in the summer. Shake a plant over a piece of white paper; if the tiny dots that fall to the paper move, they are mites. If you see white, cobweb-like secretions on a plant, you have a serious infestation. Spray the plant with insecticidal soap, especially on the undersides of the leaves.

GROUNDCOVERS
In hot, dry weather, goutweed (also called snow-on-the-mountain or bishop weed) may show

■ *Tomatoes will crack if their water supply is uneven and a surge of water bursts the skins. Try to keep the soil of tomato beds or containers evenly moist.*

■ *Wrap blueberry bushes in netting before the fruit ripens to foil hungry birds.*

brown, sunburned patches on the leaves. Make this the occasion to extirpate this invasive groundcover. You will need to dig it out thoroughly, since it spreads by underground stems, and will have to remain vigilant for new sprouts for several years.

LAWNS

If the lawn is starting to turn brown, it is going dormant, which is the natural state of grass in summer. See Plan/Lawns, June, page 102.

If your lawn is developing bare spots, find out why. Is the soil too wet? Is it too compacted by play or foot traffic? Is there too much shade for healthy grass? Address the underlying problem rather than repeatedly reseeding or laying new sod. Maybe you should plant a groundcover instead of turf in the shade, or make a path where the foot traffic goes, or plant a rain garden in the wet spot.

Don't take action against grubs unless your lawn has eight to twelve grubs per square foot. See Problem-Solve/Lawns, June, page 112.

If you decide to apply a product containing the bacteria *Paenibacillus popilliae*, which feed on Japanese beetle grubs, you must apply it in a particular pattern in late July or early August. Read the label directions carefully. You may need to repeat the treatment next year.

PERENNIALS

If hosta leaves are ragged, slugs are the likely culprit. See Care/Perennials, June, page 106.

Powdery mildew, a milky film or whitish splotches on leaves, may appear on perennial plants such as phlox

■ *If you are lucky enough to find this bright caterpillar on a fennel, dill, or parsley plant, you may soon see a black swallowtail butterfly. Some gardeners set aside a few herb plants just to support butterfly caterpillars.*

and bee balm in July, especially if they are crowded. Thin the plants to improve air circulation. If you've caught the problem early, it may help to spray with a solution of 1 tablespoon baking soda and 1 tablespoon horticultural oil mixed in a gallon of water.

When the plants are done blooming, cut them off at the ground to allow new, clean growth. Put diseased plants in the landscape waste or the trash, not the compost pile, to avoid spreading spores.

Squiggly pale lines in the leaves of columbine plants are the work of tiny insect larvae called leaf miners. Cut the plant back to the ground and the new leaves should grow in clean.

Whiteflies, mealybugs, scale, spider mites, and other pests may appear in hot weather and where air circulation is poor. If you choose, spray plants with Neem oil. Thin the plants to improve airflow.

If you see caterpillars on your milkweed, let them eat all they want. They are the caterpillars of monarch butterflies, which need all the help they can get to make their epic migration from Canada to Mexico.

ROSES

If your hybrid roses have been losing their lower leaves and the rest of the leaves are yellowish with dark spots, you likely have a fungus disease called blackspot.

Using a fungicide in July will not cure the parts of the plant that already are infected, but it can help prevent it from spreading. The fungicide will need to be applied once every seven to ten days. Some gardeners have success with a solution of baking soda. Clean up any leaves fallen from plants, since fungus spores on the leaves can spread the infection. Don't put them in the compost pile.

Consider replacing a susceptible rose. Many newer rose varieties have been selected to resist blackspot.

SHRUBS

Sometimes the normally green leaves of trees or shrubs appear chartreuse or yellowish. If you look closely at a leaf from an off-color plant, the veins may still be green while the spaces between are yellowish because the green chlorophyll has receded. This condition is called chlorosis.

HERE'S HOW

TO SOLVE TOMATO TROUBLES

Many common tomato problems have solutions, especially if you catch them early. So check over your vegetable patch often. You often can cut off the bad spot or rotted end of a tomato and eat the rest.

Lots of leaves but no fruit: The plant is probably getting too much nitrogen. Use less fertilizer, and choose one with a balanced ratio of the three major elements, such as 10-10-10, or where the middle number (phosphorus) is larger than the first number (nitrogen), such as 2-3-1.

Blossoms drop off before fruit forms: The weather may be too cool; wait for it to warm up. Blossom drop is often a problem with tomatoes planted too soon in spring.

Fruits are puckered or distorted, often with a scar on the blossom end: This can happen when nights are too cool as the fruits are forming. Look for varieties described as resistant to "catfacing" and don't plant too soon.

Cracks: Cracking results from uneven moisture while the fruits were forming. Water carefully so the moisture supply is steady, or use sub-irrigated containers. Mulch tomatoes, even those in containers.

Soft or rotten spot on the bottom: This is blossom end rot, caused by a calcium deficiency. Most often it results from uneven watering; swinging between wet and dry soil interferes with the plant's ability to use calcium. Keep soil moisture even and mulch. Fertilizers made for tomatoes usually include calcium, but steady watering is the key solution.

Wilting or yellow leaves: This might show a fungus disease, such as verticillium wilt or fusarium wilt; you can tell if you cut a stem and the interior is discolored.

Diseased plants are a lost cause; give them up and work on preventing the problem next year. Immediately remove the plants and put all parts in the landscape waste, not the compost pile. These diseases come from spores in the soil, so next spring, rotate crops and look for disease-resistant tomato varieties. If you had diseased plants in containers, dispose of the soil in the landscape waste with the plants and then wash and disinfect the containers with a solution of 1 part bleach to 10 parts water. To discourage fungus infections, don't overwater and stake plants for good air circulation.

Chlorosis can be a symptom of many plant problems. If a tree or shrub seems chlorotic, take note of all the conditions—weather, soil, water—and bring some leaves to an expert for consultation. (See Here's How to Get Help With Plant Problems, page 98.)

VINES

Be vigilant about poison ivy now that everyone is spending so much time outside. Merely brushing against the leaves can cause an excruciating rash.

Make sure you can identify the plant, a woody vine (or sometimes low shrub) with three bright green pointed leaves, one on the end of a stalk and one to either side. Before you try to remove it, dress in heavy shoes, long sleeves, heavy gloves, and eye protection. You can pull up a small plant by putting a plastic bag over your hand, pulling up the plant, and turning the bag inside out over the plant. Larger plants may need to be cut down or dug up.

Seal the plants in paper landscape waste bags. Never burn poison ivy plants; breathing the smoke can carry the rash-causing oil to your lungs.

To kill a poison ivy stump, paint on a nonselective systemic herbicide containing glyphosate or triclopyr, being careful not to splash it on other plants. It will kill any plant it touches. You will need to apply it several times a few days apart to be sure it will keep the poison ivy from resprouting.

Wash all your tools in soap and water immediately after working with poison ivy. Remove your clothing very carefully and wash it all in cold water.

Spots on stems: Brown patches on the stems, especially at the joints, can be an early symptom of a nasty fungus disease called late blight. It often occurs after wet weather and can spread from tomatoes to potatoes. Look for greasy, irregularly shaped gray spots. A ring of white mold may develop and the spots eventually dry and become papery. The fruit can also develop large, irregularly shaped, greasy spots.

Dispose of the plants immediately as described above, disinfect containers, and rotate crops. The fungus is windborne, and if the conditions are right for it there is no defense.

Spots on leaves: Tiny spots may be due to spider mites, which tend to gather on the undersides of leaves, as do tiny pale aphids. A good spray of plain water from the hose to both sides of the leaves usually will wash off these pests. If the infestation persists, try a commercial insecticidal soap (not a home-brew concoction).

Brown spots on leaves toward the bottom of the plant often are due to early blight or Septoria leaf spot—more fungus diseases. Early blight spots will be brown to black, often with a yellow border and concentric rings like a bull's-eye. They spread from leaves to stems and fruit. Septoria leaf spot shows up on leaves. The spots are tan-to-gray circles with a dark brown margin. Eventually, they can enlarge and turn the whole leaf yellow, then brown. Dispose of the plants immediately as described above, disinfect containers, and rotate crops.

Pale spots on fruit: This may be sunscald, because plants were pruned too severely and didn't have the shade of their leaves. Don't over-prune when tending and staking tomatoes. Little round pale spots are often caused by stinkbugs, which suck the sap from the fruit. You can eat the unspotted part.

Nibbled leaf edges: Look for tomato hornworms, the 2-inch-long green caterpillars of a large moth. Drown them in soapy water. If a caterpillar has white knobby growths on it, leave it be; a parasitic wasp has laid its eggs in the caterpillar, which will be eaten by the young wasps when they hatch.

Chunks bitten out: It's probably squirrels. Surround your tomatoes securely with chicken wire (including over the top), or plant enough tomatoes so the squirrels can have some. Don't eat tomatoes that squirrels have bitten.

TREES

Check magnolias closely for magnolia scale, which is a flat, round insect about the size of a pencil eraser, usually found on the undersides of branches. The scale insects suck the sap and can make the tree decline.

Often the most noticeable sign of magnolia scale is a black sooty mold on the bark. The mold, which grows on the sticky excretions of the insects, is just an indication, not a problem. If you spot scale insects, you can pick them off and squash them or drop them in soapy water.

Other possibilities include spraying with a summer-weight horticultural oil to smother them; applying an insecticide when the insect is at its most vulnerable stage in late summer; or applying dormant oil in late winter. Consult an expert before taking any of these measures, since using the wrong product or using it at the wrong time will fail to control the insects. See Here's How to Get Help with Plant Problems, page 98.

Gypsy moths, which have caused widespread damage by killing many kinds of trees in the eastern US, are starting to lay eggs. Look out for their egg masses on tree bark and other surfaces such as lawn furniture, cars, play sets, windowsills, and doorways. The masses are tan or buff-colored with a velvety surface and can contain hundreds of eggs. Scrape an egg mass off with a paint scraper or knife, drop it into a bucket of soapy water, and leave it overnight to kill the eggs.

August

It's August, and pretty much everyone and everything except the cicadas is taking it easy. We're in a beach-and-hammock holding pattern until the weather cools off.

But there's still work to do. Watering needs focus in August, because the weather can swing between drought and heavy rainstorms. It's easy to lose track of how much rain has actually fallen, so keep checking the actual soil moisture and water accordingly.

Most fall vegetable crops need to go into the ground this month, either as transplants or seed sown in the ground. They'll need steady soil moisture; water evaporates faster in hot weather, both from the soil and from plants' leaves.

Vegetables are coming fast and furious and it's important to keep them picked so the plants will continue producing. If you let a baseball-bat-sized zucchini soak up the lion's share of a plant's water and energy, you won't get as many tender young ones.

But this is best of times for the edible gardener: There are armsful of basil and the best, most flavorful tomatoes. There are summer squash, eggplant, and peppers for the grill. With a little shade, there can still be lettuce for cool salads. For the ambitious, it's time to can tomatoes and pickles.

The perennial garden is probably showing some wear and tear. Most leaves will have a hole or two by this time, but that doesn't usually indicate a problem; it's just what happens over the course of a long summer in a yard where plants coexist with insects.

Dried flower stalks and tattered leaves can sometimes be a dispiriting reminder that the summer is passing and fall soon will be here. So on a cool morning, spruce up by removing spent stalks of hostas and other perennials past their bloom, trimming off beat-up leaves, and replacing scraggly annuals in containers. It will make the garden seem fresher and newer for a few weeks and hold off the feeling that fall is on the way—at least until we hear the first distant honk of migrating geese overhead.

PLAN

BULBS

It's time to order amaryllis bulbs. You will need 10 to 12 weeks to force them into holiday bloom.

If you're ready, order spring-blooming bulbs for fall planting. See Plan/Bulbs, September, page 134.

ANNUALS & PERENNIALS

Try saving seeds from favorite annuals and perennials for next year. Save only the seeds from straight-species plants; seeds from hybrids and cultivars have gone through the sorting of sexual reproduction and won't have the same assortment of traits in the next generation.

Once seeds have formed and dried on cleome, sweet peas, larkspur, petunias, cosmos, delphiniums, and other favorites, cut the flower stems or remove the seedpods and shake the seeds into a container.

Store each kind of seed in a moisture-proof plastic zipper bag (available at crafts stores). Add a few grains of rice to absorb moisture. Store the packets in the freezer or a cool, dark place until next spring.

PLANT

EDIBLES

In the southern regions, sow a last crop of short-season bush beans for fall harvest. Pole beans would take too long, but with bush beans there should be time for a crop. See the Fall Vegetable Timing Chart on page 168. For precise timing, consult the seed packet and your average first frost date.

■ *Save seeds from plants that are straight species (not cultivars). Label them carefully.*

Sow seeds for beets and turnips. Sow staggered batches of carrots, spinach, lettuce, and other greens such as bok choy, collards, kale, and radishes.

Transplant seedlings of broccoli, Brussels sprouts, cabbage, and cauliflower to the garden. Water well when planting and mulch. Be careful to keep the soil of all seeds and transplants moist. The soil will dry out much faster than when you planted in the spring.

Greens that you start from seed in August such as lettuce, chard, and spinach will need some shelter from the hot summer sun, such as a simple hoop house or tunnel. Pin down the row cover securely against windy summer storms.

In the northern regions, full-size head lettuce may not have time to mature, so plant little heads of Boston lettuce or looseleaf lettuce and mesclun that you can harvest leaf by leaf.

CONTAINERS & HOUSEPLANTS

You can plant edible crops for fall harvest in your containers. Just remember to water them often, since containers dry out quickly.

For ornamental containers, pull out annuals that have faded or gotten leggy. Replace them with ornamental kale, chrysanthemums, or any perennials you can find in small pots, such as heuchera, hosta, or tiarella. In October, you can transplant the perennials to the ground.

LAWNS

You can reseed or resod a lawn toward the end of August, once the weather cools off. See Here's How to Reseed or Resod a Lawn, page 48.

PERENNIALS

If you purchase perennials at end-of-summer sales, plant them as soon as possible and water well. Cut back any dried or yellowed foliage or flower stalks. The plants may not bloom much next year, since they are getting such a late start on establishing their root systems in the ground.

TREES & SHRUBS

In late August, once the weather has cooled, you can start to plant trees and shrubs. See Here's How

■ *Start planting transplants of cool-season vegetables such as cabbage. Mulch to keep moisture in the soil, just as you did in spring.*

to Plant a Tree or Shrub, page 52. Be prepared to water vigilantly, especially if there's another hot spell.

CARE

ALL

Keep weeding. Many weeds are setting seed in late summer, so weeding now is an investment in less weeding next year. Dispose of any weeds that have seeds in the landscape waste, not the compost.

EDIBLES

If you keep plants picked clean, they will produce more, and you will get the fruits when they are at their best. Patrol the vegetable patch daily, and look under leaves of squash for hidden monster zucchini.

If you have extra vegetables, consider giving them to a food pantry or soup kitchen. If you are overwhelmed, make a note not to plant so many next year. Notice any vegetables that are unpopular with your family and skip them next season.

Basil is at its peak right now, so keep harvesting it. Every couple of days, pinch back an older stem right down to the soil and pinch other stems back to a leaf node. If you have an oversupply, make pesto.

To dry herbs, hang bunches inside paper bags with holes punched in them. This will keep insects and dust out. Hang them in a dark place with excellent

air circulations. In a few weeks, shake the bunch to collect the dried herb leaves. You also can save herbs by chopping them up and freezing individual portions in a little water in ice-cube trays. When they are frozen, pop out the cubes, place them in a plastic bag, label them, and you will have them to flavor soups and stews in winter.

LAWNS

Don't mow dormant lawns. If the grass still is growing, keep mowing it at 3 inches or higher.

PERENNIALS

If a clump of irises bloomed less this year, it may be crowded. Divide irises in August after they are done flowering and the leaves have yellowed. Then dig up the clump with a garden fork and shake off the soil to expose the roots, or rhizomes.

If you see any sign they've been eaten, you likely have iris borers, the larvae of a moth. Cut off any damaged part of the clump and discard it in the landscape waste, not the compost. Cut the remainder of the clump into pieces, each of which should have a fan of leaves and a few roots. Trim the leaves no shorter than 6 inches and replant the fans into soil with compost.

If you are planning to plant a new bed this fall, August is a good time to prepare the soil. See Here's How to Create a New Garden Bed, page 65.

Many perennial gardens have little bloom in late summer. Make a note, so you can remember to plant late-summer bloomers such as turtlehead, Japanese anemone, or asters next spring.

■ *Toward the end of August, refresh a played-out container with a fall-themed planting such as this combination of ornamental kale, peppers, and heuchera.*

■ *Chop up herbs, pack them in ice cube trays, fill the trays with water, and freeze them. Keep a plastic bag of herb cubes in the freezer to drop into stews or other winter dishes.*

ROSES

Keep deadheading reblooming roses, but don't do any substantial pruning for the rest of the summer. The roses are getting ready to go dormant and you don't want to stimulate new growth.

SHRUBS

Don't shear or prune trees or shrubs after the middle of August. Pruning would stimulate new growth that would not have time to harden off and would be likely to dry out and die in winter cold.

WATER

ALL

Pay attention to the moisture level in your soil. Some Augusts are very dry, while others bring waves of heavy rainstorms. Water so you're keeping the soil as moist as each plant requires. Be especially careful of anything you planted this spring.

If you're going away for vacation, provide for watering. See Water/All, June, page 108.

ANNUALS, CONTAINERS & HOUSEPLANTS

Keep watering enough to maintain steady soil moisture. Containers will need watering more often, especially now that plants are big.

EDIBLES

Water your August plantings fairly often, at least twice a week and maybe more, depending on

the weather. Tomato, pepper, squash, and other plants are large now, with lots of fruit, which takes a steady water supply. But be careful not to overwater; soggy soil leads to fungus problems.

LAWNS

A dormant lawn should start to green up toward the end of the month as the weather cools and rain increases. Water only if the weather is dry.

PERENNIALS

Water only those perennials that need it, such as astilbe. Let most Midwestern perennials get by on rainfall unless the weather is really hot and dry.

TREES & SHRUBS

Water trees and shrubs planted within the last two to three years deeply at intervals of at least a week. In hot, dry years, water established shrubs and trees too, especially trees planted in constricted spaces.

FERTILIZE

ANNUALS

Give container annuals one last feeding of a slow-release liquid fertilizer at half strength.

PROBLEM-SOLVE

ALL

Patrol the garden for places where mosquitoes might hatch. See Problem-Solve/All, July, page 121.

ANNUALS

If impatiens plants' leaves turn yellow and drop, the problem is likely impatiens downy mildew. This fungus disease has become widespread. Remove all the stricken plants and dispose of them in the landscape waste, not the compost. This fungus lives in the soil, so next year use that spot for a different species, such as begonias.

EDIBLES

A black growth that appears on ears of corn is a fungus disease called corn smut, common in hot, dry summer weather. If you cut out the black smut, the ear is still edible. Put the smut in the landscape or trash, not the compost heap.

Although some varieties are more resistant than others to this disease, any corn can get corn smut.

For tomato problems, see Here's How to Solve Tomato Troubles, page 124.

When the summer is cool and wet, basil may develop downy mildew, a fungus disease. Yellow areas on top of the leaves may be followed by brown spots; then the leaves turn brown and fall off. Undersides of the leaves may have a gray, fuzzy look.

Remove all the diseased plants and don't put them in the compost pile. If they were in containers, dispose of the potting mix in the landscape waste. If they were in the ground, don't plant basil in the same spot next year.

PERENNIALS

If clumps of tall sedums such as 'Autumn Joy' and 'Matrona' are floppy by late summer, they probably are getting too much water and fertilizer. Sedums are native to dry places, and too much water will make them grow too fast and tall. Reserve them for places in the garden you plan to neglect, with very well-drained soil. Most plants with fleshy leaves like sedums prefer soil to be on the dry side.

The same is true of prairie plants such as liatris and coneflower that have grown overly tall. Like ornamental grasses, these plants evolved to make it through the summer on average Midwestern rainfall.

Toward the end of the summer, the blue may disappear from blue-tinged leaves such as those of

■ *Once iris foliage has yellowed, dig up crowded clumps, divide and clean the rhizomes, replant them, and water well.*

Hosta sieboldiana 'Elegans'. That's because the blue is not a pigment but a waxy coating that melts off over time. To keep the blue tint longest, plant these varieties in shade.

TREES & SHRUBS

Powdery mildew often shows up in hot, humid weather toward the end of summer. It's a grayish, powdery film on leaves, commonly seen on phlox, lilacs, bee balm, zinnias, and nannyberry viburnum. It usually is only cosmetic, although severe infestations can cause a plant to decline over time. It's too late to apply a fungicide once the disease is established; a fungicide needs to be applied early in the season before the fungus appears.

The fungus prefers still, moist air, so it can help to prune shrubs to be more open for better airflow. Dispose of diseased leaves in the landscape waste. In the future, look for plant varieties that resist mildew.

Watch out for the beige, fuzzy egg masses of gypsy moths. See Problem-Solve/Trees, July, page 125.

August and September are the best time to attack magnolia scale, a sap-sucking insect that afflicts magnolias. You have to catch the insects at just the right time of their life cycle, when they are vulnerable, immature larvae crawling on the bark. Apply a horticultural oil to smother the crawlers.

If you see an area of dried-out leaves in the canopy of an ash tree in late summer, call an arborist. See Resources, page 189. The emerald ash borer, which is expected to kill most ash trees in the Midwest, does its damage by cutting off the trees' water vessels so leaves and wood dry out.

If you see this damage on your neighbor's ash tree, call an arborist before you see damage on your own ash. It may be possible to fend off the borers by injecting an ash tree with an insecticide, but the treatment must be started before the tree is too severely damaged. Ash trees that have died or are too far gone to save should be removed promptly. The dried-out wood quickly becomes brittle and unstable and branches or the whole tree can fall.

September

The early days of September can be among the sweetest of the year. Days are cooling off but nights are still balmy. The waters of Lake Michigan and Lake Erie are warm with the summer's stored sunlight. Sweet corn, tomatoes, and blueberries are still plentiful.

But fall is here. The kids are back in school and the dormant lawn is revving up again for its autumn burst of growth. Meanwhile, perennials, shrubs, and trees are slowing down and moving toward their winter sleep. The first frost may be just a month away, and there's plenty to do first.

One important task is to take stock. What worked? What didn't? Can you figure out why? Look for conditions that have changed: Perhaps the lilies you planted in full sun ten years ago are now in shade, because a sapling has grown into a tree. Or a tree that was cut down has thrown your hostas into full sun. Maybe it's time to change the garden up to fit with new conditions.

While you're at it, decide if there are plants it's time to just give up on. You don't *have* to keep bee balm that always gets powdery mildew, or an old flowering crabapple tree that has apple scab, or a viburnum that blocks the sidewalk and needs too much pruning.

It's not always easy to let go. Often a plant that has been part of the landscape for years can feel like an obligation, or a friend. Certainly a large shade tree, which takes decades to grow, should be preserved if at all possible.

But for many problems, the best solution is to be ruthless. If a perennial or shrub just doesn't thrive in your garden or needs heavy maintenance, it may be the wrong plant for you or for your conditions. There may be another that is the right size or has been selected to resist disease. Rather than undertaking another year of pruning or applying fungicides to try and make something work where it really doesn't, consider starting over with a better plan and a more appropriate plant.

PLAN

ANNUALS

Buy fall-blooming chrysanthemums and asters just as their buds are beginning to open, so they do their blooming in *your* garden and not in the garden center. The exception is when you're going to plant them in a part shade to shady location: That won't provide enough energy to prompt the plants to open tight buds, so buy them in full bloom. They should last four to six weeks, depending on the weather.

Buy pansies that are large, healthy plants in full bloom. They won't grow much before frost.

BULBS

Buy or order lily bulbs early in September. You'll need to plant them in early fall, at least a month before you plant the spring-blooming bulbs such as daffodils.

Order (and plant) bulbs of the surprise lily, also known as resurrection lily or naked ladies (*Lycoris squamigera*). This plant, which puts out a mound of foliage in spring and sends up naked stalks with pink trumpet blooms in late summer, is marginally hardy in Zone 5, so it needs to be well mulched in winter.

Order spring-blooming bulbs from catalogs or websites for October planting. Refer to your notes and photos of the spring garden to recall where there was room for improvement.

When you order bulbs, note where you plan to plant each. That way you won't wonder what you were thinking when a huge box of bulbs is delivered in October.

To improve your bulb displays, add early-blooming and late-blooming varieties or species to extend spring bloom. You can add bulbs in places where there wasn't much color. In part-sun places where bulbs didn't bloom well, you can plant species that are a little shade-tolerant, such as scilla and chionodoxa (glory of the snow). Plant these two for early bloom along later-blooming daffodils or tulips. If you had trouble with animals digging up bulbs last spring, choose plants they tend not to like, such as daffodils and alliums.

If your garden is shady, plan to plant bulbs in the least shady areas, and choose early-blooming species and varieties. In early spring, before the trees leaf out, more sun will reach the ground. Don't choose late-season bulbs for a garden shaded by trees; by the middle of May when the leaves have unfurled, there won't be enough light for the bulbs to thrive.

For a bulb garden that will be less work in years to come, order perennial bulbs that will last a long time, such as daffodils and alliums, rather than hybrid tulips that are unlikely to rebloom and need to be replanted each year. Species tulips, unlike the hybrids, often will rebloom and even spread. Alliums and daffodils also are less likely to be eaten by animals than tulips and crocuses.

Order *plenty* of bulbs, especially smaller ones such as early crocuses. They need to be planted in large numbers to make a visual impact.

Bulbs you order now will be shipped at an appropriate time for planting after the first frost in your area. If you buy bulbs early at the garden center, or if the fall is unusually warm, store them until planting in a place that is cool, dark, and dry (not the refrigerator).

Check around for bulb sales held by local garden clubs and botanical gardens. Sometimes you can find unusual varieties at these sales, and you can always find people to answer your questions.

EDIBLES

If you don't have a cold frame to extend the harvest, consider building one now. It will be useful in spring too. See Plan/All, February, page 30.

Stock up on floating row covers or old sheets to protect plants in case of an early frost.

PERENNIALS

If your garden now seems to be nothing but green by September, make a note to check out toad lily (*Tricyrtis formosana*) for a shady spot next spring. In early fall, it has tall stalks with many tiny, orchidlike flowers, often purple and streaked or spotted, that last until frost. Other alternatives for early fall flowers include Japanese anemone, turtlehead, and gentian. For sun, try asters or tall sedum, or long-blooming purple coneflower, Russian sage, and black-eyed Susan. Some kinds of hosta bloom in September too.

■ *For color in the early-fall garden, try perennials such as black-eyed Susans (top) in sun. In shade or part-shade spots, try Japanese anemones (bottom).*

SHRUBS

Don't get swept away by fall sales and buy unsuitable shrubs. Planting whatever is on sale, without making sure it fits your space and conditions, can lead to headaches later.

TREES

Fall is an excellent time to plant trees, other than evergreens (plant them in spring so they have more time to develop a good root system). But invest some time and thought to make sure you choose the right tree. A tree lives a long time, so it's a long-term, high-stakes decision. Seek expert advice; refer to Resources on page 189. The more information you can provide about the site, the better advice you will get.

PLANT

ANNUALS

Asters and chrysanthemums that you buy in September for fall color are technically perennials, but they are selected more for how easily they can be manipulated in growers' greenhouses than for cold-hardiness. They may or may not survive the winter. If you want to try, make sure you plant them in well-drained soil in full sun.

BULBS

Plant lily bulbs as soon as you buy them in soil that is well drained and thoroughly amended with organic matter. Water well and mulch after planting.

Also plant those surprise lilies (*Lycoris squamigera*) or divide crowded clumps. Mulch these bulbs well after planting; they are marginally hardy in the Midwest.

EDIBLES

Sow a last crop of radishes, looseleaf lettuce, mesclun mixes, spinach, and beet seeds.

Plant bulblets of garlic and shallots for next year's harvest. They'll take root and sprout in the fall, die back over the winter, and resprout in spring to be ready for harvest late next summer.

In a large garden, plant a cover crop in areas where the vegetables are all done. It will cover the soil and choke out weeds in fall and winter. In early spring, before it sets seed, you'll dig the cover crop into the soil to add organic matter and nutrients. For cover crop plantings in early September, choose clover or annual ryegrass. For later plantings before the middle of October, choose winter wheat or winter rye.

CONTAINERS

For a last splash of color, remove faded summer annuals and replace them with fall-blooming pansies, chrysanthemums, or ornamental kale.

■ *Plant bulblets of garlic in fall for next year's harvest. They will sprout in fall, die back over the winter, and resprout in spring.*

LAWNS

When it's a little cooler and there's likely to be more rain is an excellent time to rejuvenate a lawn.

Overseed existing lawns; in new lawns or bare patches, prepare the soil and reseed. (See Here's How to Reseed or Resod a Lawn, page 48.) Keep the new seed moist until it germinates. Assuming there is adequate autumn rain, the new grass will have time to develop roots before it goes dormant in late fall.

Don't lay sod in fall. Even with careful watering, the sod will have a hard time growing enough roots before going dormant in winter.

PERENNIALS & GROUNDCOVERS

Plant or divide perennials and groundcovers in the first two weeks of September so the plants have time to spread out a good set of roots before they go dormant for the winter. For dividing instructions, see Plant/Perennials & Groundcovers, March, page 49.

Early September is also the time to plant peonies into a bed with well-amended soil. Make sure the plant's tough root sits just 1 inch or so below the surface of the soil. Water well and mulch. Peonies often take two or three years to recover and bloom after transplanting.

TREES & SHRUBS

Plant most shrubs, other than evergreens, until your average first frost date, which will likely be sometime in October. Shrubs purchased later in the fall may be dormant.

Fall is an excellent time to plant most trees and shrubs. See Here's How to Plant a Tree or Shrub, page 52.

Trees planted before your average first frost date will have several months to settle in and grow some new feeder roots before the ground freezes. Even though the trees are going dormant, the still-warm soil will encourage roots to grow.

Next spring, you will need to remember that these trees still need extra watering. Fall will seem to you like a long time ago, but the trees' root systems will still be new.

Wait until spring to plant evergreens, redbuds, birches, oaks, or Japanese maples.

CARE

ALL

Weeds continue to set seed until frost hits. Pull them up to keep them from sprouting next year.

ANNUALS

Pull up annuals as they end their season and compost them (unless they have shown signs of disease). Mulch the area to prevent weed seeds from sprouting in late fall warmth.

If annuals are still blooming in September, leave them alone until they are killed by frost.

If you have prized annual geraniums you'd like to overwinter, there are several approaches. If the plant is in a container, bring the entire pot in as a houseplant. Or take it to a protected space such as an unheated garage, water it sparingly, and let it go dormant. In early spring, start watering it again to bring it out of dormancy. Or take several cuttings, root them, and grow new plants indoors over the winter. By late spring, you should have a couple of vigorous new plants. This also works well with begonias and coleus.

Many tender plants grown for their attractive foliage, such as coleus, begonias, Persian shield, and asparagus fern, can be potted up in good-quality potting mix and grown as houseplants during the winter.

BULBS

Dig up and divide clumps of lilies that have become crowded. You'll likely see that they have

■ *Divide clumps of lilies that have become crowded or that are in too much shade.*

produced "daughter bulbs." Gently pull away the smaller bulbs and replant in full sun, watering well. The daughter bulbs will take a few years to reach full size and flower.

EDIBLES

Clean up the vegetable garden as crops finish up. Don't compost plants that had problems; put them in the landscape waste to make sure fungus spores or insect eggs don't winter over.

Keep harvesting tomatoes, peppers, beans, herbs, and other crops that are still producing. Production will slow down as days get shorter and nights get cooler.

In late September or early October, when your average first frost is about two weeks away, harvest all the tender vegetables such as tomatoes and peppers. Put green tomatoes on a sunny windowsill to ripen (or try them sliced, battered, and fried).

Leave full-sized pumpkins and winter squash on the vine as long as possible. When frost has wilted their leaves, harvest them by cutting the stalk with a sharp knife.

Toward the middle of September, you should be able to harvest the first of the crops you sowed in summer, such as lettuce, spinach, and radishes. Harvest pak choy when the heads are small and tender.

Prolong your harvest of herbs by bringing some of the plants indoors if you have a sunny windowsill. Early in September, carefully pot them up in high-quality potting mix and water well. Keep them outdoors in a part-shade spot for a few days to lessen the shock, and then place them in your sunniest window. Many will last for several months indoors before the low light and dry, heated air do them in.

CONTAINERS & HOUSEPLANTS

If you want to overwinter shrubs in pots, make plans now. See Care/Containers, October, page 148.

In mid-September or whenever temperatures are consistently below 50 degrees Fahrenheit at night, bring houseplants back inside. Most of these plants are from tropical places and they can't stand cold.

The indoors is a very different environment for plants. If possible, help them adjust by making the move gradually, bringing them indoors for a few hours each day over a week or so.

If that's not practical, try cutting the plants back about one-third before you bring them in. That will allow more of the scanty indoor light to reach the center of the plant and will give the roots less plant to support.

Inspect houseplants carefully for insects before you bring them in. Eggs that ride along may hatch in the indoor warmth, and there will be no beneficial predator insects to keep the population down. It's a good idea to wash all the plants off with a good blast from the hose, including the undersides of the leaves.

If you still see evidence of insects, spray the plant with a commercial insecticidal soap and quarantine it away from the other plants for a few days until you are sure the bugs are dead.

Generally, it's better to repot houseplants in spring. But if you see nothing but fleshy roots through the holes in the pot in September, try judiciously root-pruning. Gently remove the plant, prune back some of the roots, add a little soil, and repot in the same pot. Prune back the top growth to about the same extent.

Place plants where they can get adequate light. It's best to identify your plants and learn their specific needs. Caladium and peace lily need bright light, right near an east- or west-facing window. Swedish ivy and philodendron can do with a little less, and snake plant and cast-iron plant can survive several feet from a north window.

Provide additional humidity for houseplants once the heating comes on. See Care/Houseplants, January, page 25. Rotate plants often so all sides are exposed to the light from the window and growth is even.

LAWNS

If you didn't core-aerate in spring, do it now (see next page). Just after you aerate is an excellent time to overseed and topdress with compost.

Dig up crabgrass before it has a chance to set seed. If you want to treat for crabgrass, the best time to do it is in early spring, before the seeds of this annual weed can sprout. See Problem-Solve/Lawns, March, page 57.

HERE'S HOW

TO AERATE YOUR LAWN

■ *Aerate your lawn in fall if you didn't do it in spring. If you plan to rent a machine and do it yourself, first flag or mark the positions of all sprinkler lines, sprinkler heads, and buried electrical, gas, or other utility lines.*

■ *Clear the lawn of debris and water it lightly a few hours before you start.*

■ *Set the depth on the machine to maximum. Run it back and forth to cover the lawn in one direction, and then shift 90 degrees and cover the lawn in the other direction.*

■ *Leave the cores on the lawn to decompose. If you prefer, wait a day before gently raking them to break them up so they decompose more quickly.*

PERENNIALS

Early September is the time to divide spring-blooming perennials such as bleeding heart and hardy geraniums. Dig up the clump, pull or cut the rootball into good-sized pieces, and replant them separately. Water well and keep the soil moist.

Divide or transplant peonies in early fall. Lift the large, fleshy root carefully from the soil and cut it into smaller pieces, each with at least three "eyes," the reddish buds that will sprout shoots in spring. Replant in well-amended soil with the root just 1 inch or so below the soil surface. Water well and spread mulch over the root zone, but keep it clear of the crown of the plant.

Don't rush to tidy up the garden. Even if they are done blooming, perennials need their leaves to gather sunlight and store food in their roots as they prepare for winter. Wait to cut them back until all green color is gone.

TREES & SHRUBS

Avoid pruning trees or shrubs at this time of year, except to remove damaged or dead wood. Pruning would stimulate new growth that would not have time to harden off and would be likely to dry out and die in winter cold. Wait to prune until the plants are dormant in late winter.

If you are treating the soil around plants such as rhododendrons or bigleaf hydrangeas to make it more acidic, apply the second half of the year's sulfur in early September. See Care/Trees & Shrubs, March, page 56.

WATER

ALL

September may seem like the end of the gardening season, but it can still be hot and you can't count on rain. Perennials, shrubs, and trees need to store lots of water in their root systems during the fall to get through winter and start up in spring.

HOUSEPLANTS

Water houseplants well before you bring them indoors. Then water often enough to keep their potting mix moist just below the surface. Once

■ *Divide or transplant peonies in September. Cut apart a tangled root mass with a sharp knife. Make sure each peony division has three to five reddish "eyes," which are the growing shoots for next year.*

■ *Plant the divisions with the eyes about 1 to 2 inches below the soil surface in well-drained soil. You can lay a rake or other tool across the hole to be sure of the soil level. Water well and mulch. The plants may take two or three years to become established before they bloom again.*

inside, their growth will slow down and they may need watering less often, but keep checking.

LAWNS

Water newly seeded lawns. Now that grass is actively growing, water established lawns if there is less than 1 inch of rain a week.

PERENNIALS

Keep watering perennials and groundcovers that you planted this year, even in spring, until the ground freezes. They still need water to establish roots.

ROSES

Water tender roses until they go dormant.

TREES & SHRUBS

Keep watering shrubs and trees that were planted within the last three years. This is especially important for evergreens in the fall. Since evergreens keep losing water through their leaves all winter, they need to store lots of water in autumn to avoid drying out. If there isn't much rainfall, water even large, established evergreens.

FERTILIZE

LAWNS

Apply a slow-release fertilizer between now and mid-October for fall growth and to help the lawn get started in spring. Choose a fertilizer that has a higher first number (nitrogen) in the ratio of major nutrients and a middle number (phosphorus) that is low or 0. See Here's How to Read a Fertilizer Label, May, page 95.

PROBLEM-SOLVE

ROSES

If you had blackspot or other disease problems this year, carefully clean up all diseased leaves and put them in the landscape waste, not the compost.

SHRUBS

Evergreens often lose a lot of needles in September. It's normal for older needles from the interior of the plant to drop.

TREES

Where deer are a problem, protect young trees that still have thin bark. Deer often rub their antlers against trees in late summer and early fall, and the rubbing can scrape the bark right off. Wrap the tree's trunk with chicken wire, wire hardware cloth, or plastic snow fencing to a height of 5 feet and secure it well. Take the wrap off in early spring.

If leaves turn color or drop early, it may be a sign that trees are stressed. Usually this is because it's been hot or dry or both. Take it as a reminder to water trees deeply and thoroughly, and hope for lots of winter snow and spring rain.

October

Autumn leaves are the gold at the end of the rainbow. As a season of color and flavor draws to an end, a treasure falls into our hands.

Falling leaves are not a nuisance to get rid of—they are a bounty. They feed fungi, microbes, and invertebrates that will digest them to make soil lighter, fluffier, and richer. In the meantime, they make splendid mulch.

Leaves are valuable even if all you do is mow them to shreds and leave them on the lawn for the worms to break down. But they also are a prime ingredient for compost, the gardener's magic.

Raking leaves on a cool, sunny day is one of the delights of autumn: the colors, the rustle, the way leaves fly through the air, the clean earthy smell. And as you mix leaves into the compost, or shred them for the lawn or to spread over perennial beds, or even collect a stash to save for spring, you are piling up treasure for your soil and your plants and banking on the promise of another gardening year.

We bury another kind of treasure in October: We plant spring-blooming bulbs. As we tuck those brown, dry-looking things under the soil, it's hard to believe that every one already has a flower secretly furled inside it. But it's true, and the proof will come in March or May when crocus or tulip opens its bloom.

Frost must come before we plant bulbs. Although we all know the average date of the first frost where we garden, we also know it can come earlier or later. A long warm autumn with a late frost gives us a little more time to get things buttoned up, but a short cold one is just as likely. Often fall, like spring, can't seem to make up its mind whether it's coming or going.

One morning, though, there will be a silver tracery of ice crystals along the veins of a fallen leaf. It may not be the end, but it's a sign. Winter is coming. Get ready.

PLAN

ALL

October is a good time to get a soil test. You can test the chemistry and nutrients of your soil any time you can dig up samples, but it's useful to get the information before you start planning for next year's garden.

There's no need to test your soil every year, but you should certainly do it when you move to a new place or start a new garden. If you've been gardening for a while, conditions may have changed and a checkup may be in order; adding compost every year for five or ten years can make a *big* difference.

If some kinds of plants or plants in a particular area are failing to thrive, a soil test can tell you whether the problem might be a nutrient deficiency. Always get a soil test before you decide whether to fertilize a tree.

Soil texture is a matter of the size of particles: large particles (sand), small particles (silt), and much smaller particles (clay). The best soil has a mixture of particle sizes, so it holds enough moisture but water and air can flow freely. It also has a substantial amount of organic matter, which adds large particles, supports microorganisms, provides nutrients, and acts as a sponge to hold and release water.

To check your soil's texture, squeeze a handful in your palm. If it sticks together and stays, your soil has lots of ultrafine clay particles. If the clump hardly holds together at all, it has a lot of sand. If it forms together but then crumbles, it's more of a mixture.

For a better estimate, do a simple test. Get a ruler and a clear jar with a tight-fitting lid, such as a Mason jar. Fill it one-quarter full of sifted soil. Fill the rest of the jar with water and add 1 teaspoon of powdered dishwasher detergent. Screw the lid on tightly and shake vigorously for several minutes. Set the jar where it can rest undisturbed for several days. The soil particles will settle out according to size.

After one minute, measure the depth of the lowest layer, the sand particles. After two hours, measure the depth of the next layer, the silt particles. After several days, when the water has cleared, measure the depth of the top layer, the clay particles.

The ratio of those three measurements is roughly the ratio of sand, silt, and clay in your soil.

If there is fluffy brown stuff floating on top of the water, that's a good sign; it means you have some organic matter in your soil.

The major way to improve your soil is usually to add organic matter, such as compost. More organic matter can help balance out the soil's pH as well as improve its texture and make more nutrients available to plants.

BULBS

Have a plan as you plant spring-blooming bulbs for the best effect and the longest bloom.

■ *To check the structure of your soil, squeeze a handful of moist soil. If it sticks together and stays, it's mostly fine clay particles.*

■ *If it hardly holds together at all, it's mostly large sand particles.*

■ *If it forms together but then crumbles, it's a mixture of particle sizes.*

HERE'S HOW

TO GET A SOIL TEST

A home test kit you buy at the garden center or online can give you a general sense of your soil's pH and major nutrients.

For a more precise and detailed analysis, send samples to a professional soil-testing laboratory. Laboratories can run a wide range of tests, with prices from $20 to $100 or more, depending on the lab and what you ask for. Ask the laboratory for a sample of its results before you order; clearly presented results that you can easily understand are worth paying extra for.

A standard soil test will determine the pH of your soil—how acidic or alkaline it is—which plays a large role in how your plants absorb nutrients. It also should assess the levels of the major nutrients potassium and phosphorus (but not nitrogen, which fluctuates constantly), and of "cation exchange capacity," a measure of how well your soil holds nutrients and makes them available to plants. Get a test that also will tell you the level of micronutrients such as calcium and magnesium.

If you are planning a new vegetable garden, test the soil for toxic lead. Widely distributed onto soil before the 1970s by emissions from leaded gasoline, lead can be absorbed by edible plants and by people. It's a neurotoxin that is especially harmful to children with developing brains.

The laboratory will give you a bag to mail the samples in and instructions for taking them. For each test, take several samples and mix them.

Do separate tests of different garden areas, because conditions vary. A lawn that has been heavily treated with chemicals is likely to have fewer available nutrients than a vegetable garden that has been heavily amended with compost. Soil near a concrete foundation or sidewalk is likely to have a higher pH, because concrete is alkaline.

A laboratory test will not tell you the texture of your soil—clay, sandy, or loam—or how well it drains, although those are things you can easily determine for yourself. The test won't tell you whether there are disease-causing bacteria or fungal spores in the soil.

To locate a soil-testing laboratory, ask a good garden center or contact your local Extension office. See Resources, page 189.

■ *A soil test can give you essential information about the qualities of your soil. Start with a clean trowel.*

■ *Test different garden areas separately. Take several soil samples from each area.*

■ *Mix samples from each area and test the soil yourself or send it to a professional lab.*

■ *Home test kits are inexpensive but will not give as accurate and detailed results as professional testing.*

loamy soil   clay soil   sandy soil

clay

silt

sand

You can explore the makeup of your garden's soil by mixing a cup of soil in a Mason jar of water. Let it settle out for several days and compare the layers that form to this illustration. If you have plenty of organic debris floating at the top of the water, you get bonus points for organic matter.

For small bulbs, buy a lot and plan to plant them in large groups. A handful of scattered snow crocuses don't make much of a visual impact. Plant all bulbs in groups of at least five to seven.

In places you tend to neglect, plant long-lasting, trouble-free bulbs such as daffodils, which will grow into larger clumps over time, or scilla, which will reseed in favorable conditions (part shade, with no fertilizing and not too much watering).

If you like the look of tiny blooms scattered in the lawn, choose the right kind of bulbs. In sunny lawns, plant crocus; in more shade, try scilla. Snowdrops aren't good candidates for lawns because they grow in dense clumps with thick, too-tall leaves. Plant them around shrubs where they can grow undisturbed.

Most tulips will not rebloom after the first year in the Midwest because our soil is too moist. Tulips come from rocky mountains in central Asia and like their summers bone-dry. To have the best chance of flowers in the second year, plant tulips in full sun among drought-tolerant perennials you don't plan to water much.

Try to place bulbs in the garden where their foliage can be masked by other plants after they bloom. That way, you will be less tempted to cut back the leaves, which the plants need. For example, you might plant ornamental onions with peonies or among shrub roses. If you plant daffodils among daylilies, their foliage will be unnoticeable because it is so similar to the daylilies'.

HERE'S HOW

BULBS WORK

For success with spring-blooming bulbs, it helps to understand these plants' life cycle.

The bulb we buy in fall is a package containing a plant, complete with flower, and food to support it while it grows. The bulb is dormant—alive but not growing.

When we plant it and water it in fall, it will grow roots until the ground freezes. Winter cold is *critical* to these plants: The bulbs have to chill below 40 degrees Fahrenheit for at least 12 to 14 weeks in order to bloom.

In spring, warmer soil and moisture from melting snow will trigger the plant to unfold out of the bulb and push to the surface to bloom.

After it blooms, the plant builds a new flower for next year. During this period of six to eight weeks after the flowers fade, the plant needs all its leaves to collect sunlight and power the bloom-building process.

When the new flower is built and packaged with food in a bulb, the plant goes dormant and the foliage turns yellow and dries up. This is the state in which we can dig up, transport, and replant the bulbs.

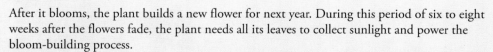

■ *When you plant bulbs in containers, use good-quality potting mix and pack them closely. Place the container in a cool, dark place such as an unheated garage, where the bulbs can stay cold for at least 14 weeks without freezing. Bring the pot out into the sun in March.*

PLANT

BULBS

Plant spring-blooming bulbs in October after the first frost. By that time your soil is probably cool enough so the bulbs won't be tempted to sprout, even while they grow roots. You can plant bulbs into November, but be careful to get it done before the ground freezes.

Plant the earliest-blooming spring bulbs, such as dwarf irises (*Iris reticulata*), snow crocuses (*Crocus chrysanthus*), and snowdrops (*Galanthus nivalis*), in the warmest, sunniest parts of the garden to encourage signs of spring to arrive as soon as possible.

You can fit different bulbs in the same space if they bloom at different times. Dig a wide hole 6 to 8 inches deep. Place large bulbs such as late-blooming daffodils or tulips on the first layer. Scatter some soil and compost over them, put on another layer of smaller bulbs such as crocuses or dwarf irises, and fill the hole. The crocuses will bloom first and then the daffodils. Don't combine early crocuses with early daffodils, whose tall foliage would shade out the crocuses.

For a more natural effect, scatter the bulbs on the bed and plant them wherever they fall. A mixture of bulbs scattered casually together can make a wildflower-like tapestry.

Save some bulbs for forcing in containers. Plant them in well-drained potting mix in containers,
packing them closely together. Water well. Then place the pot in a cool, dark place, where the bulbs will be chilled but not frozen, for at least 12 weeks. The bulbs won't bloom without this chilling.

An unheated garage or a window well full of leaves will work well to chill the bulbs (the leaves are insulation against warm spells). I also have overwintered bulbs in cardboard boxes stuffed with leaves and tucked under the back steps.

In early spring, bring the potted bulbs into the house in a sunny window or move them into the garden and start watering.

To have an amaryllis bloom indoors by Christmas, plant it by early October. It needs eight to ten weeks to grow leaves and a stalk and come into bloom. Pot it up in high-quality potting mix so the pointy end is up, with about a quarter of the bulb exposed. Make sure the pot can drain. Water well. Put the pot in a sunny window and water like a houseplant. As the foliage grows, rotate the pot from time to time so that growth is even.

TREES & SHRUBS

You still can plant most deciduous trees and shrubs in October until your area's average first frost date. Make sure you keep them watered until the ground freezes. See Here's How to Plant a Tree or Shrub, page 52.

■ *For the most effective display, plant spring-blooming bulbs in masses. Small bulbs like snow crocuses, especially, need to be planted in large numbers to make an impact.*

HERE'S HOW

TO PLANT SPRING BULBS

The basic rules for planting bulbs are simple: full sun; well-drained soil; pointy end up; deeper is better; no fertilizer.

Full sun: A few bulbs, especially early-blooming ones, can handle part shade, but for most you will get better blooming where there is eight hours of full sun in spring.

Well-drained soil: Most bulbs are native to dry, sandy, rocky places and can't stand to sit in wet soil. Organic matter such as compost is the best way to improve soil drainage. If possible, amend the whole area, not just the planting hole.

Pointy end up: The roots grow from the flat end and the stem grows from the pointy end. If you can't tell which end to place up, plant the bulb sideways. The new growth will find its way to the surface.

Deeper is better: Planting deep makes it less likely that bulbs will sprout prematurely during winter warm spells.

Eyeball the diameter of the bulb in inches, multiply by three, and dig a hole that deep. For example, if a tulip bulb is 2 inches wide, its bottom should rest in a hole about 6 inches deep. If a scilla bulb is 1 inch wide, plant it 3 inches deep.

Use a trowel to dig a hole that is just wide enough for the bulb and drop it in; tubular bulb-planting tools don't work well in heavy or sticky soils. For small bulbs, try a dibble—a pointed tool for poking holes. After you poke the holes and drop in the bulbs, fill the holes with a mixture of compost and soil.

■ *Always plant bulbs pointy end up.*

■ *To plant several bulbs, dig a wide hole of the right depth, arrange them in it, and fill it back up. Water and mulch.*

■ *For a naturalistic effect, scatter bulbs over the ground and plant them where they fall.*

If you have a number of bulbs to plant, it's often easier to dig a wide hole, amend the soil, and plant several bulbs in it. For more oomph, plant bulbs in clusters of five to seven. The smaller the bulbs, the more you will need to plant together to impress. Space the bulbs about twice as far apart as their diameter.

To plant bulbs in a lawn, try cutting a square of turf, peeling it back and spacing the bulbs out under it. Scatter on some compost and lay the turf back down.

No fertilizer: The bulb package already includes food for next year's flowers (See Here's How Bulbs Work, page 144). The best time to fertilize the plants is right after they bloom. Water bulbs well.

ALL

As leaves fall, collect them to use as mulch or in compost. Shredding leaves will help them break down faster and will make them less likely to mat down or blow around when used as mulch.

There are several ways to shred leaves. The simplest is to rake them onto the lawn in a layer a foot or so deep and run a power lawnmower back and forth over them a few times. Rake up what you want to use for compost or mulch and leave the rest on the lawn to break down and improve the soil.

Many leaf blowers also are vacuums. If you reverse the action to suction, the leaves pass through a shredding blade before being channeled into a bag that you carry over your shoulder. The bag can get heavy, but is handy for carrying the shredded leaves where you need them.

You also can buy a dedicated leaf shredder, which tears up leaves with a mechanism like a string trimmer. This is what I use, because I make such wide use of autumn leaves in my garden. The machine shreds only leaves, not sticks; it's not a wood chipper.

I use shredded leaves for mulch in the forward parts of my perennial beds, but in the back I simply rake whole leaves around the bases of the shrubs. By spring, many will have been broken down by fungi; the rest I rake up for compost.

Autumn is an excellent time to get started in the compost business. You have plenty of brown material (all those fallen leaves) and plenty of green material (the discarded annuals and other debris from garden cleanup).

See Here's How to Make Compost, page 30.

If you already have a compost pile, spread any remaining compost on beds or the vegetable garden and start over. A few handfuls of old compost or whatever remained undigested from the old pile will be enough to seed the new materials with microorganisms. By spring, you should have compost again.

ANNUALS

After frost kills the annuals, remove them from the beds or pots and compost them. If any plants, such as impatiens, had disease problems, dispose of them in the landscape waste, not the compost pile. Do the same with the potting mix from any container that held a diseased plant.

BULBS

In October, once frost has killed the top growth of tender bulbs, corms, and tubers such as gladioli, cannas, dahlias, tuberous begonias, caladiums, and elephant ears, dig them up and store them for the winter. If the foliage is yellow, remove it; otherwise, leave it attached until it turns yellow.

Brush off dirt (a paintbrush is useful for this) and let the bulbs or tubers dry in a cool, dark place. Then store them so that they will stay dry; the great enemy of stored bulbs is humidity, which can lead to mold and rot. Use cardboard boxes or paper bags rather than plastic bins. Space the bulbs out between layers of dry leaves, newspaper, or wood shavings, which will allow air to circulate and won't trap moisture. Be sure to label them (tuck in a piece of paper identifying each bulb).

Some gardeners dust bulbs with a fungicide or sulfur before storing them to help forestall fungus problems.

Place the box or bag in a place that is dry and cool, but not freezing. A cool, dry basement will work, or an unheated garage (store the bulbs along the wall against the house).

Check the bulbs from time to time over the winter, and discard any that are soft or discolored.

If you have been growing tender bulbs and tubers in containers, you can simply let the top growth die back and the soil dry out and store the whole container. However, this requires a lot more space than lifting the bulbs.

Another alternative is to think of these bulbs as annuals and leave them in the ground to die. Plan to buy more in early spring and start them in pots indoors to give them a head start on the growing season.

■ *To save tender bulbs such as cannas, wait until frost has killed foliage and dig them up with a garden fork.*

■ *Trim off the foliage.*

■ *Shake off the soil and let the bulbs dry for several days. Label the bulbs and store them where they will stay dry. Use cardboard boxes or paper bags, not plastic bags or bins.*

CONTAINERS

To overwinter a small shrub or hardy rose in a container, move the pot to a sheltered place over the winter or bury it in a pile of mulch, the compost heap, or the ground to protect the roots through the cold months. A window well or an unheated garage can provide good shelter. It also can help to slip the pot inside a larger pot filled with mulch or leaves for insulation. Water the plant and spread mulch over the soil.

If potting mix was fresh this year and there were no disease problems, you can save it and reuse it, mixing it half-and-half with fresh potting mix next year.

If you empty pots, use the discarded potting mix to fill low spots or scatter it in beds. There's no need to compost it; it's made of compost.

Empty terra cotta containers and bring them indoors to protect them from winter. The porous clay absorbs water, and when it freezes to ice it will crack the pot.

Containers and garden ornaments made of concrete—sometimes called "cast stone"—also can crack in freeze-thaw cycles. To protect them, prop them up off the ground with pot feet, bricks, or large sticks so that all water can drain away. Ideally, empty the pot of soil, which could hold moisture to expand and crack the pot. To protect a large and expensive pot, keep water out by draping a tarp over the pot and securing it with bungee cords.

Ice can even crack a concrete birdbath. Only leave the birdbath in place if you plan to use a heater to keep the water thawed (which would be a boon to the birds).

Fiberglass, high-quality plastic, lead, and stone containers can generally be left outside. Highly fired ceramic containers may be winter-worthy if they are labeled as "frostproof." Inexpensive plastic containers are likely to crack in the cold.

EDIBLES

Be aware of your average first frost date. It's not a guarantee, though, so be ready for a frost to come sooner.

Once lettuce is hit by frost, the flavor will suffer. Pull it out.

The first frost is often followed by a week or two of good growing weather, so if you protect tender plants such as tomatoes, cucumbers, and peppers when frost is predicted, you might still get more production out of them. Cover the plants with floating row cover, old sheets, or lightweight blankets in the evening. Remove the protection in the very early morning.

If you have a cold frame or can construct a simple hoop house for protection, you can keep cold-tolerant greens such as collards, kale, and spinach going a few more weeks after frost hits. Spinach may grow in a cold frame deep into winter.

Some vegetable crops in the cabbage family, notably collards and Brussels sprouts, have a better flavor if you wait to harvest them until after a frost.

Parsley and sage sometimes keep growing until Thanksgiving. Harvest other herbs before they freeze and use them or dry them.

Root crops, such as carrots, beets, radishes, and turnips, will keep in the ground for a few weeks after the first frost. But be careful to harvest them before the ground freezes; you can't pull a carrot out of a block of ice. Spread mulch or leaves over the area and the soil will freeze more slowly.

Once tender vegetables such as tomatoes, peppers, and cucumbers have finally been killed by cold, remove all the plants from the garden.

Fall, after the crops are done, is the best time to apply cow or horse manure to improve the soil of the vegetable garden. Till it into the top few inches of soil and let it break down over winter. Do this in late October or early November, or whenever you finish with the vegetable garden.

LAWNS

Rake leaves off the lawn. Shredded leaves, which quickly break down, are good for the grass because they enrich the soil. But layers of matted whole leaves can trap moisture on the lawn and lead to fungus diseases.

Continue to mow until the grass goes dormant and stops growing. Some gardeners make the last cut shorter on the theory that it may deter fungus disease, but I don't bother.

■ *Rake leaves off the lawn, but don't waste them and their valuable substance and nutrients. Add them to the compost pile or shred them for mulch.*

■ *Save leaves for later use in landscape waste bags.*

■ *You can shred leaves by running the lawnmower back and forth over a pile of them on the lawn. You also can use a leaf shredder or a blower vacuum that shreds leaves on the vacuum setting.*

PERENNIALS

If you want to try keeping fall-planted asters or chrysanthemums to see if they will survive the winter, water them consistently through the fall. Remove flowers as they fade, but leave the stems and leaves intact. Mulch around the plants, but keep the mulch clear of the plants' crowns.

Spread mulch 1 to 2 inches deep in perennial and bulb beds in late October or November. Its main purpose is to insulate the soil so it stays frozen through winter warm spells, reducing the chance that plants will sprout prematurely and be damaged by a subsequent freeze. Mulch also will enrich the soil as it decays.

You can spread winter mulch over the crowns of perennials that you have cut back, unless they are early bloomers such as hellebores. If you leave stems standing on plants such as echinacea or ornamental grasses, mulch around the plant.

ROSES

If you had roses that suffered from blackspot, prune out all the diseased canes and foliage. Dispose of them in the landscape waste, not the compost bin.

Otherwise, roses don't need to be pruned until spring unless you plan to completely cover tender hybrid varieties such as hybrid teas, grandifloras, and floribundas to protect them from cold. Wait to prune and protect these roses until November, after the plants are completely dormant.

Many kinds of roses have vivid red rose hips that add color to the winter garden. If you have enough

Many kinds of roses will form cheery bright red hips, if you stop deadheading early enough.

If you have a vulnerable evergreen shrub in a location where it is exposed to road salt or drying winds, you may be able to protect it by wrapping it in burlap. Keep the burlap open at the top.

hips, harvest them before they are blackened by frost and try making rose hip jelly (roses are related to apples). Or use the colorful hips in holiday décor.

TREES & SHRUBS

Don't prune trees or shrubs in October. Pruning would stimulate new growth that would not have time to harden off and would be likely to dry out and die in winter cold. Wait to prune until the plants are dormant in January or February.

WATER

BULBS

Water spring-blooming bulbs well when you plant them, so the water soaks deeply into the soil. If it doesn't rain, water about once a week until the ground freezes.

EDIBLES

Water the surviving vegetables and herbs as long as they are producing fruit or useful leaves.

HOUSEPLANTS

Water houseplants less often as their growth slows.

LAWNS

Lawns rarely need watering in the fall, unless the weather has been very hot and dry.

Drain an automatic sprinkler system before the water freezes inside.

TREES & SHRUBS

Keep watering recently planted trees and shrubs and evergreens until the ground freezes. Even trees and shrubs that have lost their leaves will grow roots until they are dormant. It's important that they have plenty of water stored in the root systems before winter; they need it to start growth in spring.

Evergreens are especially vulnerable to drying out over the winter. Keep watering them all fall.

FERTILIZE

HOUSEPLANTS

Houseplants slow down their growth as days get shorter and they go dormant. Cut back fertilizer to half strength for a few weeks. Stop fertilizing altogether until plants start actively growing in spring.

LAWNS

Avoid applying fertilizer in October or early November, when the grass is starting to go dormant. Late fall fertilizer applications that push new growth just before winter can contribute to problems such as snow mold.

PROBLEM-SOLVE

TREES & SHRUBS

Before the snow flies, protect evergreens in spots where they are exposed to cold winds or sprays of road salt, which can dry them out. It's unsightly but effective to stake burlap on the exposed side. Don't wrap the whole shrub in burlap; air needs to circulate.

If you have an evergreen that needs to be protected with burlap every winter, consider moving it to a less vulnerable spot or replacing it with a plant that is less sensitive, such as juniper. Consult your local Extension Service or botanical garden for suggestions. See Resources, page 189.

Antidessicant sprays can help keep broadleaf evergreens from drying out. The spray will leave a harmless coating that helps hold water in the foliage and reduces the chance that plants will be dried out and damaged by cold winter air. It may be worth spraying prized plants such as hollies and rhododendrons.

There needs to be water in the leaves for the coating to hold it in, so water the plant well the day before you spray. Follow the directions carefully and don't overdo.

In October or November, protect trees and shrubs from animal damage over the coming winter. Deer, rabbits, and voles often feed on tender bark. Small trees and new growth on shrubs are their top targets.

The best defense for a shrub is to surround it with a wide cylinder of metal hardware cloth with ½-inch mesh, well secured so the animals cannot get inside. Attach it to sturdy stakes (it's good to do this in October so you can drive the stakes before the ground freezes). Make the wire cylinder at least 3 feet high to foil rabbits that may be able to stand on deep snow to reach high into a shrub.

To protect the trunk of a young tree, wrap hardware cloth or chicken wire loosely around the trunk or use a plastic tree guard, available at garden centers. The tree guard should have lots of holes or slits for ventilation. Make a note to remove it during the spring and summer.

■ *Voles and other small mammals will eat the bark of shrubs and young trees over the winter. Protect vulnerable plants with a cylinder of small-mesh wire hardware cloth. Make sure to stake it down and overlap the ends so animals can't wriggle through.*

November

November wavers on the edge of winter. There still are touches of green in lawns and among some shrubs, but most trees have lost their leaves. In some years, fall lingers with an occasional balmy day and there still is fresh parsley to cut for Thanksgiving. In other years, big snows or harsh freezes come early and we may find ourselves with ground too frozen to plant bulbs.

As you prepare to turn the page on this gardening year, patrol the garden one last time for mislaid tools and sprinklers. Get rid of broken pots and other discards. Tidy away the bean poles and tomato cages before the snow flies. And spend a little time remembering what you enjoyed doing, seeing, and eating from the garden this year.

Take an hour to sit down and consolidate your records while you still remember some of the details. Glance through the photos to recall plants or views or flavors or tasks. Write down what you planted. Get out your sketch plan from February and note what changed this year: The new patio, for example, or the tree the neighbors cut down. Make a list of things you want to try next year, and things you are determined never to do again.

Gardeners have special reasons to be thankful now. Of course there are the canned tomatoes, dried herbs, and maybe fresh Brussels sprouts and spinach that are ready for the holiday table. But there also are memories of long days in the sun, when we forgot care in simple tasks; of children rolling in long, soft grass; of the rich smell of new compost. There's a deep satisfaction that our hard work made a small plot of earth green and productive; that we filled shady places with color and summer days with the dance of tall grasses; that we cared for the grand, green trees that give us shade; and that we provided a home and a bounty for butterflies, birds, and bees. At the feast of the harvest, we remember the feast of the soul that is a garden.

NOVEMBER

PLAN

HOUSEPLANTS
Choose houseplants that suit your conditions. For example, philodendron and pothos are tropical vines adapted to low light. Spider plants need more sun and space to dangle their trailing stems with baby plants at the end. Snake plant is a tough, stiff-leaved succulent that can handle a wide range of light conditions and doesn't like much water.

TREES
If you'd like to have a living Christmas tree that you can later plant out in the garden, you'll need to plan ahead. The important thing is to bring the tree indoors as briefly as possible to reduce stress to it and to keep it from breaking dormancy.

Pick the site and dig the hole in early November, before the soil freezes. Cover the dug-up soil with straw or a deep layer of mulch or leaves and a tarp, weighted by bricks. This will keep the soil from getting soaked and freezing.

Then buy a small evergreen that is suited to that site, space, and conditions. It probably won't be a picture-perfect conical Christmas tree. But the plant will need to live in your garden a lot longer than it spends in your house, so choose the right plant for the garden. Keep it small, so the rootball is not too heavy. A container-grown plant will be easier to manage and more likely to survive than a balled-and-burlapped one.

■ *A live Christmas tree you will plant in the garden requires planning. Buy the shrub and dig the hole in November before the ground freezes, and plan to keep the plant indoors as briefly as possible.*

Water the plant and keep it in a cool, sheltered spot where the soil won't freeze, such as a garage or porch, until Christmas Eve. Then bring it indoors and place it (in a dishpan, on a tarp to protect your floors) away from a fireplace, heating vent, or radiator. Decorate it simply.

With 48 hours, remove the ornaments and take the plant back outside. Plant it, backfilling the hole with the reserved soil. (See Here's How to Plant a Tree or Shrub, page 52.) Water it and spread mulch. Keep watering whenever there is a warm spell all winter and regularly for the next two years.

PLANT

BULBS
You can plant spring-blooming bulbs until the ground freezes. But don't dawdle too long: Some years a big snow falls or the ground freezes solid in November. See Here's How to Plant Spring Bulbs, page 146.

If you find yourself with spring bulbs and it's too late to plant, pot them up for forcing. See Plant/Bulbs, October, page 145.

CARE

BULBS
A cold frame is a good place to overwinter bulbs that you have potted up for forcing, since they need to be chilled but not frozen.

EDIBLES
Earlier in the month, pot up some parsley and sage and put them in the cold frame or keep them on a sheltered porch for Thanksgiving.

Some cabbage relatives, such as cabbages, Brussels sprouts, cauliflower, and collards (which are surprisingly hardy), taste better after a touch of frost. But harvest them before a hard freeze turns them to mush.

Pull up all the radishes. Other root crops, such as turnips, beets, and carrots, can stay in the cool soil for a while, but be sure to dig them up before the ground freezes.

A lightweight plastic cold frame such as this one can protect against frosty nights into early November. A well-built cold frame made of wood, straw bales, or rigid double-walled plastic with a transparent lid can protect late crops later into the winter.

If you have a late crop of spinach or lettuce growing in the cold frame, keep the lid open at least an inch for ventilation. Close it only on freezing nights and open it in the morning. Even when it's cold, the sun's heat trapped in a closed cold frame can cook your plants.

Fill some clear 2-liter plastic soda bottles with water and screw on the caps. Tuck them in among the plants in the cold frame. The water will store warmth during sunny days and release it to help keep the plants warm during cold nights.

CONTAINERS

If you are leaving containers outdoors, dress them up for the winter. Use the leftover potting mix to anchor an arrangement. Incorporate branches from evergreens; winterberry, with its red berries; red-twig dogwood; birch stems; or curly willow. Add in other gleanings from your garden such as interesting dried grasses and dried hydrangea flowers.

HOUSEPLANTS

Check over your houseplants to make sure they have enough soil; add a little if need be and shake gently so it fills in down the sides of the pot. Remove any brown or shriveled foliage. Provide them with deep saucers so you can water them thoroughly. Arrange them near the windows, but not against the cold panes.

LAWNS

Rake leaves and other debris off the lawn one last time before it snows, and put the mower away properly. If you do basic maintenance now, the mower will be all ready to go on that spring day when you're ready to mow.

Hose off any grass clippings and dirt. Look the machine over for loose screws or other issues. Clean fuel out of a gas mower by running it until it's out of gas or by siphoning the fuel out. Gas left in the engine over winter can turn into sticky goo that will stop the machine from operating. Change the oil. Replace the oil filter and spark plugs. Sharpen the blade (or have it sharpened at the hardware store). Before you replace it, wipe it with light oil to keep it from rusting.

PERENNIALS & GROUNDCOVERS

Don't worry if a few late leaves settle on perennials and groundcovers. Rake them off if they seem untidy to you, but they do no harm. Fungi in the soil will break down many leaves by spring.

ROSES

After your first frost, protect sensitive roses, such as hybrid teas, grandifloras, and floribundas. Use piles of leaves, mulch, or evergreen boughs, not plastic foam rose cones. The cones trap moisture that can lead to disease. During winter warm spells, the air inside them can warm up and cause the roses to start growing prematurely, with feeble growth that is easily killed.

To protect roses, first prune a few inches from the top of the bush. Clean up any fallen rose leaves that may harbor fungus spores or insect eggs. Mound mulch 6 to 10 inches up the canes to hold moisture and protect the graft union. Then insulate the rest of the plant with evergreen boughs or leaves.

Some gardeners wrap a rose bush in a cylinder of burlap and fill it with leaves around the rose canes. Leave it open at the top and don't pack the leaves down tightly; air needs to circulate.

Hardy shrub roses don't need winter protection. Some stems may be killed in winter, but you can prune out dead wood in March. Roses will bloom on new growth.

SHRUBS

If you notice a shrub or small tree growing in your yard with oval leaves that stay green after most other shrubs have lost their leaves, check to see if it is buckthorn (*Rhamnus*). This is one of the worst invasive plants in eastern North America. Its seedlings often turn up in hedges or along fence lines because birds eat the berries and drop the seeds.

Buckthorn should be removed to avoid spreading the problem further. Dig up small plants, but larger plants will need to be cut down. Then you'll need to treat the stump with a systemic herbicide such as glyphosate or triclopyr to kill the root system. For help with identification and control of buckthorn and other invasive plants, see Resources, page 189.

HERE'S HOW

TO SHARPEN MOWER BLADES

■ *Before you put the lawnmower away, do basic maintenance such as sharpening the blade. First, drain the mower of oil and gasoline. Remove the spark plug or disable the mower so it cannot turn on. Tip it on its side and brace it. Wedge a piece of scrap wood to hold the blade immobile.*

■ *Loosen the bolt that holds the mower blade and remove it.*

■ *Clamp the blade in a vise and sharpen it with a file. Then replace it. Change the air filter and put the machine away.*

■ *One way to protect a tender climbing rose against winter damage is to untie it from its support and wrap it in porous floating row cover. Do not use plastic sheeting, which would trap moisture and encourage disease and rot. Most tender roses can be protected by mounding mulch or leaves around the base of the plant, being sure to cover the graft union.*

Glossy buckthorn (Rhamnus frangula) *and its cousin* *common buckthorn* (Rhamnus cathartica) *are invasive plants that are a serious threat to natural areas such as national parks and forest preserves. These shrubs or small trees are easy to spot for removal in November because their leaves stay green after other plants' leaves have fallen.*

WATER

ALL

Before a hard freeze, disconnect the hose, roll it up and tie it, and store it in the garage or basement. Do the same with soaker hoses.

If your outdoor faucet has an indoor valve, close it. Then open the outdoor faucet and let it drain so no water will be trapped in the faucet to freeze and crack the plumbing. Leave the faucet open. If you don't have an indoor valve, wrap the outside faucet or use a foam hose cap to make it less likely to freeze. Have the automatic sprinkler system drained so water does not freeze in the lines.

Keep some buckets and watering cans handy so you can haul water from indoors to water evergreens during the winter.

GROUNDCOVERS

Any woody groundcovers you planted this year need to be watered until the ground freezes, like shrubs.

HOUSEPLANTS

Water a houseplant if the soil is dry an inch or so below the surface. Soak it thoroughly until water runs out into the saucer. But empty the saucer after 20 minutes or so and don't let the plant sit in a pool of water. Wet soil can cause roots to rot.

PERENNIALS

Water perennials you planted this year as long as they show any signs of growth.

ROSES

Water roses deeply before the ground freezes.

TREES & SHRUBS

As long as you can, keep watering evergreens. The more water they can store in their tissues before the ground freezes solid, the better. Deciduous trees and shrubs planted within the last two years can use watering too. They won't absorb water once they've gone dormant, but it will help them in spring if there's plenty of water in the soil around their roots.

FERTILIZE

HOUSEPLANTS

Fertilize less as houseplants slow their growth and go dormant. By Thanksgiving, stop fertilizing entirely.

LAWNS

If you didn't do it in early fall, scatter slow-release lawn fertilizer on the dormant lawn in late November, after Thanksgiving, or in early December. It will break down slowly and the nutrients will be available to the grass plants when they start growing in spring.

PROBLEM-SOLVE

ALL

Store garden chemicals if you haven't already. Lock them up so children and pets can't get into them. Fertilizers, herbicides, fungicides, and insecticides are all toxic to some extent. *Never* store garden chemicals in soda, juice, or milk bottles, which make them especially attractive to children.

LAWNS

Scatter leftover grass seed over the lawn; it would just dry out over the winter. Buy fresh seed in spring.

SHRUBS

Protect the bark of young trees and shrubs if you didn't do it in October. See Problem-Solve/Trees & Shrubs, October, page 151.

December

Who can see the gardening year end without a twinge of sadness? But then winter brings its magic. When the first snowfall paints the garden— making fluffy piles atop seedheads, outlining the tracery of weeping evergreens, replacing dreary brown with sparkling white—it lights up with loveliness.

Snow is a friend to plants. It's mostly air, which makes it an excellent insulator, protecting plants from winter's bitter cold and keeping it safely frozen during unpredictable winter thaws. And in spring, it melts to provide moisture just when awakening plants need it. A winter with steady snow cover—even a cold winter—is likely to be followed by a glorious spring.

We can't count on snow cover in the lower Midwest, so we mulch for backup. The purpose of mulch is not to keep the soil from freezing, but to keep it frozen, so the all-too-common sudden winter thaw doesn't prompt plants to sprout too early and then get slashed by the inevitable bitter freeze. December is not too late to make sure perennial beds, trees, and shrubs are safely tucked under a blanket of mulch.

Snow is helpful in another way: It can reveal design possibilities that we don't notice when foliage is full and we are caught up in the busyness of gardening. Snow will show up shapes, lines, and structures in the garden so you can consider its overall design and balance.

You can even use snow to try out routes and sizes for possible paths and patios. Just tramp through the snow and then photograph your footprints to consider indoors at your leisure. Or use snow to roughly pace off distances that you never got around to measuring.

This is a month when most of us are busy indoors with family and friends. Apart from the tools, books, and gloves we may put on our gift lists, the garden is scarcely on our minds. But just think: Once the winter solstice passes on December 21, the days will start getting longer. Another growing season is on the way.

DECEMBER

PLAN

ALL

If anybody asks, suggest gifts that you can really use: tools, good gloves, or even a gift certificate for a load of compost or a few hours of weeding come spring.

PLANT

ALL

The fall planting window is over for most plants; their root systems would not be able to develop in the cold soil. The ground may freeze too hard to dig anytime between Thanksgiving and New Year's.

■ *When you shovel, don't toss snow containing salt near plants. The salt dries out plant tissues, including roots, if it gets in soil. It's best to avoid using salt and other de-icers near plants.*

BULBS

Because they go in the ground dormant, you can still plant bulbs as long as you can dig a hole. Don't wait too long, though. A major snowfall, which would put an end to planting, can come anytime. If you find yourself with a few bulbs left over, pot them up for forcing (see Plant/Bulbs, October, page 145).

TREES & SHRUBS

It's best to avoid planting trees or shrubs this late. However, if you have a plant that you didn't get in the ground earlier *and* you can still dig a hole, go ahead and plant it so the soil can protect its roots through the winter. If the soil has already frozen, put the plant in a sheltered spot and bury its rootball or pot in a large pile of mulch for insulation. Water it when you can and plant it as soon as possible in spring.

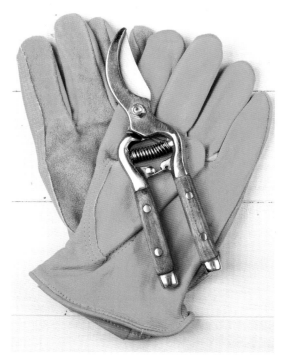

■ *If anyone asks, suggest a gift you can really use: tools, good gloves, or a gift certificate for a load of compost or garden labor in spring.*

If you have planned for a living Christmas tree, plant it as soon as possible after the holiday in the prepared hole. Fill the hole, water well, and mulch (see Plan/Trees, November, page 154).

CARE

ALL

It's a good idea to clean and sharpen tools when you put them away for the winter so they will be ready to go in spring. See Care/All, January, page 24.

CONTAINERS

Before a heavy snow makes it more difficult to move them, store containers properly so they don't crack over the winter. See Care/Containers, October, page 148.

HOUSEPLANTS

If you receive a plant as a gift, remove all the wrapping, including any foil or plastic around the pot. Place the plant in a saucer to catch surplus water and water it well. After that, water it like any houseplant, when the soil is dry an inch or so down.

Keep holiday plants in indirect light away from heating vents and radiators. They will generally last longer in a cooler room. Most gift plants have been manipulated in greenhouses for short-term holiday display and few will live long as houseplants. It's best to enjoy them while they last and then compost them.

Christmas and Thanksgiving cactus are an exception; they can be long-lasting houseplants. They do best in bright indirect light in a cool room. While the plant is flowering, the room should be dark at night, because they bloom in response to lengthening periods of darkness. Even a brief exposure to a small amount of light at night can make them flower less. Don't jostle these cactus plants; their stems are fragile.

■ *Shredded hardwood is commonly used for mulch. Use coarse mulch, such as this, around trees and shrubs and finer-textured mulch, such as screened compost or shredded leaves, in perennial beds. Avoid cypress mulch, which often is not sustainably harvested.*

Poinsettias are sun-loving outdoor shrubs, not suited for long-term life indoors. It's difficult and complex to get them to rebloom, although you can find instructions on the Internet. Poinsettias are best discarded after the holidays.

Norfolk Island pine, often sold as an indoor Christmas tree, is a tropical plant from the South Pacific. It may survive a few years as a houseplant, although it requires very high humidity. It will eventually outgrow the room. In nature, these trees can grow 60 to 100 feet tall.

Amaryllis bulbs are sold in a dormant state, either bare or potted. For forcing amaryllis, see Plant/Bulbs, October, page 145.

A rosemary topiary is another common holiday gift. Rosemary is an outdoor shrub that will dry out in a few weeks in most heated homes. Keep it watered while you use the branches in holiday dishes. When it dries out, discard it, but first shake it over a sheet of newspaper to save the dried needles for cooking.

LAWNS

Rake the last leaves off the lawn to deter fungus diseases over the winter. Put them in the compost heap or rake them onto perennial beds to serve as mulch.

PERENNIALS

Spread mulch in December if you didn't earlier. Try to buy it before home centers stow away their year's leftovers for the winter to make space for Christmas trees. Or order a load from a landscape supplier, or use the leaves you collected in October.

Whether you cut back the dried stalks of perennials for the winter is a matter of taste. If you find the stems or seedheads attractive, leave them standing where they can look lovely in snow. If that seems untidy to you, cut them back. Consider using the dried stalks in holiday wreaths or arrangements.

When it's time to dispose of the Christmas tree, you can prune off the branches to protect the perennial garden. Lay the boughs over the beds in the single layer to shade the soil and keep it from thawing in brief winter warm spells. This won't be necessary if you spread mulch on the beds in the fall to insulate the soil.

SHRUBS

In December, use clippings from your shrubs in holiday decorations. Gather boughs and branches from evergreens such as arborvitae, boxwood, junipers, and yew, as well as shrubs that have colorful bark such as red-twig dogwood. You can use cuttings from evergreen groundcovers such as myrtle and English ivy and even dried hydrangea blooms. Try tucking greenery from your garden into a plain store-bought wreath to make it your own creation.

As you cut branches from a shrub, though, keep its form in mind. Prune carefully to keep the shrub attractive and don't remove any branches that will leave unsightly holes or make the shrub look unbalanced.

A wreath of evergreens will last through the holiday season outdoors, but inside a storm door or in the house it will quickly dry out and shed needles.

■ *Cut back ornamental grasses in December, or let them stand for interest through the winter and cut them back in February.*

WATER

CONTAINERS

In early December, water any shrubs or small trees that you are overwintering outdoors in containers.

HOUSEPLANTS

Continue to water houseplants when the soil is moist an inch below the surface. Most are dormant this time of year and their growth has slowed, so they usually need watering only every two or three weeks.

TREES & SHRUBS

For safety, make sure the Christmas tree stand always is filled with water. Check the water level daily. If the bottom of the trunk dries out even briefly, it can seal with sap and will not take up more water. A dried-out Christmas tree is a fire hazard.

Throughout the winter, seize the chance of any warm spell to water trees and shrubs that you have planted within the last two years. Because they do not yet have an established root system, they cannot store much water to get them through the winter.

In the ground as in containers, evergreens are especially vulnerable to drying out. Water any evergreens in exposed locations when you can.

FERTILIZE

HOUSEPLANTS

Don't fertilize houseplants during their winter dormant season. Wait to fertilize until you see new growth, usually in late February or early March.

PROBLEM-SOLVE

ALL

Try to prevent salt damage to plants as you deal with winter snow. Salt dries out plant tissues, both when it comes in contact with leaves and stems and when it accumulates in soil, drying out the roots.

Salt used to melt snow and ice dissolves and runs off into the nearby soil. Salt in snow shoveled onto plants will dry out their leaves and stems.

Evergreen groundcovers and shrubs along sidewalks and pathways will be the first to show salt damage in the form of brown, dead foliage. Damage to perennials and deciduous plants may not show up until spring or summer, when the plants simply flag or die.

Even plants well back from a road can be damaged by salt, because cars' wheels throw up a cloud of salt spray that can travel 60 feet or more. Wrapping plants in burlap may block some salt spray but will not stop salt runoff.

Avoid planting sensitive plants such as arborvitaes, boxwoods, and evergreen groundcovers near sidewalks that are salted or heavily traveled roads. Junipers are relatively salt tolerant.

Always shovel snow first before you apply any de-icer. Consider a somewhat less harmful alternative such as calcium chloride. Apply de-icers sparingly, just enough to keep high-traffic areas clear of ice. Sweep up any undissolved crystals promptly and dispose of them in the trash.

TREES & SHRUBS

In early December, protect young trees and prized shrubs from animals. See Problem-Solve/Trees & Shrubs, October, page 151.

Double-check that mulch is not piled against tree trunks. Small animals can burrow through it to eat the bark. Spread mulch in an even layer 3 to 4 inches deep in a wide circle around the tree and keep it a couple of inches clear of the bark.

Appendix

TO CALCULATE AREA

Here are the formulas for calculating the areas of geometric shapes. Use these formulas to figure out how much soil, topsoil, mulch, grass seed, or fertilizer you need.

Square
Area = length of a side^2

Rectangle
Area = length × width

Triangle
Area = (base × height) ÷ 2

Circle
Where the R is the radius and π = 3.14:
Area = πr^2

When you need the area of a lawn or bed with a complicated shape, divide it into simple geometric shapes, measure each of them, calculate their area individually, and add them up.

As an example, suppose you have a bed like this:

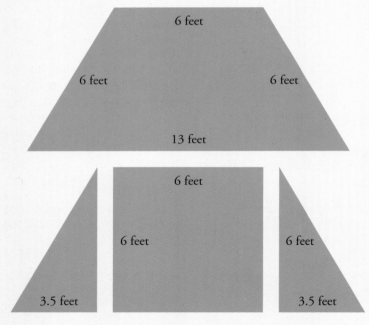

Divide the bed into a 6-foot square and two triangles, each with a base of 3.5 feet and a height of 6 feet.

Area of the square: 6 × 6 = 36

Area of each triangle: 6 × 3.5 ÷ 2 = 10.5

Total area: 36 + (10.5 × 2) = 57

PLANT	HARDINESS	SOW INDOORS	DIRECT SOW	BEST SOIL TEMPERATURE FOR GERMINATION (°F)	If your average last frost date is April 15		If your average last frost date is May 1		If your average last frost date is May 15		NOTES
					SOW INDOORS	TRANSPLANT OR DIRECT-SOW OUTDOORS	SOW INDOORS	TRANSPLANT OR DIRECT-SOW OUTDOORS	SOW INDOORS	TRANSPLANT OR DIRECT-SOW OUTDOORS	
Beans, bush	T	N	Y	60-80	---	Mid-May, June	---	Late May, June	---	June	Sow batches 1 week apart for 3-4 weeks
Beans, pole	T	N	Y	60-80	---	Mid-May, June	---	Late May, June	---	June	
Beets	H	N	Y	65-85	---	End of March, April, May	---	April, May, June	---	Late April, May, June	Sow batches 1 week apart for longer harvest
Broccoli	MH	Y	Y	65-85	Early February	Early April	Mid-February	Late April	Late February	Early May	Needs long season, must mature before summer heat
Cabbage	MH	Y	Y	55-95	Early February	Late March, early April	Mid-February	April	Late February	Mid-April	Direct-sow only short-season varieties; must mature before summer heat
Carrots	H	N	Y	60-85	---	Mid-March to mid-May	---	April, May, June	---	Mid-April, May, June	Sow batches 1 week apart for long harvest
Cauliflower, spring crop	MH	Y	N	55-80	Late January	Late March, early April	Early February	April	Mid-February	Mid-April	Needs long season
Celery, celery root	T	Y	N	60-70	Mid-January	May	Late January	Late May	Early February	June	Needs long season, must mature before summer heat
Chard	H	N	Y	50-85	---	Mid-March through June	---	April through June	---	Late April through June	Sow batches 1 week apart
Collards	H	Y	Y	55-95	---	End of March	---	April	---	Late April	Harvest spring crop as young greens
Corn	T	N	Y	60-95	---	May to mid-June	---	Mid-May to mid-June	---	Mid-May to mid-June	Only short-season varieties in June
Cucumbers	VT			65-95	Early March	Mid-May to mid-June	Mid-March	Mid-May to mid-June	Late March	Late May to mid-June	Don't transplant until soil is thoroughly warm

HARDINESS: (VT=VERY TENDER, T=TENDER, MH=MODERATELY HARDY, H=HARDY, VH=VERY HARDY)

SPRING VEGETABLE TIMING CHART

PLANT	HARDINESS	SOW INDOORS	DIRECT SOW	BEST SOIL TEMPERATURE FOR GERMINATION (°F)	If your average last frost date is April 15		If your average last frost date is May 1		If your average last frost date is May 15		NOTES
					SOW INDOORS	TRANSPLANT OR DIRECT-SOW OUTDOORS	SOW INDOORS	TRANSPLANT OR DIRECT-SOW OUTDOORS	SOW INDOORS	TRANSPLANT OR DIRECT-SOW OUTDOORS	
Eggplant	VT	Y	N	75-90	Early February	Mid-May to mid-June	Mid-February	Early June	Late February	Early June	Don't transplant until soil is thoroughly warm
Endive	H	---	Y	60-85	---	Mid-March through May	---	April through May	---	Mid-April through May	Sow batches 1 week apart
Kale	VH	N	Y	65-85	---	Mid-March through May	---	April through May	---	Mid-April through May	Sow batches 1 week apart for longer harvest
Kohlrabi	MH			65-85	---	Mid-April	---	Early May	---	Mid-May	
Leeks	MH	Y	Y	60-70	Late January	April through May	Early February	Mid-April through May	Mid-February	Mid-April through May	
Lettuce	H	N	Y	40-80	---	Mid-March through June	---	April through June	---	April through June	Sow batches 1 week apart; sow only slow-bolt varieties for summer crop and provide shade when hot
Melons	VT	Y	N	75-95	Early March	May through June	Mid-March	Late May through June	Late March, early April	Late May through June	Needs long season; don't transplant until soil is thoroughly warm
Okra	VT	Y	N	70-90	Mid-April	May through June	Late April	Late May through June	Late April	June	Don't transplant until soil is thoroughly warm
Onions (seed)	MH	Y	Y	60-70	Mid-January	Mid-March to mid-May	Mid-February	April to mid-May	Mid-February	April to mid-May	
Onions (sets)	MH	---	---		---	Mid-March to mid-May	---	April to mid-June	---	April to mid-June	
Parsnips	VH	N	Y	55-77	---	Mid-March through May	---	April through May	---	Mid-April through May	
Peas	H	Y	Y	50-75	---	Mid-March to early June	---	Mid-April to mid-June	---	Mid-April to mid-June	Sow batches 1 week apart

HARDINESS: (VT=VERY TENDER, T=TENDER, MH=MODERATELY HARDY, H=HARDY, VH=VERY HARDY)

SPRING VEGETABLE TIMING CHART

PLANT	HARDINESS	SOW INDOORS	DIRECT SOW	BEST SOIL TEMPERATURE FOR GERMINATION (°F)	If your average last frost date is April 15		If your average last frost date is May 1		If your average last frost date is May 15		NOTES
					SOW INDOORS	TRANSPLANT OR DIRECT-SOW OUTDOORS	SOW INDOORS	TRANSPLANT OR DIRECT-SOW OUTDOORS	SOW INDOORS	TRANSPLANT OR DIRECT-SOW OUTDOORS	
Peppers	VT	Y	N	68-95	Mid-February	Mid-May through June	Early March	Late May through June	Mid-March	June	Don't transplant until soil is thoroughly warm
Potatoes (seed potatoes)	--	--	--	--	--	April to mid-June	--	Mid-April to mid-June	--	Mid-April, May	
Pumpkins	T	Y	Y	70-90	Mid-March	Mid-May to June	Late March	June	Early April	June	Direct-sow only small-fruited types; for big pumpkins that take longer, start indoors
Radishes	H	N	Y	55-85	--	Mid-March through June	--	April through June	--	April through June	Sow batches for longer harvest; choose late varieties for summer
Rutabaga	H	N	Y	60-95	--	Mid-March through June	--	April through June	--	Mid-April through June	
Shallot (seed)	MH	Y	Y	60-70	Mid-January	Mid-March to mid-May	Mid-February	April to mid-May	Mid-February	April to mid-May	
Shallots (sets)	MH	--	--		--	Mid-March to mid-May	--	April to mid-June	--	April to mid-June	
Spinach	VH	N	Y	45-65	--	Mid-March through June	--	April through June	--	Mid-April through June	Sow batches; provide part shade for summer crop
Squash	T	Y	Y	70-90	Mid-March	May, June	Late March	Mid-May through June	Early April	Mid-May through June	
Tomatoes	T	Y	N	60-85	Early March	Mid-May through June	Mid-March	Mid-May through June	Mid-March	Mid-May through June	Don't transplant until soil is thoroughly warm
Turnips	H	N	Y	60-95	--	Mid-March through June	--	April through June	--	Mid-April through June	Sow batches for longer harvest
Watermelon	VT	Y	N	75-95	Mid-March	May through June	Late March	Mid-May through June	Early April	Late May through June	Don't transplant until soil is thoroughly warm

HARDINESS: (VT=VERY TENDER, T=TENDER, MH=MODERATELY HARDY, H=HARDY, VH=VERY HARDY)

FALL VEGETABLE TIMING CHART

PLANT	HARDINESS	SOW INDOORS	DIRECT SOW	BEST SOIL TEMPERATURE FOR GERMINATION (°F)	If your average first frost date is October 30		If your average first frost date is October 15		If your average first frost date is October 1		NOTES
					SOW INDOORS	TRANSPLANT OR DIRECT-SOW OUTDOORS	SOW INDOORS	TRANSPLANT OR DIRECT-SOW OUTDOORS	SOW INDOORS	TRANSPLANT OR DIRECT-SOW OUTDOORS	
Beans, Bush	T	N	Y	60–80	---	Late July to late August	---	Mid-July to mid-August	---	Early July to early August	Sow 2 batches 1 week apart
Beets	H	N	Y	65–85	---	Late August	---	Early August	---	Late July	
Broccoli	MH	Y	N	65–85	Early July	Late August	Late June to early July	Early to mid-August	Late June to early July	Early August	Start indoors to protect from summer heat
Brussels sprouts	H	Y	N	55–95	Early to mid-July	Mid-August	Late June to early July	Early to mid-August	Late June to early July	Early August	Start indoors to protect from summer heat; flavor best if harvested after frost
Cabbage, Cauliflower	MH	Y	N	55–95	Early July	Late August	Late June to early July	Early to mid-August	Late June to early July	Early August	Start indoors to protect from summer heat
Carrots	H	N	Y	60–85	---	July, August	---	Mid-July to mid-August	---	July to early August	Sow batches until 8 weeks before first frost date
Chard	H	N	Y	50–85	---	Mid-August to mid-September	---	August to early September	---	August	Sow 2 or 3 batches a week apart
Collards	H	Y	Y		---	Late August	---	Mid-August	---	Late July to early August	Flavor best if harvested after frost
Garlic, Shallots	H	N	Plant cloves or sets		---	Early November	---	Late October	---	Early October	Plant cloves after first frost.
Greens, misc.	H	N	Y	40–80	---	Mid-August to mid-September	---	Mid-July to late August	---	Mid-July to mid-August	Most greens are hardy; sow in batches until 6 weeks before first frost date; harvest as baby greens
Kale	VH	N	Y	65–85	---	Late July	---	Mid-July	---	Early July	Sow batches 1 week apart for longer harvest
Lettuce	H	N	Y	40–80	---	Mid-August to mid-September	---	Mid-July to late August	---	Mid-July to mid-August	Sow batches until 6 weeks before first frost date; harvest later crops as baby greens
Peas	H	Y	Y	50–75	---	Mid-July	---	Early July	---	Late June	
Radishes	H	N	Y	55–85	---	Mid-August through September	---	August to early September	---	Mid-July through August	Sow in batches until 1 month before first frost date.
Spinach	VH	N	Y	45–65	---	Mid-August to mid-September	---	August	---	Mid-July to late August	Sow batches until 5 weeks before first frost date; cover against frost to prolong harvest
Turnips	H	N	Y	60–95	---	Early to mid-September	---	Mid- to late August	---	Early to mid-August	

HARDINESS: (VT=VERY TENDER, T=TENDER, MH=MODERATELY HARDY, H=HARDY, VH=VERY HARDY)

Many common lawn issues can be traced to poor lawn care and can be prevented if you mow sufficiently high, don't overwater, and fertilize carefully. Here's how to deal with some common problems.

Thatch: It's normal for some old leaves and some stems to decay on the surface of the soil in a lawn, as they do around other plants. A layer of no more than ½ inch is harmless and even beneficial.

However, when this material builds up into a mat more than an inch deep, it can lead to turf problems. Thick thatch can hold water, creating a good environment for disease, and can harbor fungus spores or insects.

Thatch buildup is most common in lawns that are watered too frequently and fertilized too much, encouraging grass blades to grow fast—weak growth that readily dies. Heavy use of fungicides and insecticides can lead to thatch by killing off the earthworms and soil microbes that would normally break down dead grass.

Kentucky bluegrass, a very popular lawn grass, is especially prone to thatch buildup. Acid soil also can contribute to thatch, although most soils in the Midwest are alkaline.

Incorporate these practices into your lawn care regime:

- In a small lawn, you can remove a thatch layer with a stiff rake. Just don't rake so hard you tear up the grass. For larger lawns, you can rent a machine called a dethatcher.

- Once the thatch is removed, core-aerate the lawn to allow water and air to reach the grass roots. Core-aerating at least once a year fights thatch. (See page 130 for more on core-aerating.)

- It's a good idea to scatter compost on the lawn and rake it in. This will help replenish the population of soil microbes to break down dead plants and discourage thatch.

- Water the lawn deeply but at long intervals, no more than once a week. That way, the water will soak in and the grass roots will reach down for it, growing long, strong, and resilient, rather than short and weak.

- Fertilize with slow-release fertilizers in spring and fall, never in summer when the grass is stressed. Apply the fertilizer with a spreader, following the package directions, and do not apply too much.

- Leaving clippings on the lawn and using a mulching mower are healthy practices that do not cause thatch.

- Set the lawnmower to mow the lawn high, at least 3 inches.

- To preserve the thatch-eating underground ecosystem of your lawn, use fungicides and insecticides only if necessary to deal with a problem that you have identified for certain (see Here's How to Get Help with Plant Problems in Problem-Solve/All, May, page 98). Then use the least amount necessary in only the affected area.

Browning: It's normal for grass to turn brown in July and August. The cool-season turf grasses used in the Midwest grow most vigorously in spring and fall, when temperatures are cool and there is more rain. In the hot summer the plants naturally go dormant; the top dies back while the root system

stays alive, waiting for the cooler temperatures and rain of fall, when it will sprout new leaves. Keeping a lawn green all summer requires watering it to force it to grow and enable it to withstand heat.

Either let the lawn go dormant in summer or keep watering it, but don't whipsaw back and forth; that stresses the grass. If you decide to let the grass go dormant, water it every three weeks or so to keep the roots alive (unless there has been rain).

Grass that is cut short will turn brown faster in summer than grass that is tall with long, strong roots. Proper watering—deeply, but not too often—encourages deep roots and drought tolerance.

Thin, patchy grass: Under a tree or in other deep shade conditions, grass is usually thin with bare patches. Turf grasses evolved to grow in full sun and simply can't grow well in shade. Some species, particularly some fescues, are marginally more shade tolerant than Kentucky bluegrass, but no lawn grass can ever really thrive where there is not enough sunlight.

The best solution is to replace grass in shady areas with a shade-tolerant groundcover. Make a wide circle of mulch under trees, both to replace ugly, patchy grass and to keep grass roots from competing with tree roots. It's better for the tree.

Trees are more valuable than lawns, because they take decades to grow while they provide shade, improve property values, clean the air, absorb

stormwater, and provide many other benefits. Have a tree pruned if it needs it, but always favor the needs of a tree over the needs of the lawn.

Weeds: Mowing high enough will cut down on weeds by preventing the seeds from getting enough light to germinate in the soil. If weeds do pop up, the first line of defense should be hand-digging or pulling (do this when the soil is moist and the roots will slip out more easily). Use a weeder or garden knife to dig out the long taproot of dandelion and plantain.

Weed in spring to get out creeping Charlie and other mat-forming weeds while they are compact rosettes, before they send out creeping stems through the grass. Creeping Charlie thrives because it is more shade tolerant than grass; it may be telling you that you are trying to grow grass where there is not enough sun for it.

Pre-emergent herbicides applied in spring can keep weed seeds from germinating. However, they also will keep grass seeds from germinating, so don't use them if you are planning to reseed the lawn. Corn gluten meal is an organic pre-emergent that also supplies some nitrogen to the lawn. You likely will need to apply it for two or three years running for it to be effective.

If you have a large infestation of mat-forming weeds, your last resort may be to kill off a section of lawn with a non-selective herbicide containing glyphosate and start over. Use such herbicides very carefully, because they will kill any plants they touch; droplets of spray that stray onto garden beds or other areas of the lawn can kill desirable plants.

Cover the bare area and wait several weeks until the herbicide is no longer active before you attempt to reseed or resod.

Avoid routine use of herbicides, including "weed and feed" products. They will kill off the underground worms and microbes that keep your soil healthy and will contribute to water pollution. Used carelessly, they also can damage your lawn.

If you feel you need to use a herbicide, consult an expert to make sure you are choosing the right product to solve your problems. See Here's How to Get Help with Plant Problems, page 98.

Use the least toxic product in the least amount possible to only the areas that need it. Err on the side of using less rather than more: You can always make another application if the first is ineffective, but if you have overapplied a chemical and harmed the lawn, you will face much more work to repair the damage.

Clover: Although many people regard it as a weed, clover actually feeds the lawn. Its root system works with certain bacteria to fix nitrogen, which fertilizes the grass. If a lawn is 5 to 10 percent clover, the clover will supply almost all its yearly nitrogen needs. If you can get used to the look, clover in the lawn is actually a boon.

Grubs: Grubs are the larvae of beetles that prefer to lay eggs in moist soil. Overwatering often leads to grubs; if you let the lawn dry out thoroughly between waterings, it will be less attractive to beetles and less likely to harbor grubs.

Toward the end of June, check for grubs by peeling back a piece of turf to look for white C-shaped insect larvae. Grubs are beetle larvae, living in the

soil and feeding on the roots of grass plants. They are most common in moist soil. The best way to prevent them is to avoid overwatering the grass.

You may first notice the problem when raccoons and skunks dig for grubs in the lawn. But as the weather gets hotter and drier, grass plants whose roots have been damaged by grubs will turn brown.

Grub problems vary from year to year, and if you have only a few, there's no need to try and control them. Typically, you won't see visible damage unless there are eight to twelve grubs per square foot.

If you do decide to treat for grubs, be sure to read any product labels carefully to make sure you're using the right product at the right time of year. Products designed to prevent grubs are generally applied from late June to mid-July.

There is a bacteria, *Paenibacillus popilliae*, that feeds on Japanese beetle grubs. These products should be applied in late July or early August. You may have to repeat the treatment for several years to build up the population enough to affect the grubs.

Insects: Most insects you see in your lawn are beneficial. The list of insects that can cause problems is short, including aphids, chinch bugs, and cutworms.

The best way to combat them is by siccing insect predators on them. Ladybugs eat aphids. Ground beetles eat grubs. Some kinds of wasps lay eggs in insect larvae. Predatory nematodes, which you can buy at garden centers, will attack chinch bugs and cutworms that may stray in from the vegetable garden. You also can purchase a species of bacteria, *Bacillus thuringiensis* (Bt), that attacks many kinds of insects.

Of course, you must keep your yard free of insecticides to permit these predators to thrive and contribute to the health of your lawn.

If you have a large infestation of aphids, you can generally blast them away with a sharp spray from the hose. Break up anthills with a rake for appearances' sake, although they don't harm the grass. If the ants persist, pour boiling water on the anthill.

Core-aerating regularly will eliminate the habitat of many unwanted insects.

Digging animals: If raccoons, skunks, gophers, or a mole (there usually will be only one) are digging in your lawn, it probably means you have a large population of grubs or other insects for them to feed on. They aren't eating the grass; they're eating things that live in the soil under the grass. First, check for grubs and deal with the grub population (see Grubs) to reduce the food supply.

Roll out mole tunnels. You may need to trap the mole.

Gophers live in groups; try placing sponges soaked in ammonia in the holes to encourage the pack to leave. Avoid using poisons or baits, especially if there are children, dogs, or cats in your neighborhood.

Mushrooms and fairy rings: These do no harm to your lawn; they're the fruiting bodies of fungi that are living on decaying organic matter underground. Those fungi are a beneficial part of the lawn's underground ecosystem. Often mushrooms will appear in a ring, sometimes with dense grass growth; this is usually evidence of fungi breaking down an old tree stump. Mushrooms are harmless, but if you don't like the way they look, break them up with a rake.

Diseases: Most diseases are related to watering and overfertilization. If you water thoughtfully, fertilize carefully, and core-aerate regularly, you can prevent most of them. Water only when the lawn needs it. Although many diseases are caused by fungi, use fungicides only if the problem is severe and has been clearly identified. Overuse of fungicides kills

off many beneficial organisms that can help keep your lawn healthy.

Powdery mildew: This fungus disease creates a dusty appearance on the lawn. It is most common in shady areas, and may be a sign that you are growing grass where there is not enough sun. It rarely actually kills the grass. Don't overwater, and consider replacing grass in shady areas with a groundcover.

Rust: This fungus disease coats grass blades with reddish spores that you can rub off with your fingers. It usually appears in late summer to early fall, and most often on lawns that are already stressed. The damage is generally cosmetic. Water and fertilize carefully and core-aerate to return the lawn to health. You may want to bag clippings and put them in the landscape waste until the rust clears up to avoid spreading the spores.

Brown patch: A soil-borne fungus causes these small patches of wet-looking, brown grass. It becomes obvious in early spring or early fall, when the grass starts actively growing. Back off watering, don't fertilize, and mow the grass high; the lawn will recover.

Dollar spot: Another fungus diease, dollar spot shows up as small, round dead patches about the size of a silver dollar. It also is most common in spring and fall. Most lawns will recover, but dollar spot can develop into large areas of dead grass. If you have a large infestation of what you think is dollar spot, have the identification confirmed by an Extension agent or other expert and seek their advice about a possible fungicide application.

These plants will work well in most city or suburban gardens in Zones 5 through 7. They're grouped by the purposes they can serve and the sites where they grow well. Many of them are native to the Midwest, but native plants are not in a separate category because, as with all plants, different native species need different conditions. Choose those native plants that suit your site.

When researching perennial plants, bear in mind that "fast-growing" often means "aggressive" or "will be a problem in just a couple of years." Do your homework and think ahead to the plant's mature size. Choose plant species or cultivars (cultivated varieties) that won't spread beyond bounds, will resist common diseases and pests, and won't require more pruning, watering, staking, and other maintenance than you are prepared to provide.

FOLIAGE PLANTS FOR SHADE

These are plants whose main interest is in their leaves, although some also have attractive flowers.

Bugleweed (*Ajuga reptans*). Perennial; native to Europe. This low-growing groundcover has blue or purple flower spikes in spring but is grown mainly for its leaves, which may be green or bronzy. Ajuga is a tolerant plant that can grow in sun or part shade. It can spread aggressively.

Caladium (*Caladium*). Annual; native to South America. With their large, arrowhead-shaped leaves, caladiums give a tropical air to containers in shade. There are hundreds of cultivars with leaves of green, white, pink, red, and many combinations. Frost-tender caladiums can be started indoors from corms in spring or bought already sprouted for transplanting after soil is warm.

Coleus (*Solenostemon scutellarioides*). Annual; native to southeast Asia. A frost-tender tropical plant, coleus is grown as an annual in the Midwest for its brightly colored foliage. It can enliven shade gardens all summer because the color is in leaves, not flowers. Cultivars are available with leaves in many shades and combinations of green, chartreuse, yellow, pink, red, purple, and white. Cuttings will root easily, and coleus makes a good houseplant.

Coral bells (*Heuchera*). Perennial; native to southeastern US. There are hundreds of cultivars of coral bells, selected mainly for their mounds of colorful leaves, which range from green to nearly black shades of purple to yellow to rose to orange. They often don't get credit for their charming spikes of tiny flowers, usually pink, in May and June. Some cultivars are more hardy and vigorous than others, usually those with *Heuchera villosa* in their ancestry.

False forget-me-not (*Brunnera macrophylla*). Perennial; native to Siberia. Although the common name comes from its twinkly blue May flowers, brunnera is grown mainly for its broad, heart-shaped leaves. In some cultivars such as 'Jack Frost', the leaves are dusted with white.

Gray's sedge (*Carex grayi*). Perennial; Midwest native. Sedges' dense tufts of fine green leaves (they look like grass, but they're not) provide a striking contrast in shade. Gray's sedge has striking star-shaped seedheads in spring. It needs well-drained, consistently moist soil high in organic matter.

Heucherella (× *Heucherella*). A cross between coral bells and a different plant genus, foamflower (*Tiarella*), heucherella is a vigorous plant. There are cultivars with a range of variations on the basic maple-esque leaf shape, in often brilliant colors. Tiny white or pale pink flowers appear in spring. In warmer areas, heucherella may be semi-evergreen.

Hosta (*Hosta*). Perennial; native to Asia. Tolerant, easy-care hostas, in varieties that range from as small as your hand to as wide as a patio umbrella, are usually grown for their mounds of leaves in different shades of green. All cultivars also bloom between midsummer and September with spikes of white or purple flowers.

Japanese forest grass (*Hakonechloa macra*). Perennial; native to Japan. The mound of narrow leaves brings a grassy texture to shade. The straight species has green leaves; the cultivar 'Aureola' has a yellow stripe, and 'All Gold' has solid yellow-green leaves. The grass needs well-drained, consistently moist soil with plenty of organic matter in part to full shade.

Japanese pachysandra (*Pachysandra terminalis*). Perennial; native to Japan. This shrubby, semi-evergreen groundcover grows 8 to 12 inches tall and spreads readily by underground stems to form a dense carpet. Spikes of tiny, creamy flowers appear in spring.

Japanese painted fern (*Athyrium niponicum* var. *pictum*). Perennial; native to China, Japan, and Korea. A bit smaller and less vigorous than ostrich fern, Japanese painted fern has fronds that are frosted with silver or touched with red, depending on the cultivar.

Lesser periwinkle (*Vinca minor*). Perennial; native to Europe. Also called creeping myrtle, this groundcover with shiny green leaves and purple spring flowers spreads very aggressively in shade and is an invasive plant problem in some areas. It's best in a confined area, such as where it is surrounded by paths. The leaves are semi-evergreen, although they get tattered and discolored in colder winters.

Lilyturf (*Liriope muscari*). Perennial; native to Asia. Tufts of strappy leaves spread readily in shade. Slender spikes of white to purple flowers appear in mid- to late summer. Liriope can be a problem spreader, especially in warmer areas.

Lungwort (*Pulmonaria*). Perennial; native to Europe and western Asia. Though it has pink-to-purple late-spring flowers, pulmonaria is grown mainly for its mound of leaves spangled with white spots (or vice versa). There are many cultivars with different patterns of green and white.

Maidenhair fern (*Adiantum pedatum*). Perennial; Midwest native. The leaflets along black stems create a lovely, airy texture in the garden. It needs moist, well-drained soil rich in organic matter. It will go dormant in drought but return the following spring.

Northern sea oats (*Chasmanthium latifolium*). Perennial; native to the eastern US. The 3-foot-tall lime-green stalks with slender leaves bear flat, dangling seedheads that give this plant another common name: "spangle grass." It can handle part shade but not full shade. It reseeds heavily, though, and can become a problem in some gardens.

Ostrich fern (*Matteuccia struthiopteris*). Perennial; Midwest native. This vigorous, upright green fern thrives in shade and contrasts nicely with the broad leaves of hostas and other classic shade plants. The delicate fiddleheads are lovely in spring. It can spread aggressively through underground stems and by dispersing spores.

Pennsylvania sedge (*Carex pensylvanica*). Perennial; Midwest native. This sedge has low tufts, 6 to 8 inches tall, of fine green leaves. It's a good underplanting for hostas, ferns, and other shade-tolerant perennials. It needs well-drained, consistently moist soil high in organic matter.

Shield fern (*Dryopteris marginalis*). Perennial; Midwest native. With leathery, finely cut fronds, this fern tolerates dry shade once established. It needs protection from wind to look its best.

Spearmint (*Mentha spicata*). Perennial; native to Europe. The herb of mint juleps and chewing gum, spearmint is an upright groundcover that spreads very vigorously in part shade or sun. Keep it pinched back to make it bushier and deter the lavender flowers, which change the flavor. To prevent mint from taking over the garden, plant it in a large container.

Spotted deadnettle (*Lamium maculatum*). Grown mainly for its foliage, with green to silvery heart-shaped leaves on trailing stems, this low groundcover also has spikes of white or pink flowers in May and June. It spreads vigorously, but it is easy to control by hand-pulling.

Wild ginger (*Asarum canadense*). Perennial; Midwest native. The velvety heart-shaped leaves are the main attraction of this groundcover, which spreads happily in most soils in shade. Its interesting maroon spring flowers develop inconspicuously beneath the leaves. It's a good contrast to ferns.

FLOWERING PLANTS FOR SHADE
Plants that will flower in part shade to shade—some for just a few days, some all season.

Begonia (*Begonia*). Annual; native to tropical climates. These frost-tender plants are grown as annuals in the Midwest, though many also make good houseplants. There is a wide variety of begonia cultivars, including many hybrids, but they fall into a few notable groups. Tuberous begonias have many-petalled, roselike flowers in shades of white, pink, yellow, orange, and red. Rex begonias have green, white, pink, red, or purple leaves that are streaked, splotched, or striped, often in intriguing spirals. Wax begonias are small plants with pink, red, white, or coral flowers, often used as bedding plants. Angel wing begonias are larger, with sturdy, shiny, triangular leaves.

Bleeding heart (*Lamprocapnos spectabilis*, formerly *Dicentra spectabilis*). Perennial; native to Asia. This garden favorite is one of the sweet sights of spring, with pink flowers like little heart-shaped purses arranged along arching stems. It blooms in part to full shade. There is a white cultivar, *Lamprocapnos spectabilis* 'Alba'.

Coral bells (see Foliage Plants for Shade)

Corydalis (*Corydalis lutea*). Perennial; native to Europe. The bright yellow flowers, like clusters of little tubes, bloom above ferny green foliage in late May through June in part shade to shade. Corydalis reseeds readily and can spread.

Early daffodils (see Fall-Planted Bulbs). Species and cultivars of *Narcissus* that flower in April can be planted under trees because they will get their blooming done before the trees' leaves unfurl, while they still get more sun.

False spirea (*Astilbe*). Perennial; native to Asia. This striking plant has tall, feathery spikes of clustered tiny flowers in shades of white, pink, or red in May to June. The ferny foliage forms a low rosette below. Astilbe blooms in part to full shade, but needs consistent moisture with lots of organic

matter to thrive. Mulch to keep moisture in and check soil moisture often. Chinese astilbe (*Astilbe chinensis*) is shorter, usually with lavender or white flowers, but somewhat less finicky.

Hardy geranium (*Geranium*). Many kinds of hardy geranium, also called cranesbill, will bloom in sun to part shade, especially the Midwest native wild geranium (*Geranium maculatum*) and bigroot geranium (*Geranium macrorrhizum*), native to the Balkans. They usually have pale pink to purple flowers. Many will rebloom if you cut them back after the first flush of flowering.

Impatiens (*Impatiens walleriana*). Annual; native to tropical Africa. With white, pink, purple, or coral flowers, low-growing impatiens are hugely popular because they bloom their heads off in shade. Unfortunately, they are susceptible to a nasty soilborne disease called impatiens downy mildew. New Guinea impatiens (*Impatiens hawkeri*) is taller with larger, less dense flowers, but does not seem to be susceptible to the disease.

Jack-in-the-pulpit (*Arisaema triphyllum*). Perennial; Midwest native. The very unusual green bloom, in the form of a deep tube with a roof, that appears in spring is very striking in the shade garden. It's followed by large green leaves that eventually die away as the plant goes dormant, often leaving a stalk of bright red berries.

Jacob's ladder (*Polemonium reptans*). Perennial; Midwest native. Light blue flowers march up foot-tall stalks in late spring like the rungs of a ladder. Use it in part shade with evenly moist soil rich in organic matter. The foliage makes a nice mound.

Lenten rose (*Helleborus*). Perennial; native to Europe. Hellebores need shade. The sculptural flowers, like wax roses, appear above the clump of foliage in March to April and last a long time. Most garden hellebores are hybrid cultivars that will not bloom as early in the Midwest as they do in England. The foliage is evergreen, but will take a beating in winter; prune back tattered leaves in spring to show off the flowers.

Lily (*Lilium*). Some lilies, especially the June-blooming Asiatic lilies, martagon lilies (*Lilium* *martagon*), and the Midwest native Michigan lily (*Lilium michiganense*), will bloom in sun to part shade. In part shade, they may need staking to keep them from leaning toward the light. They need very well-drained, consistently moist soil enriched with organic matter.

Lily-of-the-valley (*Convallaria majalis*). Tiny, fragrant, white bell-shaped flowers along an arching stem are charming in spring. The plant, with pointed green leaves, spreads aggressively in part to full shade.

Ohio spiderwort (*Tradescantia ohiensis*). Perennial; Midwest native. A tall, rambling clump of foliage has three-petalled lavender flowers in May to July. Spiderwort thrives in full sun to part shade.

Siberian squill (see Reblooming Fall-Planted bulbs).

Toad lily (*Tricyrtis*). Perennial; native to Asia. Small, delicate flowers like miniature orchids, often spotted, in shades of purple or pink and white, appear on tall stems in August and September in part to full shade. There are several species.

Turtlehead (*Chelone glabra*). Perennial; Midwest native. Erect clusters of bulbous white flowers appear in late August to October. Turtlehead needs consistently moist soil with plenty of organic matter in part shade. Pink turtlehead (*Chelone obliqua*), native to the southeastern US, has similar requirements and blooms a month or so earlier.

Virginia bluebells (*Mertensia virginica*). Perennial; Midwest native. Pink flower buds rise 18 inches above the velvety foliage in spring and then open to sky-blue bell-shaped flowers. They are a perfect complement to yellow daffodils. After blooming, the foliage of this spring ephemeral wildflower dies away by mid-June to return next year.

Wild columbine (*Aquilegia canadensis*). Perennial; Midwest native. The delicate salmon-pink-and-yellow flowers nodding on tall, slender stems look like tiny rocket ships when they appear in May. Columbine thrives in part shade to shade and will reseed widely in a favorable garden. If leaves are disfigured by leaf miners in late summer, cut the foliage back. There also are a number of other US species as well as many hybrid cultivars of columbine with much more elaborate flowers in shades of white, pink, yellow, and purple. They tend to do better in part shade or part sun.

Wild sweet William (*Phlox divaricata*). Perennial; Midwest native. The dainty pale-blue to lavender blooms of this native wildflower appear in May on stems that ramble between other plants in part shade to shade.

GROUNDCOVERS FOR DRY SHADE
Plants that can survive under trees where it is shady and dry.

Barrenwort (*Epimedium*). Perennial; native to Asia. Shiny heart-shaped leaves are held on slender stems; the subtle, twinkly flowers, in yellow to red, depending on the species, appear briefly in May. Spreads, but not uncontrollably.

Creeping Jenny (*Lysimachia nummularia*). Perennial; native to Europe. With its small, round green leaves arranged along slender stems, this low groundcover spreads along the ground. Also used as a cascading plant in containers. A cultivar, *Lysimachia nummularia 'Aurea'*, also known as moneywort, has chartreuse leaves, especially in sun. Can be invasive.

Ostrich fern (See Foliage Plants for Shade)

Shield fern. (See Foliage Plants for Shade)

Spotted deadnettle. (See Foliage Plants for Shade)

Sweet woodruff (*Galium odoratum*). Perennial; native to Europe. With green leaflets that give a starry effect, this low groundcover creeps between other perennials. In May it has fluffy white flowers. Spreads, but not uncontrollably.

Wild sweet William. (See Flowering Plants for Shade)

Yellow archangel (*Lamium galeobdolon*). Perennial; native to Europe and Asia. Pointed leaves touched with silver are the main attraction, although spikes of yellow flowers appear in May. Spreads aggressively by runners and can form a dense, competitive mat. Can be invasive.

FLOWERING PERENNIALS FOR SUN

Plants that need full to part sun and will flower for one to four weeks at different times of year.

Beardtongue (*Penstemon digitalis*). Perennial; Midwest native. A tall plant bearing tubular white flowers arranged along stems in early summer. Can tolerate dry soil once established.

Bee balm (*Monarda fistulosa*). Perennial; Midwest native. Fluffy, fairylike pale lavender flowers bloom on a rangy, sometimes floppy plant in summer. Very attractive to bees and butterflies, but also prone to powdery mildew; it needs well-drained soil. It's a member of the mint family, so it spreads vigorously.

Black-eyed Susan (*Rudbeckia hirta*). Short-lived perennial; Midwest native. In the abundant blooms of this iconic prairie flower, vivid orangey yellow petals surround a chocolate brown center. The native species is tall, but more compact cultivars have been selected. Reseeds freely. Very drought tolerant once established.

Blanket flower (*Gaillardia aristata*). Perennial; central US native. Bright blooms that return all summer have concentric circles of yellow and red around an orange center. Drought tolerant once established.

Butterfly weed (*Asclepias tuberosa*). Perennial; Midwest native. Flat flower heads full of tiny orange to orangey-yellow flowers are held on hairy stalks in late summer. Like all milkweeds, it is a host to the caterpillar of the monarch butterfly. Very drought tolerant once established.

Calamint (*Calamintha*). Perennial; native to Europe. Tiny white flowers bloom in clouds around long stalks, giving the whole plant an ethereal look. Fragrant and drought tolerant, and bees love it. There are a number of species and hybrids.

Carpathian bellflower (*Campanula carpatica*). Perennial; native to Europe. This ground-hugging perennial has cup- or bell-shaped blue flowers on a low, mounded plant.

Catmint (*Nepeta*). Perennial; native to Europe and the Middle East. There are several species of catmint, all with clouds of small blue flowers on pale stems, with a spicy scent. These drought-tolerant plants are very easy-care. Cultivars such as 'Walker's Low' have been selected to be more compact and have more flowers.

Coneflower (*Echinacea*). Perennial; Midwest native. On a tall stalk, pink or purple daisylike flowers surround a high cone of seeds, adored by birds, bees, and butterflies. Purple coneflower (*Echinacea purpurea*) and pale purple coneflower (*Echinacea pallida*) are native to Midwestern prairies. Many hybrid cultivars have been selected that are shorter or bushier and have exotic shapes and colors, but they tend to be less vigorous than the straight species.

Daylily (*Hemerocallis*). Perennial; native to China. There are hundreds of cultivars of these rugged, reliable perennials. Each trumpet-shaped flower, in colors from creamy white to deep red, lasts only a day in midsummer, but the plants bear several buds on each stalk. Some compact cultivars, such as 'Stella d'Oro' and 'Many Happy Returns', have been selected to bloom repeatedly (especially if deadheaded). Daylilies are drought tolerant once established. The common orange daylily (*Hemerocallis fulva*) is invasive.

Goldenrod (*Solidago*). Perennial; Midwest native. There are many species of goldenrod in the US, native to different habitats, but all having fluffy yellow flowers arranged in long sprays in late summer. Rough goldenrod (*Solidago rugosa*) is a Midwest prairie native; elm-leaved goldenrod (*Solidago ulmifolia*) can tolerate part shade. Some cultivars have been selected to be more compact, such as 'Fireworks'. Goldenrod does not cause hay fever.

Japanese anemone (*Anemone hupehensis*). Perennial; native to China. Open-faced pink flowers bloom in late August and September on long stalks above a large, mounded plant. The plant prefers part sun to part shade and can be aggressive. Many hybrid cultivars are available, some of them smaller.

Lily (*Lilium*). Perennial; most species native to Asia. There are many species of lilies, all tall plants with large, bell-shaped flowers. Easy-care Asiatic lilies bloom in June, followed by LA hybrids, a cross between Asiatic and longiflorum types. The trumpet lily (*Lilium longiflorum*) has long, fragrant blooms in July or August. Martagon lily (*Lilium martagon*) has many blooms with curved petals on one stalk. Oriental lilies are hybrids that bloom in late summer. All lilies need well-drained soil; many prefer part sun or even light shade.

Meadow sage (*Salvia nemorosa*). Perennial; native to Europe. Purple spikes of bloom rise above a clump of foliage in late May to June; cut them back back after flowering and the plant will rebloom. Drought tolerant once established. There are several species and many hybrids and cultivars of perennial sage.

Monkshood (*Aconitum carmichaelii*). Perennial; native to Russia. Striking blue to purple flowers bloom on tall stalks in fall. Grows in sun to part shade.

New England aster (*Symphyotrichum novae-angliae*). Perennial; Midwest native. Fine-petalled, daisylike purple flowers bloom on a tall, robust plant in late summer. There are many cultivars in shades of pink and purple, some selected to be more compact for garden use.

Oswego tea (*Monarda didyma*). Perennial; Midwest native. Scarlet flowers with a fluff in the middle bloom in summer on a tall, somewhat coarse and rangy plant, also known as wild bergamot and sometimes called bee balm. It's a member of the mint family, so it spreads vigorously. Somewhat prone to powdery mildew, it needs well-drained but consistently moist soil. There are a number of cultivars that have a more compact habit.

Peony (*Paeonia*). Perennial; native to Asia. Peonies are long-lived perennials that form large, wide, showy flowers in shades of pink, white, red, yellow, purple, and apricot on a substantial, mounded plant in May or early June. Cultivars have been bred with so many petals that the flowers may weigh down the stems, especially in the rain, and need support.

Phlox (*Phlox paniculata*). Perennial; Midwest native. Tall stems, up to 4 feet, bear oval clusters of small white, pink, lavender, or purple flowers in midsummer. Very attractive to butterflies. Susceptible to powdery mildew.

Russian sage (*Perovskia atriplicifolia*). Woody perennial; native to the Himalayas. Fragrant dusty blue-green stems are lined with a cloud of pale blue flowers. Very drought tolerant and durable once established. The straight species is a large plant, but smaller cultivars have been selected.

Sky blue aster (*Symphyotrichum oolentangiense*). Perennial; Midwest native. Pale blue daisylike flowers bloom on a tall, robust plant in early fall. Drought tolerant once established.

Spike speedwell (*Veronica spicata*). Perennial; native to Europe and Asia. This plant has pert, upright spikes of blue flowers in midsummer. Many cultivars have been developed with blue or purple flowers.

Swamp milkweed (*Asclepias incarnata*). Perennial; Midwest native. The large tufts of tiny pink flowers bloom from July through August on a tall plant. Like all milkweeds, it is a host to the caterpillar of the monarch butterfly. Drought tolerant once established.

Tall sedum (*Hylotelephium spectabile*). Perennial; native to China. Tightly packed flattish flower heads include hundreds of small flowers above tall stalks and fleshy leaves. The plant is very drought tolerant once established. There are many cultivars, of which 'Autumn Joy', 'Vera Jameson', and 'Matrona' are popular.

Yarrow (*Achillea millefolium*). Perennial; native to Europe and Asia. Flat flower heads have hundreds of tiny flowers in yellow, red, or orange in summer. Very drought tolerant once established.

SHRUBS FOR SHADE

Some shrubs that tolerate part to full shade.

Bottlebrush buckeye (*Aesculus parviflora*). Southeast US native. This very large shrub has handsome dark green leaves, spectacular footlong white flower clusters around the Fourth of July, and yellow fall color. It does well in part shade.

Dwarf fothergilla (*Fothergilla gardenii*). Southeast US native. This small shrub grows well in partial shade and will stay compact and tidy, rarely exceeding 3 feet tall and wide. It has bluish green leaves, vivid fall color, and fluffy bottlebrush flowers in early summer.

Fragrant sumac. See Shrubs for Sun.

Hybrid yew. See Evergreen Shrubs.

Japanese spirea. See Shrubs for Sun.

Korean boxwood. See Evergreen Shrubs.

Oakleaf hydrangea (*Hydrangea quercifolia*). Southeast US native. With large, oak-shaped leaves that turn burgundy in fall, large white flower clusters in summer, and decorative, peeling coppery bark in winter, this is a handsome shrub. It can grow large in warmer climates, but often dies back in severe Zone 5 winters. It's a large shrub, but smaller cultivars are available.

Panicle hydrangea (*Hydrangea paniculata*). Native to Asia. Reliably hardy, this large shrub has white flowers in oval clusters in mid- to late summer. Limelight is a popular cultivar with large greenish flowers. Some newer cultivars such as Bobo have been selected for small size, and other have pink-tinged blooms.

Smooth hydrangea (*Hydrangea arborescens*). Midwest native. White fluffs of flowers bloom on tall stalks in midsummer in part shade. The most popular cultivar is 'Annabelle', with large, white globes of bloom so heavy they can bend the stalks. 'White Dome' is more upright with flatter, domed flower clusters. Hills of Snow hydrangea (*Hydrangea arborescens* 'Grandiflora') has smaller blooms but sturdier stalks. Some newer cultivars have pink blooms.

Spicebush (*Lindera benzoin*). Midwest native. Spicebush is a large shrub with fragrant green leaves, subtle yellow flowers in early spring, and yellow autumn color. If you have both male and female plants, you may get red berries. Spicebush does well in part shade.

Virginia sweetspire. See Shrubs for Sun.

EVERGREEN SHRUBS

Shrubs that keep their leaves and usually their green color through the winter.

Chinese juniper (*Juniperus chinensis*). Native to Asia. This extremely tough, hardy, drought-resistant evergreen has prickly gray-green foliage. It's a large tree, but cultivars are available in many shapes and sizes.

Creeping juniper (*Juniperus horizontalis*). Native to Canada. Tough, hardy, and drought tolerant like most junipers, this North American species of the prickly evergreen spreads wide and creeps along the ground. It's useful as a groundcover in a difficult place.

Eastern arborvitae (*Thuja occidentalis*). Eastern US native. A very common evergreen used for privacy screens, with flat, feathery sprays of foliage. An arborvitae can grow to be a 70-foot-tall tree in time. The most popular cultivar is the narrow Emerald Green (*Thuja occidentalis* 'Smaragd'). Shrub-sized cultivars include 'Hetz Midget', 'Golden Globe', and Mr. Bowling Ball™. Tall, slender cultivars include 'Techny', 'Wintergreen', North Pole™, and 'DeGroot's Spire'.

Eastern red cedar (*Juniperus virginiana*). Eastern US native. Not, in fact, a kind of cedar, this juniper species is prickly but extremely tough, surviving cold, heat, drought, and even salt-tainted soil. It's a large shrub, but there are smaller cultivars including 'Blue Mountain' and 'Grey Owl'.

Giant arborvitae (*Thuja plicata*). Western US native. This evergreen with flat sprays of scaly green foliage is used for privacy screens; it's thought to be more resistant to deer than Eastern arborvitae. It can grow to be a large tree, more than 70 feet. 'Green Giant' is a popular fast-growing cultivar; 'Spring Grove' is extra hardy.

Hybrid yew (*Taxus × media*). Hybrid of plants native to Europe and Asia. Surviving from sun even to deep shade, this nearly indestructible evergreen has flat, dark green needles. It can be sheared as a hedge. Unlike other evergreens, it will eventually resprout if cut back severely. Keep a yew pruned or it will grow into a large, spreading tree. 'Hicksii' is an upright, narrow cultivar, useful for hedges.

Japanese yew (*Taxus cuspidata*). Native to Asia. Similar to *Taxus × media*, it has relatively narrow cultivars that are good for hedges: 'Nana Pyramidalis' and 'Columnaris'.

Korean boxwood (*Buxus microphylla* var. *koreana*). Native to Asia. This species of the evergreen shrub is especially winter hardy, where other species are not, and somewhat shade tolerant. There are many popular cultivars, including 'Wintergreen' and the small 'Green Gem'. Two very winter-hardy hybrid boxwoods are Chicagoland Green (*Buxus* 'Glencoe') and Northern Charm™ (*Buxus* 'Wilson').

SHRUBS FOR SUN
Some shrubs that do well in full sun in the Midwest, including flowering shrubs.

Arrowwood viburnum (*Viburnum dentatum*). Midwest native. A large, upright shrub with shiny green summer leaves, flat clusters of white flowers in spring, and red fall color. It does well in sun or part shade.

Black chokeberry (*Aronia melanocarpa*). Midwest native. This elegant medium-sized shrub has delicate white flowers briefly in spring, red berries that later turn purple, and glossy green leaves that turn red in fall. Iroquois Beauty black chokeberry (*Aronia melanocarpa* 'Morton') is compact with more flowers.

Buttonbush (*Cephalanthus occidentalis*). Midwest native. Found at the edges of marshes and wetlands, this large, rangy shrub does well in wet sites. It has glossy green leaves and fragrant, small, ball-shaped clusters of white flowers in July.

Common lilac (*Syringa vulgaris*). Native to Europe. The glorious fragrance and spectacular flowers of a blooming lilac are among the thrills of spring. The rest of the year, though, a lilac is a large, rangy shrub prone to powdery mildew. Prune it regularly to keep it from becoming congested. A smaller, more shade-tolerant species is Meyer lilac (*Syringa meyeri*, native to China), which blooms a little later. Some newer lilac cultivars bloom again later in the season.

Forsythia (*Forsythia*). Native to China. The arching stems of golden bloom are the proof of spring in places with cold winters. After that, the shrub has shiny green leaves for the rest of the season. Forsythia needs regular pruning to keep it from becoming a tangle. There are several species and hybrids, some larger, some smaller.

Flowering quince (*Chaenomeles speciosa*). Native to China. In early spring, this shrub is covered with vivid coral-orange blooms. It does well in sun or part shade and can tolerate clay soil.

Fragrant sumac (*Rhus aromatica*). Midwest native. This low-growing shrub has glossy green leaves that turn brilliant red in fall. A sturdy, tolerant plant, it can handle part shade as well as full sun. A popular compact cultivar is 'Gro-Low'.

Japanese spirea (*Spiraea japonica*). Native to Japan and China. This easy-care shrub fits easily into gardens in part to full sun, with a dense, compact habit and clusters of tiny pink or white flowers in late spring or summer.

Koreanspice viburnum (*Viburnum carlesii*). Native to Korea and Japan. The fluffy white flower clusters are extremely fragrant as they change from pink to white in spring. This medium-sized shrub, which grows well in sun to part shade, has dark green leaves that turn dull red in fall.

New Jersey tea (*Ceanothus americanus*). Midwest native. Relatively compact and dense in its habit, this native shrub has rounded puffs of white flowers. It prefers well-drained soil but is tolerant of drought.

Ninebark (*Physocarpus opulifolius*). Midwest native. An upright, spreading shrub that has peeling bark and clusters of small pink or white flowers in late spring. The straight species has green leaves that turn yellow in fall, but some newer cultivars such as 'Diablo' have coppery purple foliage or a more compact size.

Rose-of-Sharon (*Hibiscus syriacus*). Native to Asia. Large, showy flowers, often pink, appear on this tall, vase-shaped shrub for a long period in the summer. Many cultivars are available.

Shining sumac (*Rhus copallina*). Midwest native. This shrub is also known as flame-leaf sumac after its vivid fall color. It's large, with fronds of smooth, slender, shiny dark green leaves. The native species only grows in sandy, acid soil, but a selection, Prairie Flame shining sumac (*Rhus copallina* var. *latifolia* 'Morton'), tolerates a wider range of situations.

Staghorn sumac (*Rhus typhina*). Midwest native. A large shrub noted for its conspicuous drupes, or clusters, of hairy dark red berries that often persist into winter. It's an aggressive spreader. A cultivar, 'Laciniata', has finely cut leaves and spreading branches. Tiger Eyes staghorn sumac (*Rhus typhina* 'Bailtiger') is a popular dwarf selection.

Virginia sweetspire (*Itea virginica*). Southeast US native. Sweetspire is a medium to large shrub that offers fragrant white flowers and red leaves in fall. It grows well in both sun and shade. Scarlet Beauty sweetspire (*Itea virginica* 'Morton') is especially hardy with beautiful fall color, and Little Henry® sweetspire (*Itea virginica* 'Sprich') is a compact cultivar suitable for a city garden.

SHADE TREES FOR URBAN SITES

Some shade trees that tolerate air pollution and the poor soils of cities and suburbs.

Accolade hybrid elm (*Ulmus japonica × wilsoniana*). Hybrid of Chinese species. This handsome, upright tree is resistant to Dutch elm disease, which has killed most American elms.

Bur oak (*Quercus macrocarpa*). Midwest native. This large, stately oak has deeply ridged bark, spreading branches, dark green leaves, and large acorns with fringed caps that feed birds and other wildlife.

Ginkgo (*Ginkgo biloba*). Native to China. The elegant fan-shaped leaves on this large, spreading tree turn sparkling yellow in fall and drop all at once. Pest resistant, resilient, and popular in US cities, it is endangered in China. Buy a male tree to avoid the messy (and bad-smelling) fruit.

Hackberry (*Celtis occidentalis*). Midwest native. This sturdy, tolerant shade tree has green leaves, yellow fall color, and gray bark. A common pest, hackberry nipple gall, which causes bumps on the leaves, is harmless.

London planetree (*Platanus × acerifolia*). Hybrid of US and Asian species. With beautiful gray-brown peeling bark and broad leaves, London planetree is especially resistant to air pollution. Exclamation planetree (*Platanus × acerifolia* 'Morton Circle') is a cultivar that is especially disease resistant.

Swamp white oak (*Quercus bicolor*). Midwest native. This large tree has beautiful, lustrous green leaves with silvery white undersides, golden yellow fall color, and big acorns that are a boon to birds and other wildlife.

SMALL TREES FOR TIGHT SITES

Trees that will fit into small gardens or city courtyards.

American hornbeam (*Carpinus caroliniana*). Midwest native. A slow-growing small tree that tolerates shade and has interesting rippled gray bark, giving rise to its other name, musclewood. The fall color combines yellow, orange, and red.

Apple serviceberry (*Amelanchier × grandiflora*). Midwest native. Several species of large shrubs or small trees are called "serviceberry" or "Juneberry," but this naturally occurring hybrid is the one most often found in nurseries. It has billows of fluffy white flowers in spring, handsome gray bark, edible dark purple berries in summer, and vivid red-orange color in fall. Cultivars include 'Autumn Brilliance' and 'Forest Prince'.

Eastern redbud (*Cercis canadensis*). Midwest native. Lilac-pink flowers seem to grow right out of the dark bark of this pretty small tree in spring. The leaves turn yellow in fall.

Flowering crabapple (*Malus*). Native to Europe and Asia. There are hundreds of cultivars of crabapple trees, in a range of sizes, with white-to-pink-to-scarlet flowers, green-to-purple foliage, and fruit in various sizes. It's crucial to get one that is selected to be resistant to apple scab, a lingering, disfiguring fungal disease.

Kousa dogwood (*Cornus kousa*). Native to China. This elegant small tree has a vase form and white flowers in late spring.

PLANTS FOR DRY SITES
Some sun plants that, once established, need little watering except in hot, dry periods.

Beardtongue. See Flowering Perennials for Sun.

Black-eyed Susan. See Flowering Perennials for Sun.

Chinese juniper. See Shrubs for Sun.

Coneflower (straight species). See Flowering Perennials for Sun.

Creeping juniper. See Shrubs for Sun.

Daylily. See Flowering Perennials for Sun.

Epimedium. See Groundcovers for Dry Shade.

Hybrid allium. See Reblooming Fall-Planted Bulbs.

Little bluestem (*Schizachyrium scoparium*). Perennial, Midwest native. The stems of this grass are bluish green in midsummer and coppery red in fall. 'Carousel' is a little more compact and 'The Blues' has especially strong color.

Meadow sage. See Flowering Perennials for Sun.

Prairie dropseed (*Sporobolus heterolepis*). Perennial, Midwest native. This fine-textured grass has pale pink summer flower heads, golden late summer color, and a lovely fragrance. 'Tara' is a dwarf cultivar.

Russian sage. See Flowering Perennials for Sun.

Sky blue aster. See Flowering Perennials for Sun.

Switchgrass (*Panicum virgatum*). Perennial; Midwest native. A tall, handsome, upright grass has weeping flower heads in late summer. 'Shenandoah' a bit shorter, has a reddish tinge, and turns purplish in autumn; steel-blue 'Northwind' is especially upright, sturdy, and storm resistant.

Tall sedum. See Flowering Perennials for Sun.

Yarrow. See Flowering Perennials for Sun.

PLANTS FOR CLAY SOIL
Some shrubs and perennials that can tolerate clay soil once established.

Arrowwood viburnum. See Shrubs for Shade.

Black-eyed Susan. See Flowering Perennials for Sun.

Chinese juniper. See Evergreen Shrubs.

Daylily. See Flowering Perennials for Sun.

Fragrant sumac. See Shrubs for Sun.

Grape hyacinth (*Muscari armeniacum*). See Reblooming Fall-Planted Bulbs.

Kousa dogwood. See Small Trees for Tight Sites.

Large-flowering crocus (*Crocus vernus*). See Plants for Early Spring.

Leichtlin's quamash. See Reblooming Fall-Planted Bulbs.

Lily-of-the-valley. See Flowering Plants for Shade.

Lilyturf. See Foliage Plants for Shade.

New England aster. See Flowering Perennials for Sun.

Ostrich fern. See Foliage Plants for Shade.

Prairie dropseed. See Plants for Dry Sites.

Purple coneflower. See Flowering Perennials for Sun.

Snowdrops (*Galanthus nivalis*). See Reblooming Fall-Planted Bulbs.

Switchgrass. See Plants for Dry Sites.

Swamp milkweed. See Flowering Perennials for Sun.

Swamp white oak. See Shade Trees for Urban Sites.

Turtlehead. See Flowering Plants for Shade.

REBLOOMING FALL-PLANTED BULBS
Some fall-planted bulbs that usually rebloom the next year in Midwestern weather and soils.

Daffodil (*Narcissus*). Yellow to white bell-shaped flowers.

Glory-of-the-snow (*Chionodoxa luciliae*). Small, sparking white flowers touched with blue in early spring.

Grape hyacinth (*Muscari armeniacum*). Bright blue flower spikes in mid-spring.

Hybrid allium. *Allium* 'Summer Beauty'. Pink flowers and handsome shiny leaves in summer. Similar but smaller: *Allium* 'Millenium'.

Leichtlin's quamash (*Camassia leichtlinii*). Tall, pale blue flower spikes in mid-spring.

Siberian squill (*Scilla siberica*). Bright blue flowers in early spring; shade tolerant; reseeds.

Snowdrops (*Galanthus nivalis*). White dangling blooms in very early spring.

Species tulip. Low wild-type tulips that tend to return year after year. *Tulipa dasystemon*: open-cupped yellow flowers. *Tulipa batalinii*: tight red blooms. *Tulipa clusiana*: open, starry yellow blooms.

PLANTS FOR EARLY SPRING
Plants that may lift the spirits by blooming when there is still snow on the ground.

Bloodroot (*Sanguinaria canadensis*). Midwest native. Pristine white flowers emerge from the rolled-up leaves in early spring. After the flowers fade, the large, silky, kidney-shaped leaves persist for months, making a handsome groundcover.

Sharp-lobed hepatica (*Hepatica acutiloba*). Midwest native. One of the first spring wildflowers are the lilac-blue blooms of this mounding perennial. The plant will go dormant and fade away in a few weeks.

Snow crocus (*Crocus chrysanthus*). Native to Europe. Tiny, delicate blooms in pastel colors appear two or three weeks before the large-flowered crocuses (*Crocus vernus*).

Snowdrops (*Galanthus nivalis*). Native to Europe. Planted in fall as bulbs, snowdrops develop into dense clumps with dangling white flowers in very early spring—sometimes as early as February, depending on the weather.

Vernal witch-hazel (*Hamamelis vernalis*). Midwest native. This large shrub or small tree has subtle yellow blooms in late winter or early spring.

Winter aconite (*Eranthis hyemalis*). Native to Europe. Golden buttercuplike flowers open above a fringe of leaves scattered along the ground and are often covered by snow. They reseed freely in sun to part shade.

It's important to monitor your plants for evidence of damage from diseases and pests, but it's also important not to overreact. Most insects in the garden are harmless or beneficial, and many diseases, though they create cosmetic imperfections, don't do plants any real harm. The wisest course is to get expert help to diagnose a problem and advise you on what alternatives might be available to control it—if you decide it's serious enough to require any action at all. (See Here's How to Get Help with Plant Problems, page 98.)

DISEASES AND SYMPTOMS

Browning evergreens: It's normal for the oldest needles in the interior of an evergreen to turn brown and drop; as long as this occurs evenly on branches near the trunk, there's nothing to worry about. Evergreen needles also can turn brown if twigs or branches have been dried out and killed by a harsh winter. Prune them out in spring to let the shrub fill back in, and the following fall, water regularly until the ground freezes so the plant can store water for winter. If the plant is near a road, drive, or sidewalk, salt used to melt snow may be a factor. You can try flushing the soil with water to rinse out salt, but a better long-term solution is to replace the plant with a more salt-tolerant species.

Bark damage: Tree bark can be sliced and gashed by lawnmowers or string trimmers. Create a wide circle of mulch around the trunk to keep the power tools away. Bark on young trees and shrubs can also be damaged by deer rubbing or by animals chewing during winter. Protect vulnerable plants with a cylinder of wire mesh with ½-inch openings. Hold it down with wire staples so animals can't get beneath.

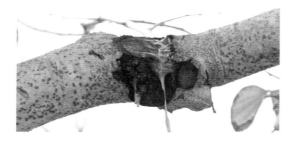

Cankers: These sunken or raised spots on the bark of trees and shrubs are usually dark and dry but sometimes oozing. They can be caused by a range of bacterial, fungal, and viral diseases depending on the plant species. The canker-causing organisms can be spread by insects or the wind or can be transported on a gardener's tools. There is no practical cure. If plants are small enough, dig them up and dispose of them. Prune out growth with cankers in winter, when the plant is dormant. Destroy the pruned leaves and twigs. Disinfect your tools between plants with a disinfectant spray that uses benzalkonium chloride as an active ingredient or with alcohol wipes. For new plants, seek out disease-resistant varieties.

Chlorosis: Leaves sometimes turn yellow between the veins, leaving veins green. This condition, chlorosis, can be a symptom of many different problems, so if you see yellowing leaves, you may need expert help to sort through the possibilities. Some plants, such as birches, show chlorosis because of the alkaline soil common in the Midwest. You can amend the soil with sulfur to make the soil more acid, or start over with a plant more tolerant of alkaline soil.

Crown rot and root rot: These diseases are caused by soilborne fungi, bacteria, and nematodes. Wet, poorly drained soil encourages them. Crown rots occur at the soil line, blackening the stems, and the infection spreads until the plant wilts and dies. Wet soil often leads to root rot, causing discolored and wilting leaves. By the time you see the evidence, it is too late to save the plants. Dig up all rotted plants and destroy them. Remove and destroy potting mix from containers that held plants with rot. Always let soil dry out before watering. In a garden, improve the drainage. Look for disease-resistant plants.

Damping off: New seedlings can die back because of a soilborne fungus that infects the stems just at soil level. If you start seeds indoors, use a sterile, soilless seed-starting mix that has no live fungus spores. When you sow seeds outdoors, make sure the soil is well drained. Don't fertilize until the seedlings have a couple of sets of leaves; nitrogen encourages the fungi.

Failure to flower: A plant that does not flower as expected may be in too much shade, or may need dividing or deadheading. Too much nitrogen fertilizer may lead to lush green growth at the expense of flowers. On shrubs that bloom on old wood, pruning at the wrong time may have removed flower buds.

Fireblight: This is a bacterial disease that affects all members of the rose family, such as pears, apples, mountain ash, crabapples, and many other plants. It blackens the leaves and twigs as if they have been burned. To avoid spreading the disease, prune susceptible plants only in winter, when they are dormant, while the bacteria are overwintering in the bark. Prune well below the discoloration. Destroy the pruned leaves and twigs. Disinfect your tools between plants. For new plants, seek out disease-resistant varieties.

Leaf spots: Many fungal and bacterial diseases cause various kinds of spots on leaves. Usually these infestations are not serious, especially toward the end of the growing season when most plants have already stored the bulk of their food for the year. In general, you can deter fungal diseases by keeping foliage dry. Get an expert ID on any leaf spot problem before you attempt to treat it. To deter infections, avoid overhead watering, such as with a sprinkler, and water at soil level, such as with a soaker hose. In fall, collect all diseased leaves and destroy them or put

them in the landscape waste rather than composting them. Home compost piles usually cannot destroy bacteria or fungal spores. Fungicides are usually ineffective once you have seen symptoms; they must be applied as a preventative starting in spring.

Powdery mildew: This fungus disease and other mildews deposit a white or gray powdery film or patches on leaves of many types of plants. Eventually, leaves and flowers blacken and curl. Mildews are unsightly but, except in severe cases, they do not seriously harm plants. To deter an infection, avoid overhead watering. Prune plants to improve air circulation. Collect and destroy all infected fallen leaves. Fungicides are usually ineffective once you have seen symptoms; they must be applied as a preventative starting in spring. Some plants, such as bee balm, phlox, and lilacs, are particularly prone to mildew; seek out resistant cultivars or other species that are mildew resistant.

Rusts: Some fungi cause yellow, orange, or black spots that appear on the undersides of leaves. Growth is stunted and leaves turn yellow and drop off. The rust fungi need hours of moisture to infect plants, so avoid overhead watering and watering in the evening. Collect and destroy all infected fallen leaves and stems. Look for resistant varieties.

Stretched or distorted growth: Plants in too much shade may stretch toward the light. Late spring cold or frost may damage plants that were set out too early. Protect plants at night until it's warmer. Growth also may be distorted by pesticide sprays, which can drift onto plants that were not targeted—even from next door or across the street.

Viruses: These organisms disrupt plant cells, causing a wide range of symptoms that can include stunting, distorted growth, dead spots, and mottling, ring patterns, or bumps on leaves. Viruses can be spread by insects or the wind or can be transported on a gardener's tools. Dig up infected plants and dispose of them; there is no practical cure. Seek out varieties selected to be resistant to common viruses such as tobacco mosaic virus, which affects tomatoes, peppers, and potatoes. Use floating row cover to keep insects off plant, and control weeds, which often harbor viruses such as aster yellows.

Wilting: This can be a symptom of underwatering or overwatering. Check the soil. If it's dry, water; if it's wet, let it dry out. If the soil is consistently wet, such as in a low spot, move the plant to a new location, then deal with the soil drainage. If the site is dry, try more drought-tolerant plants. Wilting also can be caused by some disease or insects infestations, such as borers that disrupt fluid transport in trees.

Yellowing: Sometimes leaves turn yellow all over, including the veins. This is often caused by lack of nitrogen. Try increasing fertilizer, but do so slowly and carefully (excess nitrogen can contribute to many diseases and other problems).

COMMON INSECT PESTS

It's normal for insects to feed on plants, and few plants are seriously harmed by them. Only a few insects cause the kind of damage that can affect plants' health, and then only if the infestation is severe. The vast majority of insects in any garden are harmless, and many are useful predator insects that help control the populations of problem insects. If you overuse insecticides, you will kill predators, leaving your garden more vulnerable. When you see an unfamiliar insect, get expert help to identify it before you take any action (See Here's How to Get Help with Plant Problems, page 98). Decide whether you can live with the level of damage. Toward the end of the summer, most plants will have some dings, but they already will have done most of their growing and stored food for the winter. If you decide to try and control the insect, use the least-toxic alternative and use it only on the problem plant, according to the label directions. Even organic pesticides are toxic to some degree.

Aphids: These insects suck the juices from many plants. Leaves may be pale or spotted and may turn yellow or brown. Check for a sticky residue called honeydew, a byproduct of aphids' feeding, and look on the undersides of young leaves for the small, soft-bodied bugs. Give plants a stiff daily spray with water to blast off the aphids. If an infestation is heavy, try a commercial insecticidal soap. You may want to purchase beneficial insect predators such as lacewings or ladybugs.

Borers: Borers are insect larvae that burrow beneath the bark of trees, creating tunnels that cut off the flow of water and nutrients. The emerald ash borer, which has killed millions of ash trees in the Midwest, is a notorious example. Borers are usually the larvae of beetles, and include the bronze birch borer, rose cane borer, and lesser peach tree borer. You may not notice the infestation until a large part of the tree or shrub wilts and dies. If an ash tree is heavily damaged, an insecticide applied regularly to the soil may control emerald ash borer; consult a professional arborist (See Resources, page 189). Borers often attack weakened trees; for example, birches stressed by alkaline soil are especially vulnerable to the bronze birch borer. Choose the right plant for your site and keep it healthy.

Beetles: Many beetles affect plants, both as larvae and as adults. They eat leaves, stalks, flowers, and sometimes plant roots as well as bore into stems, flower buds, and fruit. They can skeletonize leaves, eating the green tissue and leaving on the veins behind. Common garden pests include black blister beetle, tiny jumping flea beetle, Japanese beetle, rose chafer, asparagus beetle, carrot weevil, Colorado potato beetle, cucumber beetle, flea beetle, harlequin bug, and Mexican bean beetle. The viburnum leaf beetle is a serious emerging pest of viburnum shrubs, especial arrowwood viburnum. Pick off larger beetles when you see them and drown them in soapy water. For substantial infestations, seek professional help for advice on insecticides; the right product and the right timing are critical to reach the insects at a vulnerable point in their life cycle. Since many beetles lay eggs in soil, cultivating gently around shrubs or applying a thick layer of mulch may deter them.

Caterpillars: The larvae of moths and butterflies, caterpillars (and cankerworms, which are small caterpillars) can do substantial damage to some plants by eating soft leaf tissue. The large green tomato hornworm, for example, may feast on peppers, eggplant, and potatoes as well as tomatoes, while other caterpillars are so small they can burrow between the layers of a leaf. Inspect plants often and remove caterpillars when you see them, drowning them in soapy water. (If a tomato hornworm has white ricelike eggs on its back, it has been hijacked by a parasitic wasp; leave it alone so the wasp's eggs can hatch and eat the hornworm.) Search for leaves with egg masses and destroy them. The beneficial bacterium *Bacillus thuringiensis* (Bt) is effective against many

types of caterpillars. Don't kill every caterpillar, though; leave some to feed the birds and other wildlife and to turn into moths and butterflies. If you find striped monarch butterfly caterpillars on milkweeds, leave some plants for them to feed on to fuel their next generation (you can move the caterpillars to a few sacrificial plants, if you like). Do the same for swallowtail caterpillars on parsley. Avoid insecticides; they will kill the butterflies too.

Cutworms: These are caterpillars that feed on young plants' shoots and buds at night. Control them in the vegetable garden by cutting cardboard paper towel tubes into 3-inch lengths and placing one over each tender transplant to fence out cutworms. Once the plants grow big, they can resist cutworms.

Galls: These bumps or growths form when an insect lays its eggs inside plant tissue, or as a response to insect feeding or infections. Galls rarely do harm to the plant and there is no practical control. Some plants, such as hackberry, nearly always have harmless galls from a gall-forming insect.

Japanese beetles: This iridescent green beetle, about ½ inch long, feeds on many plants including rose-of-Sharon, maples, plums, cherries, and crabapples, but their favorite food is roses. Watch for the beetles in June and try to hand-pick the first ones and drown them in soapy water while there are just a few. The more beetles are in one place, the more will be attracted. Pheromone traps can actually make the situation worse by drawing beetles from all over the neighborhood. If you have Japanese beetles, be careful not to overwater the lawn; they like to lay their eggs in moist soil, and the eggs hatch into grubs.

Leafhoppers: These small insects hop or fly away when disturbed. Both the nymph and adult stages feed on plants, causing leaf stippling, stunting, and distortion of leaves and stems. Check for their sticky honeydew. Use floating row cover to help keep them off valuable vegetable crops. Keep weeds down. Encourage birds that eat insects by providing food, water, and shelter.

Leaf miners: These are the larvae of flies, moths, or beetles that lay eggs on the undersides of leaves. The larvae tunnel between the surfaces of leaves, feeding on the inner tissue. Columbine leaves often show curly leaf miner tracks. Check the undersides of leaves for small, chalky white eggs. Pick off the leaves and destroy them. Remove affected leaves and destroy them. Keep weeds down.

Plant bugs: Chinch bugs, harlequin bugs, squash bugs, stink bugs, four-lined plant bugs, and tarnished plant bugs all can harm garden plants when the nymphs and adults suck plant juices. Leaves may have white or yellow blotches, and they may wilt, curl, and turn brown. Injured areas may turn black. The damage these bugs do is mostly cosmetic, so try to live with it if you can. Keep weeds down to make it harder for bugs to travel. Protect valuable crops with floating row cover.

Scale insects: These sucking insects have oval, flat, armored bodies that lie immobile against tree stems and bark. They move only when they first hatch, when the young "crawlers" search for spots to settle down. The damage to magnolia and other woody plants may show up as yellowing leaves or when sticky honeydew attracts ants or becomes covered with black mold (which itself is harmless). Scrape off minor infestations. For a serious scale problem, wait until the crawlers have hatched—in late August through September for magnolia scale—and spray with horticultural oil. Only the tender crawler stage is vulnerable; the adults are impervious.

Slugs and snails: These soft-bodied creatures eat plant leaves, stems, and fruits, usually near the soil, where they live. They emerge from the soil and eat only at night, so they are hard to spot. Hand-pick them early in the morning. Lay damp newspaper on soil overnight to collect slugs. Try trapping them by sinking a shallow dish of beer level with the soil. Or spread diatomaceous earth—a product made of tiny, sharp shards of fossil animals' shells—around plants such as hostas. The sharp shards pierce the skin of slugs. Slugs and snails also avoid crossing copper strips or copper wire placed around plants.

Spider mites: These tiny arachnids suck plant juices, causing leaves to become stippled. Severely infested leaves will be bronzy and curled. Spider mites create a fuzzy white webbing. To detect the tiny creatures, hold a white piece of paper under a branch and tap it; mites will fall onto the paper as moving specks. Spider mites prefer hot, dry conditions, so they affect houseplants in winter and garden plants in midsummer. Remove and destroy affected plant parts. For a severe infestation, try insecticidal soap or horticultural oil. On outdoor plants, natural predators often will control mites.

Squash vine borers: These caterpillars feed on pumpkins, gourds, cucumbers, and melons, tunneling into the main stem. This can cause all or part of a vine to wilt. Cut the damaged vine open to reveal the fat white caterpillar with a brown head. To deter the caterpillars, keep weeds down. Protect crops with floating row cover until they start to flower. Remove and destroy all damaged plant parts. Apply Bt (*Bacillus thuringiensis*) early in the season and again at weekly intervals.

Resources

BOTANICAL GARDENS

Chicago Botanic Garden (Glencoe, IL):
    www.chicagobotanic.org/plantinfo

Missouri Botanical Garden (St. Louis, MO):
    www.missouribotanicalgarden.org/gardens-
    gardening.aspx

The Morton Arboretum (Lisle, IL):
    www.mortonarb.org/trees-plants/
    tree-and-plant-advice

Cincinnati Zoo & Botanical Garden:
    www.cincinnatizoo.org/plants

GETTING HELP
WITH PLANT PROBLEMS

Cook County Ask a Master Gardener Online (IL):
    www.web.extension.illinois.edu/units/survey.
    cfm?sID=368&UnitID=467

Ohio State University Master Gardener Program:
    www.mastergardener.osu.edu

Purdue University Master Gardener Program:
    www.hort.purdue.edu/mg/index.html

University of Illinois Master Gardeners:
    www.web.extension.illinois.edu/mg

BOTANICAL GARDENS
WITH ADVICE SERVICES

Chicago Botanic Garden Plant Information
    Service (Glencoe, IL): www.chicagobotanic.org/
    plantinfoservice

Missouri Botanical Garden (St. Louis, MO):
    www.missouribotanicalgarden.org/gardens-
    gardening/your-garden/help-for-the-home-
    gardener/advice-tips-resources.aspx

Taltree Arboretum & Gardens (Valparaiso, IN):
    www.taltree.org/our-gardens-and-yours/
    horticulturalist-qa

The Morton Arboretum (Lisle, IL):
    www.mortonarb.org/trees-plants/
    tree-and-plant-advice/plant-clinic

FINDING A
PROFESSIONAL ARBORIST

International Society of Arboriculture:
    www.isa-arbor.com/publicOutreach/
    treesAreGood/index.aspx

Illinois Arborist Association:
    www.illinoisarborist.org

Ohio Chapter, International Society of
    Arboriculture: www.ohiochapterisa.org

INVASIVE PLANTS

General information (US National Arboretum):
    www.usna.usda.gov/Gardens/invasives.html

Chicago Botanic Garden (plants found to
    be invasive at the garden, with suggested
    alternatives): www.chicagobotanic.org/research/
    identifying_threats/invasive

Illinois Invasive Species Month Species of Concern:
    www.invasive.org/illinois/SpeciesofConcern.html

Indiana's Most Unwanted Plant Pests (Indiana
    Cooperative Agricultural Pest Survey):
    www.extension.entm.purdue.edu/CAPS/plants.html

Indiana Department of Natural Resources:
    www.in.gov/dnr/naturepreserve/4736.htm

Midwest Invasive Plants Network:
    www.mipn.org/MIPN%20redraft2.pdf

Ohio Department of Natural Resources Invasive
    Plants List: www.ohiodnr.gov/portals/0/pdfs/
    invasives/ohio-invasive-plants-r0400.pdf

Ohio DNR Alternatives to Invasive Plants:
    www.ohiodnr.gov/portals/0/pdfs/invasives/
    Alternatives_to_Ohio_Invasive_Plant_Species.pdf

LAST/FIRST FROST DATES

National Oceanographic and Atmospheric
    Administration website: www.ncdc.noaa.gov

Plantmaps.com (search by ZIP code):
    www.plantmaps.com

NATIVE PLANTS

Cincinnati Zoo (recommended native shrubs, grasses, and perennials): www.cincinnatizoo.org/plants/#symple-tab-native-plants

Lady Bird Johnson Wildflower Center (comprehensive national native plant database): www.wildflower.org

Plantnative.org (consortium urging use of native plants in mainstream landscaping; has suggested plant lists and retail sources): www.plantnative.org

Wild Ones (national nonprofit dedicated to landscaping with native plants; find local chapters on website): www.wildones.org

PLANT HARDINESS ZONES

USDA interactive map: www.planthardiness.ars.usda.gov

RAIN GARDENS

Central Ohio Rain Garden Initiative: www.centralohioraingardens.org

SELECTED PUBLIC GARDENS TO VISIT

Cantigny Park (Wheaton, IL): www.cantigny.org

Chicago Botanic Garden (Glencoe, IL): www.chicagobotanic.org

Cincinnati Zoo & Botanical Garden: www.cincinnatizoo.org

Cleveland Botanical Garden: www.cbgarden.org

Dawes Arboretum (Norwalk, Ohio): www.dawesarb.org

Franklin Park Conservatory & Botanical Gardens (Columbus, Ohio): www.fpconservatory.org

Garfield Park Conservatory (Chicago, IL): www.garfield-conservatory.org

Holden Arboretum (Kirtland, Ohio): www.holdenarb.org/home

Indianapolis Zoo White River Gardens: www.indianapoliszoo.com/plan-your-visit/white-river-gardens

Lurie Garden (Chicago, IL): www.luriegarden.org

Missouri Botanical Garden (St. Louis, MO): www.missouribotanicalgarden.org

Taltree Arboretum & Gardens (Valparaiso, IN): www.taltree.org

The Morton Arboretum (Lisle, IL): www.mortonarb.org

SOIL TESTING

Purdue University soil testing explanation and list of laboratories: www.ohioline.osu.edu/hyg-fact/1000/pdf/1132.pdf

University of Illinois Extension list of soil testing labs (can mail samples from any state): www.urbanext.illinois.edu/soiltest

UNIVERSITY EXTENSION OUTREACH WEBSITES

Buckeye Yard and Garden Online (Ohio State University) gardening e-newsletter: www.bygl.osu.edu

Purdue University Extension: www.extension.purdue.edu

University of Illinois Extension Hort Corner: www.urbanext.illinois.edu/hort

UNIVERSITY EXTENSION PLANT CLINICS

Submit samples for laboratory analysis of plant problems; fees range from $20 to $60.

Ohio State University Extension Plant Clinic: www.plant-clinic.bpp.oregonstate.edu

Purdue Plant & Pest Diagnostic Laboratory: www.ppdl.purdue.edu/ppdl

University of Illinois Plant Clinic: www.web.extension.illinois.edu/plantclinic

Glossary

Acidic soil: On a soil pH scale of 0 to 14, acidic soil has a pH lower than 5.5. Most garden plants prefer a slightly acidic side. Most soils in the Midwest are somewhat alkaline, although this can vary.

Afternoon sun: A garden receiving afternoon sun typically has full sun from 1 to 5 p.m. daily, with more shade during the morning hours.

Alkaline soil: On a soil pH scale of 0 to 14, alkaline soil has a pH higher than 7.0. Most soils in the Midwest are somewhat alkaline, although this can vary.

Annual: A plant that germinates (sprouts), flowers, and dies within one growing season.

***Bacillus thuringiensis* (Bt):** An organic pest control based on naturally occurring soil bacteria, often used to control harmful caterpillars such as cutworms, leaf rollers, and webworms.

Balled and burlapped (B&B): Plants that have been grown in field nursery rows and dug up with some of their roots in a ball of soil. The rootball is wrapped with burlap, which must be removed at planting. Most plants sold balled and burlapped are large evergreen plants and deciduous trees.

Bare-root: Shipped dormant, with no soil around the roots. Roses are often shipped bare-root.

Beneficial insects: Those that perform valuable services such as pollination and pest control. Ladybugs, soldier beetles, and bees are examples. Most garden insects are beneficial.

Biennial: A plant that sprouts during its first year, blooms during its second year, and then dies.

Bolting: When a plant such as lettuce switches from leaf growth to producing flowers and seeds, it bolts. Bolting often occurs quite suddenly and is usually undesirable, because the flavor usually changes and the plant soon dies.

Brown materials: Materials for a compost pile that are high in carbon, such as brown leaves and grass, woody plant stems, and sawdust.

Bud: A small, undeveloped shoot, protected by overlapping leaves, that will eventually produce a flower or side stem. Usually found at a branch tip or along the side of a branch.

Bulb: A large, underground storage organ containing a plant, flower, and food supply. Examples of plants with bulbs are tulips, daffodils, and hyacinths. Bulbs usually are sold and planted when dormant. Those that flower in spring are typically planted in fall.

Bush: *See* "shrub."

Cane: A stem on a shrub. A term commonly used for rose, blackberry, or raspberry stems, and sometimes for blueberry plants and shrubs with long, arching stems, such as forsythia.

Cellpack: A container with four, six, or eight small plants, often sold in flats of 24, 36, or 48 plants. Most common for herbs, vegetables, and bedding annuals.

Central leader: The upright center stem of a tree. Usually, the best structure for a tree is to have a strong central leader and several side branches.

Chilling hours: Hours when the air temperature is below 45 degrees Fahrenheit; chilling hours are related to fruit production in orchard trees. Chilling for several weeks or months also is necessary for some perennials and for spring-blooming bulbs.

Chlorosis: A lack of chlorophyll, usually seen as yellowing of the leaves. Chlorosis can be a symptom of many different problems, from overwatering or underwatering to disease.

Cold frame: A box with a transparent lid that can be opened for ventilation, used to protect plants against cold, harden off new plants, grow cool-season crops, and overwinter plants.

Common name: A name that is generally used by gardeners for a plant, as opposed to its scientific or botanical name; the common name for *Echinacea purpurea* is "purple coneflower." Common names are imprecise because they vary by region. Some plants have several common names, and some common names, such as "snow-on-the-mountain," may be used for several different plants. *See* "scientific name."

Compost: Humus, or decayed plant matter, used to improve soil. Compost is made in a pile or a bin by providing plant materials for insects and microorganisms to digest. It harnesses the natural processes of plant decay and imitates the humus that naturally forms from dead plants.

Contact herbicide: A herbicide that kills only the part of the plant that it touches, such as the leaves or the stems.

Container: Any pot or vessel used for planting. A container can be ceramic, clay, steel, or plastic—or a bucket or barrel—and must have a drainage hole.

Container garden: A garden that is created primarily by growing plants in containers instead of in the ground.

Container grown: A plant that is grown, sold, and shipped while in a pot.

Cool-season annual: A flowering plant, such as snapdragon or pansy, that thrives during cooler months.

Cool-season vegetable: A vegetable, such as spinach, broccoli, and peas, that thrives during cooler months. Often called hardy or very hardy.

Core-aerate: To create many holes in a lawn by removing plugs of turf, allowing air and water to reach the grass plants' roots. It is done with a special machine.

Cover crop: Plants are grown in the vegetable garden to enrich the soil, prevent erosion, suppress weeds, and control pests and diseases over the winter.

Cross-pollination: The transfer of pollen from one plant to another plant to produce a fruit and seed. *See* "pollination."

Cultivator: A tool with three or four curved tines that is used to break up soil clods or lumps before planting, rake soil amendments into garden beds, or scratch out weeds. There are hand-held and long-handled versions. Sometimes called a "four-tined claw" or "three-tine claw."

Cut back: To remove the ends of stems all over a plant, to encourage bushier growth and more blooming.

Dappled shade: Bright shade created by high tree branches or tree foliage, where patches of sunlight and shade intermingle.

Day-neutral plant: A plant that flowers when it reaches a certain size, regardless of the day length.

Days to harvest: On seed packets or in catalogs, a number stating how long the variety usually takes to flower or provide ripe fruits. Note that in some cases it is counted from the time the seed is sown in the ground and in others it is counted from the time a seedling is transplanted outdoors.

Deadhead: To remove dead flowers in order to encourage further bloom and prevent the plant from going to seed.

Deciduous plant: One that loses its leaves when they are no longer needed, typically in fall or early winter when the plant is dormant. Many trees and shrubs are deciduous.

Diatomaceous earth: A natural control for snails, slugs, flea beetles, and other garden pests consisting of ground-up fossilized remains of sea creatures. It has too many sharp edges for slugs' tender skin.

Dibber or dibble: A pointed tool used for poking holes in the ground so seedlings, seeds, or small bulbs can be planted.

Disease resistant: Plant varieties that are disease resistant have been selected to be less likely to get diseases that often afflict plants of their kind, such as black spot for roses or powdery mildew for lilacs.

Divide: A technique consisting of digging up clumping perennials, separating the roots, and replanting. Dividing plants encourages vigorous growth, as well as producing more plants, and is typically performed in the spring or fall.

Dormancy: The period when plants normally stop growing in order to conserve energy. This happens seasonally, usually in winter.

Dripline: The area defined by the outer reach of a tree's branches, where rain drips off. Many roots that absorb water and nutrients are found within the drip line, although most mature trees' roots extend farther.

Dwarf: A tree or shrub whose growth is constrained so it stays smaller than normal. In conifers, it usually refers to varieties that grow very slowly. In fruit trees, it refers to a tree that grows no taller than 10 feet, usually because it was grafted to a dwarf rootstock.

Edge: To make a neat, even edge on turf. It can be done with a sharp spade, a string trimmer, or a dedicated tool called an edger. There are hand edgers and power edgers with electric or gasoline motors.

Evergreen: A plant that keeps its leaves year-round instead of dropping them seasonally.

Fertilizer: A preparation that provides nutrients to plants to supplement the food they make through photosynthesis. There are organic and synthetic fertilizers.

First frost date: The date in fall on which, on average, the first frost is most likely to have occurred in a particular location.

Floating row cover: Lightweight fabric that can be used to protect plants from pests. Usually white.

Floricane: A second-year cane on a blackberry or raspberry shrub; floricanes are fruit-bearing.

Flower stalk: The stem that supports the flower and elevates it so that insects can reach the flower and pollinate it is the flower stalk.

Frost: Ice crystals that form when the temperature falls below freezing (32 degrees Fahrenheit). Can also refer to temperatures below 32 degrees Fahrenheit.

Fruit: In common use, a sweet-tasting edible part of a plant. In reference to vegetable crops, a "fruit" is the individual tomato, squash, ear of corn, or bean. "Fruiting" refers to a plant producing its edible seed-bearing organs, such as tomatoes, squash, ears of corn, beans, or berries.

Full sun: Areas of the garden that receive direct sunlight for six to eight hours a day or more, with no shade, are in full sun.

Fungicide: A chemical compound used to control fungal diseases by killing the organisms that cause them.

Gallon container: A standard-sized nursery container for plants. However, many nursery pots referred to as "gallons" are actually smaller.

Garden fork: A garden tool with a long handle and tines, used for loosening and turning soil or a compost heap.

Garden knife: A hand-held garden tool with a broad, semi-sharp blade, used for digging, weeding, cutting twine, and other jobs. Sometimes has one serrated edge. Derived from a Japanese tool called a hori-hori. Also called "soil knife."

Garden lime: A soil amendment that lowers soil acidity and raises pH. Rarely necessary in the Midwest.

Garden soil: The existing soil in a garden bed, evaluated by its nutrient content and texture. Garden soil is also sold as a bagged item at garden centers and home-improvement stores or in bulk from garden centers and landscape suppliers. Compare to "topsoil."

Germination: The process by which a plant emerges from a seed or a spore; sprouting.

Grafted tree or shrub: A tree or shrub composed of two parts: the top, or scion, which bears fruit or flowers, and the bottom, or rootstock. Usually the rootstock is hardier or more disease resistant. Roses often are grafted.

Graft union: The place on a trunk or stem where the rootstock and the scion have been joined. Typically appears as a line in the bark or a crooked or knobby place at the bottom of the trunk near the root flare.

Granular fertilizer: Fertilizer in a dry, pellet-like form rather than a liquid or powder. There are organic and synthetic granular fertilizers.

Grass clippings: The parts of grass that are removed when mowing. Clippings are a valuable source of nitrogen for the lawn or the compost pile.

Green materials: Ingredients for compost that are high in nitrogen, such as grass clippings, kitchen fruit and vegetable scraps, pulled weeds, or manure.

Hardy: Able to tolerate cold or frost. Some plants are hardier than others or are only hardy in places with milder winters. Contrast with "tender."

Hardening off: The process of slowly acclimating seedlings and young plants that have been grown in an indoor environment to the outdoors.

Hardiness zone: A geographic area that shares a range of average minimum temperatures in winter, based on a map prepared by the USDA. Hardiness zones are crucial to choosing appropriate plants. In the latest (2012) version,

North America is divided into 12 hardiness zones. Ohio, Indiana, and Illinois are mostly in Zones 5, 6, and 7.

Hard rake: A tool with a long handle and rigid tines. It can be used to move a variety of garden debris, such as soil, mulch, leaves, and pebbles.

Heirloom: A plant variety that was more commonly grown pre-World War II.

Herbicide: A chemical compound used to kill plants. There are selective herbicides, which kill only a certain type of plant such as grasses or broadleaf weeds; non-selective herbicides, which will kill any type of plant; contact herbicides, which kill only the part of a plant they touch; systemic herbicides, which are absorbed to kill the entire plant; and pre-emergent herbicides, which prevent seeds from germinating.

Hoe: A long-handled garden tool with a short, flat steel blade, used for breaking up hard soil and removing weeds.

Hose bubbler: A device that screws onto the end of a garden hose to disperse the flow of water. Used where slow, deep watering is desired, such as for young trees.

Host plant: A plant such as milkweed grown to feed caterpillars that will eventually morph into butterflies.

Hybrid: A plant produced by crossing two genetically dissimilar plants. Hybrids often have desirable characteristics such as disease resistance.

Insecticide: A substance used for destroying or controlling insects that are harmful to plants. There are organic and synthetic insecticides. Their toxicity varies, but all are toxic to some degree.

Invasive: A plant that is naturalized and that reproduces so freely and spread so aggressively that it overtakes natural areas, outcompetes native plants, and disrupts ecosystems is said to be invasive. Most invasive plants originate in gardens, and many common garden plants are invasive. Invasive plants are a huge problem in state and national parks and other natural areas.

IPM: Integrated Pest Management, a gardening philosophy that focuses on keeping plants healthy so they can resist pests and diseases themselves. Pesticides are used only as a last resort and in the smallest possible amount and the least toxic form.

Irrigation: Any system of watering the landscape. Irrigation can be an in-ground automatic system, soaker or drip hoses, or hand-held hoses with nozzles.

Jute twine: A natural-fiber twine used for gently staking plants or tying them to plant supports.

Kneeling pad: A padded cushion for protecting the knees while weeding and planting. Kneepads are another kind of cushion strapped to each knee.

Landscape fabric: A synthetic fabric that is laid on the soil surface to control weeds and prevent erosion. It is not necessary beneath mulch.

Last frost date: The date in spring on which, on average, the last frost is most likely to have occurred in a particular location. This date can vary by location even within a USDA hardiness zone.

Larva: The immature stage of an insect that goes through complete metamorphosis; caterpillars are butterfly or moth larvae.

Leaf rake: A long-handled rake with flexible tines, used for collecting leaves or removing debris from lawns.

Liquid fertilizer: Plant fertilizer in a liquid form. Some types need to be mixed with water and some types are ready to use from the bottle. There are organic and synthetic liquid fertilizers.

Long-day plant: A plant that flowers when the days are longer than a critical period. Long-day plants typically flower in early summer, when the days are still getting longer.

Loppers: Pruners with longer handles and larger blades for more leverage to cut larger branches. Choose bypass loppers and use them for pruning branches 1 to 3 inches in diameter.

Morning sun: Areas of the garden that have an eastern exposure and receive direct sun in the morning hours are in morning sun.

Mulch: A material that is spread over the soil surface around the base of plants to suppress weeds, insulate roots, and retain soil moisture. Mulch always should be made of plants, such as compost, leaves, bark, straw, or chipped or shredded wood.

Mulching mower: A power mower that chops up grass clippings into small pieces that will quickly break down on the lawn.

Native plant: In general, a plant that evolved in the region of your garden. Native plants are part of an ecosystem with native wildlife.

Naturalized: Introduced into an area but now spreading widely beyond gardens, as opposed to being native to the region. "Naturalizing" also can mean using plants such as daffodils in large informal masses to give a naturalistic effect.

Nectar plant: Flowers that produce nectar that attract and feed butterflies. Chosen for a succession of blooms throughout the season.

Nematodes: Microscopic, wormlike organisms that live in the soil. Most nematodes are beneficial, while some are harmful.

New wood: The new growth on plants. It's usually a lighter or brighter green and is more flexible than older, woodier growth.

Node: The place where one part of a plant grows out of another, such as a leaf node or a branch node. Flowers are often pinched back to a leaf node and shrubs are often pruned back to a branch node.

Nozzle: A device that attaches to the end of a hose and disperses water through a number of small holes; the resulting spray often can be adjusted to cover a wider or narrower area.

Nutrients: Chemical elements that plants need to supplement the food they make through photosynthesis. There are 14 essential nutrients, but the three primary nutrients are nitrogen (N), phosphorus (P), and potassium (K). In many situations, the soil provides sufficient nutrients.

Old wood: On woody plants, growth that is more than one year old. Some fruit plants and flowering shrubs produce on old wood. If you prune these plants in spring before they flower and fruit, you will cut off the wood that will produce fruit or flowers.

Organic: In reference to gardening products, derived from naturally occurring materials instead of those that have been synthesized or derived from chemical processes. In reference to plants, grown using organic products.

Own-root: Grown on its own roots rather than grafted; used in reference to a tree, shrub, or rosebush.

Part shade: Areas of the garden that receive three to six hours of sun a day are in part shade. Plants requiring part shade will often need protection from intense afternoon sun, either from tree leaves or from a building.

Part sun: Areas of the garden that receive three to six hours of sun a day are in part sun. Although the term is often used interchangeably with "part shade," "part sun" places greater emphasis on plants' minimum sun requirements.

Perennial: A plant that lives for more than two years, keeping its roots alive through the winter. Examples include trees, shrubs, and some flowering plants.

Pesticide: A category of chemicals used to kill insects, plants, or disease organisms in the garden. The category includes insecticides, fungicides, and herbicides. There are synthetic and organic pesticides. They vary in toxicity, but all are toxic to some degree.

pH: A measure of the acidity or the alkalinity of garden soil, which affects plants' ability to use nutrients. It is measured on a scale of 1 to 14, with a pH of 7.0 being neutral.

Photosynthesis: The process by which plants convert sunlight, carbon dioxide from the air, and water into food, which they store as sugar and starch. The green color of plants comes from chlorophyll, a chemical necessary for photosynthesis.

Pinch: To remove the unwanted part of a stem by pinching it with your fingers. To "pinch back" is to remove the ends of stems all over the plant, which can promote bushier growth and increased blooming.

Pitchfork: A tool with a long handle and sharp metal prongs, typically used for moving loose material such as mulch or straw.

Plant label: The label or sticker on a plant container that names and describes the plant and provides information on its care and growth habits.

Pollination: The transfer of pollen for fertilization from the male pollen-bearing structure (stamen) to the female structure (pistil), usually by wind, bees, butterflies, moths, or hummingbirds. This process is required for fruit production in orchards and vegetable gardens.

Potting mix: A mixture used to grow flowers, herbs, and vegetables in containers, usually containing compost and vermiculite or perlite to improve drainage in a base of peat moss or another organic material. Some potting mix contains slow-release fertilizer. Sometimes called "potting soil."

Powdery mildew: A fungal disease characterized by white powdery spots on plant leaves and stems, this disease is worse when plants have poor air circulation.

Power mower: A lawnmower with an engine that spins a blade parallel to the ground to cut grass. Some power mowers are self-propelled and others are designed to be ridden. There are gasoline, electric, and rechargeable models.

Pre-emergent herbicide: A kind of weed-killer that works by preventing weed seeds from sprouting.

Primocane: A first-year cane on a blackberry or raspberry shrub. A primocane doesn't produce fruit, except on everbearing varieties, which produce fruit on the tops of primocanes.

Pruner: A hand tool used for light pruning, clipping, and cutting. Bypass pruners have two sharp, curved blades that work like scissors to slice cleanly. Anvil pruners have one sharp blade that strikes a flat surface and crushes wood; use them only for dead wood.

Pruning: The practice of removing dead, overgrown, or unwanted branches on a tree or shrub to improve its structure and form, control its size, and allow better air circulation to prevent disease.

Pruning saw: A hand tool for pruning branches and limbs has a serrated edge that may be fixed or may fold into the handle. Some versions cut on both the pull and push stroke.

Push mower: A lawnmower without an engine, propelled by the user. Usually a reel mower.

Reel mower: A lawnmower in which five to eight blades are arranged as a cylinder that spins to cut the grass with a scissoring motion.

Rhizome: An underground horizontal stem that grows side shoots. Some aggressive plants, such as mints, spread by rhizomes.

Root flare: The place at the base of a tree or shrub where the trunk or stems flare out to become roots. The root flare should be just above soil level.

Rootball: The network of roots and soil clinging to a plant when it is lifted out of the ground.

Rootstock: The bottom part of a grafted shrub or tree. The rootstock is usually a different variety that can impart pest or disease resistance, make a plant more cold hardy, or cause a fruit tree to be a dwarf.

Runner: A stem sprouting from the center of a strawberry plant. A runner produces fruit in its second year. *See* "stolon."

Scaffold branch: On a tree, a horizontal branch that emerges almost perpendicular to the trunk.

Scientific name: The unique name that precisely identifies a plant, consisting of the genus name and species name, such as *Rudbeckia hirta*. Sometimes called "botanical name." Compare to "common name."

Scion: The top, fruit-bearing part of a grafted tree or shrub. The lower part is the rootstock.

Seed packet: The package in which vegetable and flower seeds are sold. It typically includes growing instructions, a planting chart, and harvesting information.

Seed-starting mix: A sterilized, fine-textured blend of perlite, vermiculite, peat moss, and other ingredients, formulated for growing plants from seed.

Self-fertile: A plant that does not require cross-pollination from another plant in order to produce fruit is self-fertile.

Shade: Full shade is the absence of any direct sunlight in an area, usually due to tree foliage or building shadows.

Shearing: The practice of trimming a shrub or hedge all over to create a solid, defined mass. Also called "hedging."

Short-day plants: Plants that flower when the days are shorter than a critical period. They typically bloom during fall, winter, or early spring when days are short.

Shovel: A tool with a broad, flat blade, often rounded, and slightly upturned sides that is used for digging and moving soil and other garden materials. It may have a long handle or a shorter shaft with a D-shaped handle.

Shrub: A woody plant that is shorter than a typical tree and has multiple stems. In general, multi-stemmed plants smaller than 15 feet high are referred to as shrubs. Also called "bush."

Shrub rake: A long-handled rake with a narrow head to fit easily into tight spaces between plants.

Sidedress: To sprinkle slow-release fertilizer along the side of a plant row or plant stem.

Slow-release fertilizer: Fertilizer that releases nutrients slowly over a period of several months. It needs to be applied less often and is less likely to cause pollution. All organic fertilizer is slow release. Slow-release pellets of synthetic fertilizer have a coating that slowly breaks down.

Snips: A smaller version of pruners with longer, pointed blades, used for deadheading, snipping small stems, and harvesting fruits, vegetables, and flowers.

Soaker hose: A porous hose, usually made from recycled rubber that allows water to seep out slowly into garden soil.

Soil test: An analysis of a soil sample to determine the level of nutrients (to identify deficiencies) and detect pH.

Spade: A tool with a sharp, rectangular metal blade, used for cutting and digging soil or turf.

Spreader: A tool for evenly distributing grass seed or fertilizer. A drop spreader distributes the material directly beneath the spreader. A rotary spreader distributes it over a wider area.

Stolon: A creeping side stem on the surface of the soil that helps a plant spread; creeping Charlie and strawberries are examples. Sometimes called a "runner."

String trimmer: A power tool that whips a plastic line in a circle to trim grass or cut weeds. Use with caution.

Succulent: A type of plant that stores water in its leaves, stems, and roots and is acclimated for arid climates and soil conditions. Cacti are a kind of succulent.

Sucker: An unwanted stem growing from the base or root system of a tree or shrub. On trees they often are a sign of stress. On grafted trees or shrubs, they may sprout from beneath the graft. Many shrubs naturally spread by suckers. Remove suckers to prevent a shrub from spreading or to keep them from diverting energy from desirable growth.

Systemic herbicide: A chemical that is absorbed by a plant's tissues to destroy all parts of the plant, including the roots.

Taproot: An enlarged, tapered plant root that grows straight down.

Tender: Easily damaged by cold or frost. Contrast to "hardy."

Thinning: The practice of removing excess seedlings to leave more room for the remaining plants to grow. Can also refer to the practice of removing some fruits when still small from fruit trees so the remaining fruits can grow larger.

Top-dress: To spread fertilizer or compost on top of the soil. Top-dressing is common in established perennial beds, raised beds, and lawns.

Topsoil: The top layer of undisturbed soil. In most city and suburban developments, the topsoil has been removed and replaced with a thinner layer of lower-quality soil. Do not buy "topsoil" in bags for gardening purposes; buy garden soil, with good texture and ample organic matter. *See* "garden soil."

Transplants: Plants grown in one location and then moved to another, such as seedlings started indoors or nursery plants.

Tree canopy: The upper layer of growth, consisting of the tree's branches and leaves.

Tropical plant: A plant such as an eggplant that is native to a tropical region of the world so it is acclimated to a warm, humid climate and is not frost hardy.

Trowel: A small, shovel-like hand tool that is used for digging or moving small amounts of soil.

Turf: Grass and the surface layer of soil that is held together by its roots.

Variegated: Having differently colored areas on plant leaves, usually white, yellow, or a brighter green.

Vegetable: A plant or part of a plant that is used for food; usually applied to food crops that do not taste sweet. Compare to "fruit."

Warm-season annual: A tender annual flower that thrives during the warmer months of the growing season.

Warm-season vegetable: A tender vegetable that thrives during the warmer months, such as tomatoes, okra, and peppers.

Watering wand: A sprinkler with a long handle for watering plants beyond reach.

Weeder: Any of many hand tools designed for weeding. A fork-tongued weeder or snake-tongued weeder is designed to remove plants with deep taproots, such as dandelions. A crack weeder is a flat tool designed to remove weeds between bricks.

Weed and feed: A product containing both a herbicide for weed control and a lawn fertilizer.

Weeping: A growth habit in trees and shrubs that features drooping or downward-curving branches.

Index

Photo Credits

Cathy Barash: 149 (bottom)

Beth Botts: 54

Heather Claus: 116

iStock: Cover

Tom Eltzroth: 14 (bottom), 17 (right), 32, 33, 40, 44 (top middle), 84 (bottom left and right), 135 (bottom left)

Katie Elzer-Peters: 10 (all), 12, 22 (right), 25 (both), 34 (left), 45 (both), 44 (top left and right), 47 (top, middle), 53 (right), 55 (top, middle), 58 (left), 63 (top), 66 (all), 69, 70 (left, both), 78 (right), 83 (all), 87 (left), 90 (left, top three), 91 (bottom), 94, 96 (left), 97 (all), 102, 105 (all), 106, 112 (left), 119 (left), 122 (top right), 129 (left), 145 (left), 146 (top, bottom), 170, 172 (left)

Bill Kersey: 19, 23, 31 (bottom right), 36, 50, 53 (left), 77, 93, 144 (both)

Tom MacCubbin: 172 (right)

National Garden Bureau, Inc.: 42 (right)

Jerry Pavia: 16, 17 (left), 44 (bottom left and right), 84 (top middle)

Shutterstock: 6, 8, 11, 13, 14 (top), 20, 22 (left), 27, 28, 34 (bottom right), 37, 38, 42 (left), 43, 44 (bottom middle), 45 (bottom), 46, 47 (bottom), 57, 58 (right), 59 (both), 60, 62, 64 (all), 69, 70 (right), 72 (bottom), 73 (both), 74, 76, 78 (left), 84 (top left and right, bottom middle), 86 (both), 87 (right), 88, 91 (top), 92 (both), 96 (right), 99 (both), 100, 103 (all), 107 (right), 108 (both), 109, 110, 111 (all), 112 (right), 113, 114, 118 (left), 119 (right), 122 (left, bottom right), 123, 126, 129 (right), 130, 132, 135 (right, top left), 136, 140, 145 (right), 150 (left), 151, 152, 154, 155, 156 (right), 157, 158, 160 (both), 161, 169, 171 (both), 186 (both), 187 (both)

Neil Soderstrom: 55 (bottom), 85, 90 (bottom left), 128, 131, 139 (both), 150, 162

Lynn Steiner: 63 (bottom), 184 (both), 185 (right), 188 (both)

Meet Beth Botts

Beth Botts is an award-winning writer who has contributed hundreds of articles about gardens and nature for publications including the *Chicago Tribune, Organic Gardening, Country Gardens* and *Chicagoland Gardening*. Raised on the South Side of Chicago by an organic gardener and environmentalist, she now gardens in a leafy suburb on the edge of the city. A University of Illinois Extension Master Gardener and a volunteer tree steward, she was a longtime editor and reporter for several newspapers, with more than 20 years at the *Chicago Tribune*. She now is a senior writer at the Morton Arboretum, a 1,700-acre public garden near Chicago, as well as a freelance writer and speaker. Her website is www.thegardenbeat.com.